CAROL D. LEVINE

PANIC CHILD

AuthorHouse™
1663 Liberty Drive
Bloomington, IN 47403
www.authorhouse.com
Phone: 1-800-839-8640

First published by AuthorHouse 3/19/2010

ISBN: 978-1-4490-5029-0 (sc)
ISBN: 978-1-4490-8908-5 (hc)

Library of Congress Control Number: 2009912191

Printed in the United States of America
Bloomington, Indiana

This book is printed on acid-free paper.

This book is dedicated to all of those children who didn't survive

and also to those who did and suffered.

I want to thank all of the people who champion for justice

in the name of abused children.

— This is my story.

CHAPTER 1

Hurry, Hurry, Hurry!!!

I was running as fast as my little feet would allow me. My brother, who was almost five years my senior was far ahead of me. He was yelling in the wind, "You'd better do better than that; Daddy's coming down the street towards the house. I can see him!" I thought, "Oh my God, he'll surely hit us." Our care was left in the hands of Maude the babysitter who just simply didn't watch us. Mommy got home from her job after Daddy got home. My mind was racing.

Maude was standing in the doorway with a look of fear and anger on her face. We had stayed with our friends too long. We were just reaching the steps that led up to our house when Daddy saw us. "Hey," he screamed! "What are you two doing down here on the sidewalk?" "We were just playing daddy," I said. "Get in the house!" He yelled. We both ran up the steps forever grateful that he believed me. As he passed Maude, he glared at her, but said nothing. When he was out of her sight she held her nose and made a face. We knew what that meant, Daddy smelled again of alcohol.

Our father was a full-blown alcoholic who was as mean as the day was long. Almost every night my mother and father would yell and fight scaring the hell out of us. Sometimes, I would creep down the stairs to see if Daddy was going to kill Mommy. He certainly said he would many times. I wasn't sure what that actually meant; after all, I was only five years old. My brother was very frightened of my father, and would pull the blankets up over his head and pretend that he was sleeping when my parents fought. One night as I watched with horror, my father had a heavy black skillet in his hands and he was yelling "Now I'm gonna bash you in the head!" My poor mother was helpless. She fell down to the floor holding her head waiting for the possibly fatal blow from the frying pan. My father stood over her and mocked her calling her very bad names. I stood in the hallway that faced the kitchen and started to scream at this monstrous man who was almost six feet tall. I screamed "Stop Daddy, stop!" He spun around and saw me. He had an ugly look on his face that made me stiffen; I felt like I couldn't breathe. Oh my God, what have I done? Now he's going to get me! I stood frozen with fear not knowing what to expect next. He came over to me and pinned my little body against the hallway wall. He was hurting me, but said nothing. Suddenly he let me go and left the house. I honestly believe I saved my mother's life that night. I looked at my mother who was a small woman in stature, and even though I was only five, I knew this was very wrong. She called to me and said, "I'm so very sorry you had to see that." I thought to myself, "So am I." In the hallway was the phone that stood on a little table. Mommy said, "Come here my brave little girl, I want to show you something." She took me by the hand over to the phone and taught me how to call for the police. In those days the phone was quite simple to use, lift the receiver off and dial 0. Perfect! Now I get to put Daddy in jail the next time he's bad! That's what Mommy said! What is jail?

I loved the daytime when Mommy and Daddy were at work. It's true that Maude didn't watch us the way she should have. We would get up in the morning and put on the clothes that Mommy laid out for us, get dressed, push down some hot cereal that Maude had made, [yuck] and off we would go. It was summer and when you are very young, every day is a new day that is filled with wonder and excitement. I had a friend who lived quite a few blocks away from our house, and every day I'd go to her house and we would play for a while in her yard. Then we'd backtrack and go into town. We loved going into town. In those days storeowners would take damaged merchandise and put it out back of their stores to be carted away. One of our favorite stores was the stationary store. Many a day we would sneak around the back of the property and go through boxes of thrown out goods. We did this very quietly because we didn't know if we were doing anything really wrong or not. Oh, what treasures! I remember many pencils and crayons not to mention paper of all sizes. "Mission accomplished!" My friend yelled. "Shhh," I said. "Someone will hear us!" We grabbed our treasures and ran down the many blocks back to my friend Amy's house. On the way back we ran into my brother. He said, "Hey dope head, don't be late today, remember how Daddy gets!" He went on to tell me that he saw Daddy put a bottle of booze under each couch pillow, and tonight might be really bad. My friend shuttered, "Why does your father drink so much?" she asked. I just looked at her and said nothing. After all, how would I know? The whole block knew that he was a drunk. I was too young to feel shame, or maybe I was just numb. I thought to myself, if I get home earlier today, I'll throw out Daddy's bottles of booze and that'll make things better. I did just that! At day's end, I walked into the house right past Maude and gathered up Daddy's bottles. Maude stood there with a look of shock. "What are you doing?" she asked. I didn't answer her. I took the bottles outside to the ally way that ran alongside of our house, and proceeded to smash them against the wall. Maude followed me out of the house and watched in horror as I destroyed daddy's bottles. She yelled, "You're crazy! Your father is going to beat the hell out of you!" She was probably right. Suddenly what seemed to be a good idea, turned out to be a bad one?

I went to my bedroom and sat on the bed feeling very frightened. What was I thinking? Even though I was only five years old, I could visualize how Daddy would respond to this and I started to cry. Oh, why didn't I think about this first? I knew that Daddy would be home soon. There was nothing I could do but wait and pray to God that Daddy would only hit me once or twice. I had an aunt who was very religious. She had told me that if you close your eyes really hard and ask God to help you, he would hear your prayers. I closed my eyes and said, "Lord, this is Carol here; I promise you if Daddy doesn't hit me very hard, or not at all, I'll never take his bottles again." I heard a door slam. It was only my brother. He came running into my room and started to yell at me. "What are you nuts? Maude just told me what you did." I told him "It's your fault; you said tonight would really be bad because Daddy had bottles of booze under the couch pillows, so I got rid of them!" We stood there looking at each other each with our own thoughts and feelings of doom when sure enough Daddy came into the house. My brother went to his room. He was not going to be a part of this!

I stood in the upstairs hallway, I couldn't move. I heard Daddy tell Maude that she could go for the day, and my mother would pay her for the week when she got home from work. "Be back on Monday" he said. I was quite sure Maude was thinking "Yes, if I'm needed." I stood in the   hallway waiting for Daddy to discover the missing bottles, and of course his screaming, screaming in the morning, screaming in the evening, screaming all day long. I wondered at times if his throat ever hurt him. It seemed like I stood in the hall forever. I was actually starting to get tired of standing there. Suddenly I heard what sounded like a loud gasp! Uh oh, here it comes! "Carol, come down here right now!" he shouted. I thought, "Why didn't he call my brother too?" Very slowly I started to go down the steps expecting to get thrashed. He looked at me. I found it very painful to look at his face. I was so filled with fear. I certainly couldn't look into his eyes, as I was afraid of what look he would have on his face. "Carol?" he asked, "Did you take my bottles of wine?" I felt like I was going to pee my pants. I actually felt myself start to shake. "Yes Daddy," I whispered. For what seemed to be an eternity, there was a silence that was so thick it could cut the air. Finally I heard him sigh. He said, "Don't ever do that again, or I'll hit you so hard that you'll never walk again. Go to your room and *do not* expect to eat tonight." That was it? Wow, there really is a God! No beatings like he gave Mommy.

My father left the house leaving my brother and I unsupervised. My brother crept out of his room and actually seemed disappointed that more didn't happen. "Boy, you sure got off easy." It was true, if my brother Jimmy had done that, he would have gotten hit. My father liked me better than my brother. We both knew this but never spoke about it. However, my father's main target for abuse was my mother, and like clockwork that night was no exception. I stayed in my room that night and only heard a little of what was said. I did hear him mention my name, and of course I knew why.

————

CHAPTER 2

Saturday! Saturday was actually almost always good times and a good day! We would all get into the car looking our very best, and go to my grandparents' house. These were my fathers' parents. My grandfather was a very successful florist and considered to be one of the best flower growers in the world! I actually have pictures of him posing with well-known movie stars. They lived in a house that was like a mansion. I loved going there. Every room was like an adventure. Their living room was called the ballroom. It was a huge room with highly polished floors, and had a beautiful chandelier that lit up the room. I loved to go and look at it and imagine I was a beautiful lady, dressed in a gorgeous gown, dancing the waltz with a handsome partner, spinning me ever so gently around. The dining room was a long wide room with a beautiful dining room set. The table had clawed feet, as did the chairs. My grandmother would have many fancy dinners in that room, with hired help of course. Everything had to be perfect! On one particular night that I'm sure was the topic of many a conversation for years to come, a certain little girl waited for all the grownups to finish their meals and go to the ballroom. Then I walked around the table and every glass that had wine or a mixed drink left in it, I sampled! All of a sudden, I felt like I could fly! I ran out of the dining room and went into the ballroom, where everyone who was anyone was dancing. I started to dance too! I spun around and around. I felt exhilarated and free. I shouted, "Look Mommy, look what I can do!" All of a sudden I fell to the floor and threw my guts up. My head was spinning. There was a silence, and then a roar of laughter. This isn't the attention I wanted. My mother came over to me and pulled me to my feet roughly. "What did you do," she asked? I pointed to the dining room, and then to the glasses. "Oh my God" she said, "She's drunk!" I heard another roar of laughter. "Where are the maids?" my mother asked. "Why didn't they clear the table?" Looking back, I hardly think they had time to. My mother calmed down and said, "Well, I guess I know where we're going." She went and got our coats and home we went. She was very sad. I never did that again.

On sunny summer Sundays we would go swimming. My parents had one spot in particular that they would take us to. Over the years my grandfather had purchased a log cabin in upstate New York. We all loved going to the cabin, it meant more good times for the most part. You see, even though my grandfather was very successful, he too was an alcoholic. My father and he would drink and have awful arguments. My mother and grandmother would take my brother and me out for a ride to get away from the fighting. When my grandmother insisted on driving, it was always an adventure. The lady did *not* belong behind the wheel of a car. One day she pulled into a gas station to get gas, and when she put the car in gear to leave, she accidentally put it in reverse hitting all the cans of stacked oil! The cans went flying and rolled everywhere! My brother and I looked out the back window and saw the gas station attendants screaming and yelling, shaking their fists at us. At first we were humiliated, but then we started to laugh hysterically. My mother didn't think it was so funny, and my grandmother went gaily on as if nothing happened. One thing about my grandmother, nothing ever bothered her. She was probably one of the funniest people I ever knew, and she was afraid of nothing. I would have loved to be just like her. She brought me a lot of joy just by being herself.

CHAPTER 3

The summer was almost over and that meant school. My brother loved school and I had not yet gone, so I was a little worried or maybe even a little scared. I had a new dress to start the big event and new shoes as well. However the shoes were horrible! I told Mommy that I hated them and that they didn't fit right, and she said, "Don't worry, no one will notice." Daddy had taken me for a walk the day before school started and he saw them in a window. "Carol, don't you think those are great shoes?" he asked. I looked into the window and felt shocked at what he thought was nice. "No Daddy," I answered. "I don't like them!" I could see that he was getting mad. He grabbed my hand and said, "You're getting those pretty shiny black shoes!" I thought, "I won't wear them, I'll show him!" My father marched us into the store and went over to the sales person. He demanded that he get the shoes from the window display. No one asked about size or whom they were for. The man simply said, "Your wife will love them." He paid and we left. Now you can imagine how big they were! At that moment I felt a new feeling for my father. I couldn't quite put a label on it, I knew it wasn't fear; it was something else, something not good.

I went into the school by myself, like a big girl, to a teacher who was waiting for all the new arrivals. We were all filled with anticipation. Everything was going well until we were told to get on the floor and form a circle. It was story time. Under ordinary circumstances this would have been fun. I looked down at my new shoes that flopped as I walked. I could barely keep them on. I knew that someone was going to see them and surely make fun of me. We all did as we were told and formed a small circle. Before the teacher could start, I heard a little girl start to laugh and point at my shoes. I tried to pull my dress down over them so no one else could see them, but try as I might it was impossible. I heard more laughter coming from someone else. I felt like running, but had nowhere to run to. The teacher came over to me and bent down. She pulled my head up which was looking down at the floor and whispered in my ear, "It might be a good idea not to wear those tomorrow." I wanted to die. How could I tell her I had no other shoes to wear? I thought the day would never end. Mommy showed up and I told her what had happened with my shoes. She sighed, and said, "I'll see what I can do." That didn't sound very promising. I walked into the house, had a few cookies and went to sit on the steps outside.

Suddenly Maude walked by. She looked at me sitting on the steps and stopped. "Hey pumpkin head how was your first day at school?" I looked at her and started to cry. She said, "Hey, you never cry, what's wrong?" I started to tell her and she got a look of anger on her face. "Stay here" she said. Lucky for me Maude had sisters younger than herself who always looked nice and well dressed. She came back soon with a pair of shoes that fit pretty darn well. I felt oh so relieved and grateful. To me that was one of the kindest things anyone had ever done. I ran into the house and said "Mommy look!" "Maude gave me these!" Mommy was happy too, but didn't know how Daddy was going to take it. What will I say when your father asks about the other shoes? I thought for a minute and took off to my room. There they were the ugly black shoes that caused me so much grief. I bent down and picked one up. I didn't know quite what to do. Then it dawned on me. Daddy couldn't expect me to wear shoes that were broken. I took one shoe into my parents' room and found the scissor. The shoes had a thin strap that went across the foot that would have been all right on someone who took a women's size six. I took the scissor and cut the strap in several places. Done! No more ugly shoes.

The next day, everything went well in school for me. I missed my friend Amy because she went to a private school. Her mother and father had more money than we did, and a lot more kids to care for. They all went to a Catholic school. I came from a family that was much divided. Some of the people in my family were Catholic and others were Protestant. This caused a lot of division amongst family members. Most of my friends were Catholic. As far as I was concerned I felt at home in the Catholic Church. Somehow it felt natural for me. Thinking back to Amy, I longed for the days and times that we would run the streets like wild little Indians. Those days were gone, but never forgotten.

One day after I came home from school, I knew that I wasn't feeling well. Maude was still our babysitter, but only for an hour after school, which kept me close to home. She looked at me and told me to go and lay down. I heard her go over to the hallway phone and call my mother at work. She told her that she believed that I was very sick. She was right. My mother came right home and immediately drove me to the hospital. Several doctors examined me very closely and the prognosis wasn't good. I had polio. They told my mother that there had been a lot of people sick this week with the very same disease. In the early 1950's there was a polio epidemic. They told my mother that I would actually do better at home, but I would be very sick for some time. The doctors gave my mother medicine and written instructions for my care. We went home.

When my mother told my father what had happened, he took off. He was gone for many weeks. My brother was sent to my mothers' parents to stay away from me, so he wouldn't get sick like me. It has been told that my mother walked the floors with me night and day trying to comfort me. I had a very high fever for many days. I wasn't paralyzed from this awful disease, but I did have trouble pronouncing certain alphabetical letters for many months. I was absent from school for quite some time and fell far behind. To make matters worse, I had to attend a class for the speech and hearing impaired at my school when I did return. Kids were not nice back then either. They all called this class the dummy class.

I was determined to practice my L's and E's and F's. On the weekends, I stayed in the house and practiced all day long and well into the evening. My mother thought that I was over doing it and expressed concern. She had no idea what it was like going into that classroom. It was because of this humiliation that I practiced day and night for a condition that was to take around a year to change. I was out and "normal" in less than six months. I also suffered from weakness in my legs and stumbled a lot. I completely recovered from that in time.

One day my father came back home. I hadn't seen him for quite a few weeks. He looked at me for a few minutes and said to my mother that I had lost too much weight. What did he expect, I had been very sick. With that he went into the living room and poured himself a glass of beer, a new drink for Daddy. Mommy fed us and put us to bed earlier than usual. My brother and I knew better than to say anything, but we were hurt. We had no real reason to like my father, but thought that maybe he would act like he missed us and spend a little quality time. That of course, was wishful thinking.

It was too early for me to go to sleep, so I played quietly in my room. All of a sudden I heard a loud smashing sound. It sounded like glass. Here we go again. Daddy's home! I rushed into the hallway and went to the top of the stairs as usual. I heard it all. My mother accused my father of seeing other women, one in particular. He didn't try to deny it. My mother told him to leave. He laughed and said no. He told *her* to leave, saying "You and your bratty kids." He called her ugly and told her that no other man would want her. As soon as the fight started, it ended. I ran to my room and got into bed. I started to cry very hard. I knew that my father was bad, but I still wanted him to love me. I felt so alone and unloved.

The next day Daddy was gone. I didn't want to talk to Mommy about it. She didn't want to discuss it either. Mommy sat on the couch with her one leg crossed over the other swinging it wildly. My brother and I knew that she was really mad. I can't say that I blamed her. All of a sudden Mommy ordered us to get dressed. It was Saturday and we were still in our pajamas. We ran to our rooms and did as she instructed. Was Mommy going to take us out? Were we going to grandmothers' house or something? When my brother and I came down stairs, we were shocked at what happened next. My mother told us to go outside and get into the taxi! I had never been in a taxi before and suddenly started to feel scared. I looked at my brother and he just shrugged. The taxi man opened the car door for us to get in, and we drove away.

It was a cold rainy day. We had no idea what was happening, or to where we were going. My mother had always been pretty good to us, but this was weird and didn't feel right. My mother was never a loving type of person, but I sure needed a hug now. I looked at my big brother and thought, "Why isn't he scared too?" The driver had nothing to say to us either. After driving for what seemed like a long time, the driver pulled into a lengthy driveway that was very bumpy. It was a dirt driveway. Now I was really scared, and I could tell that my brother was too. We looked at each other with a feeling of desperation. Where are we?

Suddenly, we saw a house and some pens that housed dogs. I wondered if we were at some kind of farm like my books showed in school. The driver stopped the car and ordered us to get out! It was raining pretty hard and I was cold and starting to get wet. My brother and I looked at each other and we both started to cry. What had Mommy done? Surely this has to be a mistake. The dogs were barking very loudly and they looked nasty. I looked towards the house and decided to go to the front door. After all, what else was there to do? I knocked on the door, but no one answered. The door wasn't locked so I went in. My brother was still outside. This may have been a nervy thing for me to do, but I was cold, wet and scared. I stood in a big room that was empty and thought to myself, "Where are all the people?"

As I stood looking around the big room, I suddenly became aware of strange sounds coming from behind a door off of what I guessed to be the living room. I didn't know what to do, and I didn't know what the sounds were that I heard. I really needed to see and talk to someone. I was *very* scared. I decided to enter the room that I heard the noises coming from. I walked over and turned the doorknob and walked inside. To my amazement, there was Daddy lying on the bed with no clothes on! He was not alone. A lady with short black hair was on the bed too, and she had no clothes on either. "Holy Shit!" my father said. "That's my daughter standing there." He looked at me with big eyes and screamed at me to go outside. Outside I ran! I felt horrified and scared again. My brother saw the look on my face and knew that there was something very wrong. I was crying very hard and I told him what had happened, and also what I saw. We both stood there in the pouring rain shocked, scared, and lost. All of a sudden, for no reason at all, my brother knocked me down to the ground, and now I was full of mud. I started to scream and ran back inside the house. This was not funny. Is that what he thought? I went right over to the same door that I was at before and flung it open and screamed, "Daddy, I'm cold and wet and I want to go home!"

The lady still wasn't dressed, so she wrapped the sheet from the bed around her and got out of the room. Daddy glared at me, and asked me where my brother was. I told him and he ordered me out of the room. He had a small blanket on him, so he wasn't totally indecent this time. That day I learned what big people looked like without clothes on.

My fathers' car was parked on the other side of the house. I walked around back and saw it. It wasn't locked so I got in. It was something that looked familiar. I started to wonder where my brother was. He was nowhere in sight. As it turned out he was hiding not too far from the house. He knew that he had done something wrong by knocking me down, and he was afraid of what Daddy would do. After what seemed to be a lifetime, my brother and father approached the car and got in. My brothers' face was red on one side. My father had slapped him. On the way home, not a word was spoken. The silence was deafening, but I didn't really care. What was I going to say to my father anyway? Of course, I had many questions to ask, but didn't dare. I wanted my mother. I don't know why she sent us over there, but I knew that I wanted to be in my house, my room, and the few toys that I had, suddenly became very precious to me.

Children are always the real victims, and the ones that can't really speak. How many times did I want to say, "Please don't fight, please let us live like Amy's family." To me she was a little girl who had a wonderful life, pretty clothes, and lots of toys. She didn't know what it was like to have parents always screaming and yelling at each other. Quite frankly, even though I may have envied her, I liked her far too much for her to have to go through what my brother and I came to know as just another day. There was no family help or intervention. In those days everything was hush-hush, and if you had a bad marriage, it was your problem. Times were different. People were different. I don't mean to say that people were Saints; I just mean that as a child if people were engaged in what was considered to be adult conversations, children were ordered out of the room to play elsewhere, and voices were lowered. Perhaps a better way to describe an adult conversation was to say they whispered a lot. That is what my grandparents did. I must say, that my brother and I learned to eavesdrop a lot. How else would we know anything?

────

CHAPTER 4

My mother and father no longer spoke to each other. At least it was quiet. My brother said that this too was wrong. He and I sat in the upstairs hallway and had conversations that children our age should never have. He was sure that something was about to happen in our lives, but he wasn't sure what it was. He was right.

My fathers' mother had three sisters. I knew them pretty well. They of course would be my aunts. All three of them were rather likeable, but very different. Aunt Connie was a school teacher who lived and worked in New York City. She was a very jolly acting person and also very religious. One day she took me into the city to a very large convention. We were to see Billy Graham. And so we did. There were a lot of people. Everyone was being saved, even me! I actually liked all of the excitement, and to see so many happy people was quite a sight to see. I got to shake hands with Billy Graham after the convention was over. I remember he gave me a bible. That was something I'll never forget.

After we left the building Aunt Connie approached construction workers on the street and started to preach to them. She told them that they had to repent and be saved. No matter whom she spoke to, they didn't respond to her kindly. Then there was Aunt Ruby. Her mother named her well. Aunt Ruby had beautiful long red hair. She was a very nice and kind acting lady. I suspected that she too had problems at home, because she and Uncle Don yelled at each other a lot. They didn't care who heard them either.

17

However, no one said anything. Last but not least, there was Aunt Glady. Aunt Glady was a wonderful piano player. She gave lessons at her house and made a little extra money doing it. She was married to a man named Clifford who always had a cold manner about him. I was very frightened of him. You know the old saying, "Dogs and kids can tell when something is wrong with a person — they can just sense it." This was no exception.

It was my sixth birthday. School was almost out. The month of May is a strange month. The days can be cold or very warm. On this particular day it was nice and warm. My birthday celebration was held over at Aunt Gladys' house. All of the family was there. In those days I had a large family. My mother was one of four children, my father only one of two. But, I had lots of aunts, uncles, cousins, and other extended family members. I was quite happy with this party. My aunt and Uncle Cliff lived in a very pretty stone house on a nice piece of property. I remember doing lots of cartwheels and summersaults down their hill, and having a wonderful time with my cousins. This particular day was a success. The day came to an end and it was time to go home. My mother told my brother and me to go to the car. She and my father, who also attended the event, needed to talk to Aunt Glady for a minute. I had no idea of what was soon to happen.

My parents came back to the car and we drove home. My parents still weren't speaking to each other; instead they spoke at each other, and only when it was necessary. I had no idea that my parents were about to separate. Everything was kept from my brother and me. We were completely unprepared for what was about to happen the following weekend. I noticed that my mother started to go through our drawers and closets to look at our clothes. I thought that maybe she was looking at them to see if they were still good to wear. I didn't ask and she didn't offer any explanations.

The rest of the week went by as usual. I was looking forward to summer, so Amy and I could once again run and play as we had the previous year. Our relationship was a little strained because of separate schools, but summer was almost here and I thought we could pick up where we left off. I was very wrong. The weekend was almost here and my mother said to me "Do you remember how much fun you had at your birthday party?" I answered, "Yes." "Well you're going to go to Aunt Gladys' house again this weekend," she said. "Why?" I asked." "Because I want you to," she said. I knew better than to ask any more questions by the tone in her voice. I suddenly remembered what my brother had said not long ago. I felt that he was right, something was about to happen. I went to his room and walked in. He was reading one of his comic books. I told him what had just happened and what Mommy had just said. He just told me to wait and see what happens next. I'm sure that he had no idea that his life was about to change so much as well.

The weekend came. Brother and I got up and got dressed as usual. We went downstairs to have breakfast. Mommy was busy in the kitchen making us eggs. She seemed a little different, and kind of nervous. "I have something to tell both of you" she said. "I don't want you to be afraid, but I have spoken both to Aunt Glady and Grandma and Grandpa Myers. We've spoken in great detail about how much we care about you kids. Jimmy, you know how very much grandma and grandpa love you, and Carol your aunt Glady and Uncle Cliff have expressed how fond they are of you. Mommy has tried very hard to make a life with your father, but we just can't be together anymore. You both know that we fight too much, and this isn't good for anyone. I guess what I am trying to say to is Jimmy, you're going to stay at grandmas' for a while, and Carol you are going to stay at Aunt Gladys'. I have to get a lot of things straightened out." I felt myself stiffen. All of a sudden I felt very frightened. She went on to say that she would be able to take both of us to school for the remainder of the year, because the school year was almost over. We would be starting our new school in the fall. My heart sank. I looked at my brother and he looked like he was going to throw up. I knew that Mommy was right that she and Daddy were like poison to each other, but this was a change, a very big change.

We finished our breakfast. She told both of us to go back to our rooms and gather up some of our favorite toys, and come back downstairs to the living room, and wait until it was time to leave. My brother and I were silent as we did what we were told.

I still felt stiff and funny. Aunt Glady was an all right person, but to live there? How come Jimmy got to go to grandma and grandpa's house? Didn't they love me too? My brother and I didn't speak. This was going to be the last time that we lived together for a long time to come. Mommy came into the living room and told us it was time to go. We silently left the house and got into the car. I took one last look at the house. It was an ugly house that had not much yard at all. The furniture store was right next door. It actually separated the alley from our house, but to my brother and me, it was what we had come to know as home.

First we went to grandma's house where my brother was now going to live. Mommy gave us a little hint that our new living arrangements were going to be for some time, because she said that we would be starting new schools this fall. Even though my first experience of school was bad because of those darn shoes, and also being ill, I did adjust, and make some friends in school. I was feeling comfortable and now this! Only God knows what my brother was thinking. I knew that he got the better end of the deal because grandma and grandpa favored him. He looked like their side of the family, where as I looked like my fathers side. They seemed to hold that against me. I would hear my grandparents say, or I should say whisper, how much I resembled them. They would then shake their heads. I used to think how dumb, my father and his mother were good looking people, and to this day I'm glad I look like them. We stayed there for some time. We were told to go outside and play. There were kids on their street that were our age and like kids do we were able to forget our problems for a short time and enjoy ourselves.

We suddenly heard Mommy's voice. She was telling us to come back to the house because it was time to eat. I will say that this grandmother was probably one of the best cooks in the world. Everything she made was from scratch and just simply delicious. My brother and I ate heartily. Very soon after we ate it was time for Mommy to take me to Aunt Gladys' house. We said our goodbyes and we left. I looked at my mother as she drove. She was staring straight ahead and silent. It was a bad silence. I said "Mommy, I don't want to go to Aunt Gladys house to live." She just simply said that was the way it was going to be. Then I asked her how long this new living arrangement was going to be for. She didn't answer me at first, and then finally she said that she didn't quite know. I again felt my little heart sink. I thought to myself, why and how did this all happen? I knew in my heart of all hearts that my mother was always being physically hurt and yelled at by my father, and that is no way to live, but no one could make me like it or really accept it. I was going to live with Aunt Glady and creepy Uncle Cliff.

All of the relatives lived pretty close to each other; some only a few miles apart so it didn't take us long to get there. We pulled into the driveway and parked the car. I took a deep breath and got out. My aunt greeted us at the door and let us in. All of a sudden while standing in her kitchen, I grabbed a rag and wet it at the sink. I started to wash off the counters and anything else that I could see. My aunt grabbed my arm and asked, "Why are you doing that?" My mother looked at me with amazement. My thought was I don't know these people that well, so I had better show them that I could be good and helpful, so they will like me. At that point Uncle Cliff came into the kitchen and he gave me a funny look and then smirked. He and I weren't going to get along. I started to softly sob as I knew that Mommy was going to leave me here very soon, and I wouldn't see her until Monday. My mother apologized and said that it had been a long day for me and I probably should go to bed. She didn't care that I was frightened and just wanted to run. I looked up at her and had bad feelings for her that I couldn't put into words.

Up the stairs we went and walked into my new bedroom. I had to admit the room was nicely decorated and had pretty paper on the walls. It wasn't decorated for me; it was just a nice room. "See Carol," my mother said. "See how nice this room is?" It didn't make me feel any better, because now I knew that I had lost my naughty father and I was about to lose my mother too. My mother put down my suitcase and went over to the bed. She pulled the covers down and told me to get my clothes off and prepare for bed, as it was getting late. No bath tonight. I did as I was told and climbed into bed while my aunt and mother stood in the room and spoke. Uncle cliff poked his head in the doorway and again looked at me and smirked. I felt myself stiffen again. Why did this man act like that? "Look Carol," my mother said "Your bedroom is right across from Aunt Glady and Uncle Cliff's room." Was this supposed to thrill me or comfort me? How dumb. I climbed into bed feeling very lost and alone. This was a feeling that at my young age I was already familiar with.

My mother tucked me in and Aunt Glady left the room to leave the two of us alone. I looked at my mother with one last pleading look and said "Please Mommy, don't leave me here." She had lost patience with me and said in an angry voice, "I'll be back Monday morning to take you to school and once school is out, I'll see you once a week on weekends." She then shut the light and left me alone in the dark. I felt alone and abandoned. I didn't like being completely in the dark. Even at our house that we just left, Mommy always left the door open a crack, and a light on in the hallway. To this day that hasn't changed, I still sleep that way. I didn't think that I was going to be able to sleep, but the truth is I was completely exhausted, and even though I tried to stay awake to see if I could hear anything coming from downstairs, or even in the hallway outside my door, I just simply fell asleep.

———

CHAPTER 5

Morning had come. I opened my eyes and felt totally disoriented. For a minute I forgot where I was. Then reality set in. My last thought of my mother was that she was angry with me and she didn't really say goodnight. She just left in a huff. I started to feel a lump in my throat. I was about to cry again. I thought to myself, for a person who supposedly doesn't cry a lot like Maude once said, I'm really turning into a crybaby. I composed myself and decided to get up and at least get dressed. I was just putting on my shoes and in walked Aunt Glady. She said, "Well, I see you are up and about. I want you to come downstairs and have some breakfast." I wasn't really hungry yet. I think that I was still too upset about the change in my life.

Once I got downstairs she took me into the dining room and sat me down. I started to eat my cereal when all of a sudden the kitchen door opened, and in walked Uncle Cliff and their beautiful German Shepherd whose name was Ginger. I looked at the dog and immediately fell in love with her. She came over to me and licked my hand. Then I looked up at Uncle Cliff and he again had that strange smirk on his face. I don't know why, but I felt like hitting him. He suddenly walked away. Aunt Glady was standing nearby and I could see that she appeared nervous and jumpy all of a sudden. Aunt Glady almost never smiled, and she was not smiling now. She glanced into the living room where my uncle had gone and just sighed. I heard him order the dog to lie down. I went back to eating my breakfast and Aunt Glady sat down at the end of the table. She cleared her throat and said, "Carol, I have a surprise for you." I thought sarcastically, someone has a surprise for me? "There is a little girl who lives right down the road from here and she is about your age." She continued to say that she very much wanted to meet me. I suddenly felt happy. If all went well, I would have someone to play with, someone I could tell my secrets to. I became very excited and pushed my cereal down my throat like I used to do when I would get ready for a days adventure with Amy.

I finished my all too familiar breakfast and down the road we went to meet my new friend. Aunt Glady knew these people very well and they greeted us warmly. "Hi, come on in!" the lady said. We went into the house and I looked around the living room waiting to meet my new friend. In a short time out walked a little girl who was about two years older than me. We looked at each other very shyly. I'm not usually shy, but today I felt awkward. We were introduced. "Carol, this is my daughter, Peggy." We smiled at each other and then started to giggle the way little girls do. Peggy said, "Let's go outside and play." Out we went. At first we ran around her yard in circles with her dogs running at our sides. Then we went over to the chicken coop that was located at the rear of the yard. We were out of breath and happy. I thought, this is going to be a good friendship and we're going to have a lot of fun. We started to really talk and get to know each other. Peggy listened to what I had to say and she just shook her head. She said at times her parents fought too, but never anything like what I had described.

Peggy was one of three children and the youngest. I was six and she was eight years old. We became good friends right from the start. I was starting to feel happy. She and I were going to go to the same school in the fall, and we would walk there together. I felt some relief for once. Maybe I could be happy here? But, something in the back of my mind told me that Uncle Cliff was strange, and to be careful, but careful of what? I pushed the thought out of my mind and off we went to play. We ran and ran and then we went over to a swing hanging from a large tree. It was one of those tire swings and swing we did. I had a great time with my new friend.

Too soon, Aunt Glady came outside and told me it was time to go. I felt bad and wanted to stay. Peggy's mom told me not to be sad because I would be able to come back the next day after church. She also said that I could stay for dinner. I immediately thanked her and looked at Aunt Glady for her approval, she nodded and I thanked her too.

Mommy took me out for a ride that night, but we hardly spoke. There just wasn't much to say. I didn't need more vague answers to simple questions. There was a definite lack of trust that had developed between mother and daughter. I noticed that my mother was looking really good. Her clothes were pretty, actually *she* was pretty, which was good, but she seemed a million miles away. I no longer felt like I knew her. Our visit was a short one.

I thought the next day would never come. I was so excited about seeing my new friend again. I was informed by Aunt Glady that while living in their house; I had to go to Sunday school. I wasn't sure if I was going to like it or not, but had no choice. Mommy never made me go or even spoke to me about God. I was dressed in my Sunday best and off Aunt Glady and I went. The church was not like the church that Amy went to. I had once gone with her and her parents. Amy's church was very big and the man who stood up at the front of the church was dressed in a long robe. I didn't understand what he spoke about, but I felt quite comfortable sitting there. People even turned around at one point and shook your hand and wished you well. I liked her church. Anyway, this was to be my new church, my new Sunday school. Peggy went to church too, but not every Sunday.

After church was over, Aunt Glady told me that next week I would be downstairs with kids my age and I would learn about the Lord. This seemed all right to me. We were finally back home. I took off my Sunday dress and changed. I was free to play. I could hardly wait and after saying goodbye to Aunt Glady, out the door to my new friend's house I ran. I knocked on the door and Peggy came out. We were very happy to see each other. For a while we hung out in her yard and then she told me about a special place that she went to every day. We would also be going to walk that way to school when the time came. It would be good for me to learn the way. Peggy had already told her mother that we were going to go there, so we left.

What Peggy was talking about was a place called the glen. The glen had a rather large brook in it and also a road, that if followed, went out to the street that led to our school. I already liked the glen. It was hard not to. The glen was very secluded and heavily wooded with flowers scattered all about. It looked like something out of a fairytale. I immediately removed my shoes and ran over to the brook. Peggy removed hers as well. The brook had a lot of rocks, but there were areas that had hardly any. Those areas were deeper, but neither one of us felt threatened by them. We played and played. What a wonderful time! I actually forgot about my problems for a while. Finally it was time to go back to Peggy's house. We were starving. We walked in the house, and that day I met Peggy's brothers. They were older, but seemed nice. We ate our Sunday dinner, which was very good, and had dessert made out of chocolate pudding and chocolate cake.

After we finished eating, we went out to play. Suddenly, Peggy's father came out of the house and told me that Aunt Glady had called, and that it was time for me to go home. Peggy and I parted our ways and I reluctantly went home. Peggy promised me that we would see each other in a couple days. We both had to finish out the school year. I got back to the house and did my best to avoid Uncle Cliff. I didn't feel like being smirked at again. Aunt Glady told me it was time for me to take a bath. My mother would be by the next day to take me to school. She would first pick my brother up and then swing by to get me. I had funny feelings about seeing my mother again. I knew that I loved her, and of course I missed her, but she hadn't called me on the phone to see how I was doing, or to even say goodnight. I guess I was kind of mad at her. I had no feelings for my father that I was aware of. There had been no mention of when he might visit me, or if he even wanted to.

I went into the bathroom and removed my clothes. My bath was ready for me. The tub was a very old one, and not too comfortable. It seemed kind of dirty. Mommy kept our tub nice and clean. I took my bath in silence, and when I was done, Aunt Glady gave me a towel and helped me out. She then fixed my hair, but not like Mommy used to. My hair was long and blonde, but if not brushed right it was full of tangles. I started to yell, "Hey you're hurting me!" Aunt Glady seemed mad and said "If I had my way, you would have short hair." I looked at her with horror. I certainly didn't want my hair to look like hers! I immediately shut up and let her continue; as I felt it was the best thing to do. By the time I went to bed my head was sore. She pulled the covers down and told me to go to sleep. Instead, I started to cry softly. "Oh Mommy, why am I here? Why did you leave me here?"

The next morning Aunt Glady came into my room and said it was time to get up. "Your mother will be here soon. Get dressed right away and come down stairs." I jumped out of bed and did what I was told. I asked her where Uncle Cliff was and she told me that he gets up very early to go to work. She went on to say that she gets up first and comes down to make his breakfast, and now that I was here, she would get me up after he leaves and make mine. Good, I knew he'd be gone all day.

Mommy walked into the house just as I was finishing up my eggs and toast. "Hi" she said in a happy voice. I looked at her and felt a strange combination of joy and anger. "How is everything going?" she asked. Aunt Glady quickly told her that I had already made a new friend, and that things were going well. Before I could say a word my mother took my Aunt into the doorway that separates the dining room from the kitchen, and they started to speak in a whisper. I thought, gosh I hate that. I was able to see though. My mother handed my aunt what seemed like a lot of money and my aunt put it in her apron. Oh, I thought, Mommy is paying her to keep me. I got up from the table and prepared to leave for school.

My brother and I only had a couple of school weeks left. I looked at my mother as we approached the car. She had a different look about her. I thought she actually looks good. It's amazing what a couple of days away from the old man can do. She again had on pretty clothes. In the car sat my brother. He looked at me and stuck his tongue out. That was typical behavior for him. On the way to school I asked Mommy again how long would I be living at Aunt Gladys' house, and again she was very vague. My brother said nothing; it actually was a very quiet ride to school. We approached the school and finally Mommy told us to meet her out front the minute school was over. The day was uneventful. The teacher spoke of summer vacation and places she was going to visit over the summer. She went around the room and asked each one of my classmates if they knew what they were going to do over the long summer. She came to me. It was my turn and I felt very uncomfortable. I just said that I was going far away, but I wasn't sure where. I heard a few snickers but chose to ignore them. I could tell them some really wild stories. That's for sure. I'm not certain that it would be kid stories though.

Mommy was sitting outside of the school when school was over. My brother was already sitting in the car. We first went to my grandmother's house to let Jimmy off. Once there, my mother and I stayed for a little while. No one asked me how I was doing at Aunt Gladys'. There was a lot of whispering going on as usual. I was really starting to get annoyed. Suddenly it was time to go back to Aunt Gladys'. The rest of the week was boring. I asked if I could see Peggy, and aunt Glady told me that when school was over, I could see her every day. I could hardly wait. Our friendship at this point in my life was the only thing I had to look forward to.

I started to notice that at mealtime I never felt really full when I left the table, but I was afraid to ask for bigger portions or seconds. My aunt was not the best cook, but what she served was all right, and I wanted more to eat. Also, no one spoke at the table. We ate in silence. One time I started to say something and my uncle who sat at the end of the table looked up with anger on his face and stared directly at me. I looked at Aunt Glady and she put a shush finger to her mouth. I was shocked! No one was allowed to speak! After dinner aunt Glady told me that Uncle Cliff liked to eat in silence, and on Fridays he ate a huge bowl of ice cream for dinner, because in his religion he couldn't eat meat that day, and he didn't like fish. I wasn't to stare at him, and I was *not* allowed to ask for any ice cream. I thought to myself "No ice cream?" Wait until I tell Mommy on Saturday!

Mommy came to pick me up Saturday evening at around five. I had waited all day for her, but was told that she went to see my brother first. I was really hungry when she arrived and when she asked me what I wanted to do, I said, I don't want to go and see grandma, I said, "Let's get something to eat." Off to the diner we went. I ordered spaghetti and meatballs, my favorite food. After eating that, I ordered an ice cream sundae! My mother looked at me with amazement. "How can you eat so much?" she asked "Mommy, I'm really hungry," I replied. I was afraid to tell her that I was being underfed. Mommy was acting differently towards me. She was acting distant. She only asked me a little about my new friend, and didn't seem to care. On the way home I suddenly felt sick to my stomach. I knew that I was going to throw up. I yelled, "Pull over Mommy I'm going to be sick." Sure enough, that's what happened. My mother seemed annoyed with me. "Why did you eat so much?" she asked. I felt like screaming at her. Why couldn't she see that even though I had a new friend that I like very much, Aunt Glady is cold acting, Uncle Cliff is weird, and I am *not* happy! We got back to the house and my mother told Aunt Glady that I was sick, so to bed I went. Mommy tucked me in and said she would see me next week on Monday to take me to school. She reminded me that school was almost over, and she was making plans for my new school in the fall. She promised me again that she would continue to pick me up on Saturday evenings, and we would spend a little time together. My mother then gave me a peck on the cheek and left.

The next day I got to see Peggy. It was Sunday, and again I was over their house for dinner. At Peggy's house everyone was happy, and at the dinner table they ate heartily and joked around. Boy, I wish I could live here. The house was actually too small and not big enough for them. The brothers had to share a bedroom, and Peggy's room was pretty small, but at least she had privacy. Nonetheless, everyone got along well. Peggy's house truly became my home away from home. It also became my safe place. This routine remained the same until the very end of school.

I saw Mommy on Saturdays, and continued to over eat and get sick to my stomach most of the time on the way home. What was she thinking? Why didn't she get it? She and I had very little to talk about when we were together. I once asked her if we could go over to Grandma Myers house to eat, instead of going to the diner. She said that maybe we could. I didn't really miss my brother. We were just too far apart in age, and he was my grandparents' favorite. I guess that I was just curious. I was sure that he didn't miss me either. I had to wonder who he had to tease now. When we lived in Westwood my brother made it his business to tease me all of the time. Sometimes he would hold me down and tickle me until I almost went pee in my pants. This was not horseplay, because he had an angry look on his face. I think my brother secretly despised me because he wanted to be the only child.

———

CHAPTER 6

It finally happened, school was out. It was over in the middle of the week, and this meant more time to play with Peggy. We were both very happy about that. My Aunt started to do something very strange in the mornings. She would come into my room and get out of her nightgown and put her housedress on. This seemed odd to me because this was something new. One day she caught me watching her and she gave me a dirty look. After that she used her own room, which made me feel better. I mean who needs to see that? I felt funny about going downstairs to breakfast because I didn't know what she was going to say. She said nothing and acted as though nothing had happened. I was really getting tired of the same old food. I was going to have either one hard-boiled egg with toast or a bowl of hot cereal with toast. No pancakes in this house or scrambled eggs. On that particular day, I asked if I could have two pieces of toast with jelly on it. She seemed shocked and gave me one egg and 2 pieces of toast. At least today my tummy felt better. I had enough to eat for once. Peggy and I spent most of our time in the glen. We had a blast. Sometimes other kids would show up and we would all play together. We stayed in the glen until lunch time, which for me was usually peanut butter and jelly. Then we would meet again after we each had our lunch, and play again until around five. Peggy's older brother would come to the glen and tell us tomorrow is another day. I hated going home, but I knew I had to.

One morning something happened that would change my life forever. My aunt got out of bed as usual to go down and fix Uncle Cliff's breakfast. Instead of my uncle going downstairs, he came into my room with only his underwear on! I looked at him and I felt myself freeze. He had that weird smirk on his face again as he came towards my bed. To my amazement he climbed in and lay next to me. "Oh no!" I thought. Suddenly, he turned and faced me and started to feel my body all over with his hands. He whispered in my ear, "Someday you're going to like this." Then after feeling my little body all over, he jumped out of bed and stood looking down at me. He had an ugly look on his face and said, "If you tell anyone about this, I *will kill* you! Do you hear me?" I could hardly breath I was so scared. I did manage to nod. I lay in my bed feeling stiff and I couldn't think at first. What my uncle had just done I knew wasn't right, and yet I didn't know what to do. Should I have screamed? Would that have been the right thing to do? I lay there thinking of all the dirty things he said to me, and also of his threat. I didn't feel close enough to Aunt Glady to tell her. Actually, I didn't feel close enough to anyone. My friend Peggy and I are close, but is this the type of thing you share? What if she told her mother? I completely believed my uncle when he said he would kill me if I told. This is something I'm going to have to keep to myself. I got out of bed and crept into the hallway. I wanted my uncle to get out of the house. It wasn't quite time for Aunt Glady to call me for breakfast, but I knew that I wasn't going to have an appetite today. I felt sick to my stomach. Like clockwork Aunt Glady yelled up the stairway a few minutes later, and told me to get dressed. Aunt Glady had a schedule for everything. You could almost set the clock by it. I suppose that was good because I knew what to expect from her, no surprises. I went downstairs and sat at the table. Aunt Glady had made cereal and toast for me. I just stared at the food and said nothing. She noticed that I wasn't eating and she asked me what was wrong. I told her that I didn't feel well, that my stomach hurt. She took the food away and said that maybe I should stay inside today instead of playing with Peggy. A part of me wanted to just get up and run, and yet another part of me just wanted to hide. I chose to go up to my room. I knew that I was safe until my uncle came home. Peggy came by and Aunt Glady told her that I wasn't feeling well, and that she was sure that I would be better tomorrow. For the rest of the day I stayed in my room and drew pictures. I just wanted to be very quiet. How can I look at my uncle again? And what did he mean when he said that someday I would like what he did? Aunt Glady checked on me from time to time to see if I was all right.

The day went too quickly for me. I knew that any minute that scary man was going to walk into the house like he did every day. Was he going to look at me differently? I felt my stomach start to knot up as he walked into the house. I walked quietly into the hallway to see if I could hear them talking. I could hear fragments of sentences. I heard my aunt mention my name, and I knew she told him that I stayed in all day because I wasn't well. I couldn't hear what he was saying. Suddenly I heard my aunt call me down for dinner. I went down the steps and entered the dining room. I looked at Uncle Cliff with fear in my heart. He said nothing but gave me his usual smirk. He had me where he wanted me. I silently ate my dinner. I wasn't allowed to speak anyway, and for once it didn't matter. I managed to eat.

After dinner the three of us went into the living room to watch TV. I don't know what I was watching because I felt like my uncle was looking at me. I was afraid to ask to go to my room early because maybe he would come upstairs again, and I didn't want to draw attention to myself. I again felt like hiding. I sat on the floor next to Ginger. I felt safe next to Ginger.

That night I couldn't sleep because I had missed a couple of meals. I was actually very hungry. My aunt and uncle were fast asleep and I could hear both of them snoring. There was no such thing as snacks in this house, and I was told never to go to the fridge by myself. I was feeling really hungry, and yet I was afraid to go against their rules. My tummy was growling I was so hungry. I thought what could I eat? I crept out into the hallway and slowly went downstairs. Ginger was in the kitchen. She wagged her tail when she saw me, and I bent down and hugged her. I thought maybe she would like a milk bone. I got one out of the cupboard for her, and looked at all the bottles of coke that were there. I was so hungry so I opened up a bottle of coke, and took out two milk bones, one for Ginger and one for me. Well, I thought as I chewed it down, I'm no longer hungry. I looked at the clock and got a shock, it was after three in the morning. I went quietly up the stairs to my room and got back into bed. I thought could dog bones hurt people? What are they made of? Ginger sure liked them. I managed to fall into a restless sleep. I had horrifying dreams that woke me up. I wished my mother was here. I felt so strange and alone. I thought is uncle going to come into my room again? I'm very frightened, this I knew. Is he going to feel me all over again and say threatening things? I felt very creepy and dirty. I think I felt ashamed. I started to cry quietly as I lay alone in the dark. I had a window in my room and I looked out the window. I would close my eyes and then open them again. It wasn't long before the sky was no longer dark, and I remember as I lay there looking at the sky from my bed, I could hear the birds chirping. It was the beginning of a new day, but I didn't feel joy.

Peggy was standing at the foot of my bed. She said to me, "Hey sleepy head are you going to sleep all day?" I looked at her with shock. I had gone back to sleep. I should say I *went* to sleep. I jumped out of bed and felt a feeling of happiness to see my friend standing there. Uncle Cliff hadn't come into my room early this morning. I thought maybe he has decided to leave me alone. I got out of bed and got dressed feeling much better. Peggy always had a way of making me feel good. She was a good friend who was a little older than me, and she had a way of making me feel like everything was going to be all right. But, I still couldn't share my dirty secret with her. Anyway, it might be dangerous. I hurried up and ate some toast and juice and out we went. We went directly to the glen. Once we were in the glen, I forgot about my problems and we had a great day. There was another young girl who lived by me. Her name was Sandy. She was a little older than both of us. Sandy was nice, but she had a way about her that Peggy and I didn't like. She thought that she was better than us; we could tell by the way she acted and treated us. But even so we all had a great time that particular day. It's a great place to forget all problems. Peggy and I could spend all of our time in the glen and never get bored. The only time that wasn't possible was if there were storms. We would then play at her house, or in the beautiful sunroom that was off of our living room. I preferred her house though. We could be a little loud without getting into trouble. Aunt Glady was so structured and boring. She was nothing more to me than a baby sitter.

My mother continued to visit on Saturdays for a short amount of time. I continued to eat too much at the diner and at times get sick. It really amazed me that she didn't figure out that there has to be something wrong. To top it off, my pretty golden hair started to turn brown, and my eyes went from blue to green! I was shocked and asked my mother why this happened. She had no answer and agreed that no one in the family had green eyes. The relationship between my mother and I was very strained. We never really had much to say. She mentioned that my brother was doing well, and sometimes we would go over to Grandma Myers house. He did seem very happy. I bet he was being treated like a prince, I thought with sadness. I didn't wish poor treatment on my brother, but I knew in my heart that he always had good days and lots of attention. I also know that he saw my cousins a lot more than I did. Because I looked like the other side of the family, I was the black sheep. I was left out of a lot of good times at grandma's house because when I did see my cousins, I could tell by their conversations that I had missed their birthday parties and my brother had not.

It was Monday morning. A new week was starting. Of course to Peggy and me every day was a holiday. We had our usual day planned, and were looking forward to starting a new week of fun and games. Suddenly, I heard my doorknob turn. What time is it? I was still very sleepy and not sure. In walked Uncle Cliff! Oh no, here he is! I sat up quickly and looked at him with horror in my heart. He gave me a threatening look that made me want to scream. He approached my bed and pushed me back down. "Here we go again I thought, "What should I do?" I felt myself start to stiffen because I knew what was about to happen. He climbed in bed with me and again he started to rub me all over. I wanted to cry and yell and hit him, but instead I just laid there totally stiff. I couldn't move a muscle. I felt like there was nothing that I could do. He would touch me in my private places and make funny noises. He said nothing this time, he just made noises. Suddenly he jumped out of bed and started to leave the room, but not without looking at me with a look of anger on his face. I guess this was to remind me to keep my mouth shut. I thought that I was going to throw up. I just lay in bed holding my stomach and I curled up into a ball, and didn't move until Aunt Glady called me. I knew that uncle was gone by this time. I didn't know if I could go downstairs and look at her. I just wanted to go over to her and scream at her and say, "Don't you know what's going on? Don't you know that uncle is rubbing me in funny places and making strange noises?" In my heart I was sure that she didn't have the faintest idea, but that didn't make me feel better. I felt like asking her why she fed me so little. Didn't she understand anything at all? Ginger and I ate dog bones together on quite a few occasions. When I did have the nerve to ask her for more food, she would sigh and say that there wasn't much to eat. I knew better. I do have eyes and believe me I knew that I was pretty thin. What was wrong with everyone? I already didn't have much respect for the adults in my life that I was supposed to look up to. Then again, why should I?

CHAPTER 7

Early one morning I heard a loud bumping noise and then a moan. I was very sleepy and I thought that maybe I had dreamed it. Then I heard the moaning sound again. I was pretty scared, but didn't feel like getting out of bed to investigate it. What could it be? Suddenly I heard Aunt Gladys' voice. She was making strange whimpering noises. Finally I heard her call to me. "Carol help me!" she pleaded. She sounded like she was in a lot of pain. In my heart I knew what had happened, she had fallen down the stairs and she is begging me for help. I laid there and didn't move. I thought to myself, "If this is bad, maybe Mommy will take me back and we can live together again." My anger towards my mother was because I felt deserted, this could bring us back together again, and then I wouldn't have to be touched by scary Uncle Cliff. She would have to take me back wouldn't she? As I lay there and pondered this thought, I heard my Aunt continue to cry and ask for my help. I sighed and got out of bed. I knew that I had to do the right thing, and that was of course to help her. I walked to the head of the stairs and looked down. There she lay in a crumpled heap. I was so shocked at how old and frail she looked. Suddenly I felt ashamed that I took so long to get out of bed and I apologized. She said "It's alright," but I had to go and get help. She knew that Peggy's mother wasn't home right now, and told me to go to the neighbor's house right at the end of our driveway across the street. She said that the ladies name was Rose, and that she was very nice and she would help us.

I immediately ran over to her house and in a very excited voice told her what had happened. We both ran back to the house and looked at Aunt Glady. "Oh my God!" she exclaimed. "I think this is very bad Glady, I'm going to call for an ambulance. You have to go to the hospital." That's exactly what happened. My aunt moaned and told Rose that I was in her care and that my mother had to be called at work. I hate to say this, but I felt a little sense of joy. I thought no more being hungry and no more Uncle Cliff! My mother was called and arrived soon afterwards. I stayed with the nice lady called Rose until she arrived. My Aunt was taken away to the hospital, and my mother and Rose started to talk. My mother explained that I lived with my Aunt Glady because she was in the process of getting a divorce from my father. The lady looked startled and said she understood. In those days getting a divorce was hardly heard of. It was frowned upon. People always thought that marriages should be worked out and not gotten rid of. I never really held it against my mother because I was a kid who saw too much. I didn't hide under the covers and hope for the best.

After the lady spoke to my mother for some time, it was agreed upon that she would care for me until my aunt was better. Rose had a large house with plenty of bedrooms. She actually lived alone at this point in her life. Her husband had died and her children were grown. This lady could use the extra money and the company. "There, we're all settled!" my mother said with satisfaction. I was crushed. What I thought was going to happen just simply didn't. My mother looked at me and said that I could still play with Peggy all day, but Rose was going to take care of me for a while, and that I should be a good girl and behave. My mother and I walked over to Aunt Gladys' house to retrieve a lot of my clothing, and she promised that she would be back this weekend. Well, I thought, at least I will be away from creepy Uncle Cliff for a while, so that made me feel a little better.

My aunt had not broken any bones or anything as it turned out. However, the hospital kept her for a couple of days. When they released her, they put a back brace on her, and she was ordered not to do any lifting or any other kind of work around the house for at least two weeks. She was to stay quiet and rest. I actually felt relieved that she wasn't hurt more, even though I thought it would help my cause if she was. I knew that she had no idea what uncle was doing to me.

Rose was a nice person, but she was distant acting. To her this was a job and that was all, I could tell. I ate well during those weeks and was kept clean. I had to take a bath every night at her house instead of once a week at Aunt Gladys. I didn't see my uncle at all during that time, and felt very much relieved. Rose offered me a place to live and very little chit-chat. Every day I played with Peggy as usual, but I had to be back a little earlier than before. I could live with that. Rose also advised me that my hair which was turning browner all the time really did need to be trimmed or cut. She explained it in such a way that I understood and I allowed her to cut my hair. She did a good job. I wasn't disappointed. I was sorry that my hair had turned darker and my eyes changed as well. I told Rose about this and she simply said that happens at times, but she was a little surprised that my eyes turned green from blue. I felt cleaner and better after she was done. I thanked her. Everything was so polite and crisp between us, but I knew that I was in good hands. I didn't go to visit Aunt Glady at the house because she needed her rest. Quite frankly, I was relieved to hear that I shouldn't visit her because I really didn't want to, and I was away from uncle.

The weeks went by. Mommy came on the weekends as usual. She liked my new haircut and took me to the store one evening to buy me some new clothes. Some of the clothes were for the rest of the summer, and other clothes were for the fall. Summer goes by so quickly, and soon I would be starting a new school. I was scared about starting a new school again, but knew that I had no one to talk to about this either. I had come to accept the fact that this was the way I had to live for now and prayed that it wouldn't be forever. I knew that things were just not going to change, at least not for a long time. I knew that I would soon be back at Aunt Gladys' house, and by now I knew that things wouldn't change there either.

I was right, and sooner came too quickly, because it was time to go back to Aunt Gladys' house that evening. Aunt Glady liked my shorter hair of course! But she probably would have liked it better still if it was even shorter. Uncle Cliff had his usual smirk but made no comment and that was fine with me. The only one I missed there was Ginger. I knew that Ginger was true to her master and wouldn't help me, but she still gave me comfort. I looked around the house that I came to hate so much, and just sighed with resignation. I looked at my clothes and decided to take them up to my room, and as I walked past Uncle Cliff I could have sworn that I heard him snicker at me. I wonder what would happen to me if I found a way to poison him. Would I go to jail if I told everyone how he was touching me? Would anyone care?

It didn't take long for uncle to start in again. I thought, what did he do without me? He came in my room two days after I had returned. Aunt Glady was able to move around by now; she just didn't do as much housework. She did however get up and make the monster his breakfast every morning, so in he came. I just lay still, made no sounds and took whatever he dished out to me. He always felt me all over and said strange things in my ear. On one day in particular he told me that my breasts were getting bigger, and I would love to have them felt when I got older. He then left the room. I always felt like I was going to vomit afterward, and he always remembered to say something threatening to keep me in line. It worked, but I knew that some day under the right circumstances, I would tell on him. I would actually plot and plan how this would come to be. I believe it was one of the things that help keep me sane.

———

CHAPTER 8

School was going to start in a few days. I was very upset. I was at least happy to have Peggy to walk with, but she was two years older than I, and we wouldn't be in the same grade. Peggy hadn't moved around to different towns and only went to one other school. Mommy had made all of the arrangements and I was the new kid on the block. I wasn't happy. Peggy was getting all of her new clothes together and while we played in her room she proudly displayed them. She asked me what I had gotten. I had only about half of what she had, and believe me that wasn't enough. I didn't have any pencils either and no notebook. If we were back in the old house, my friend Amy and I would have taken a walk to the stationary store, and I would have plenty, I mused. I told Peggy that I needed paper and pencils and like the good friend that she was, she gave me a small notebook and two pencils. She also found an old pencil box from the year before which she gave me. I felt a little better. A little more prepared.

I went back home and decided to go to my room until supper. I didn't feel like looking at either of my keepers. They both made me sick, each in their own way. I looked at the three new dresses that I had and thought I guess that I can wear each one twice a week. I did have two pair of shoes, and they fit. Yea! I was truly thankful for that. Mommy had gotten me one cardigan sweater to start with, and she did mention that she would get me another one soon. Every time I saw her she had on a new outfit, so this meager pile of clothes did *not* impress me. I also needed some more socks. I had a few pair but they were not new. I went downstairs and asked Aunt Glady if I could call my mother on the phone and she asked me why. I told her that I know that Mommy is very busy working so that she can buy her divorce, but school was going to start and I felt that I needed socks, another sweater, and maybe another new dress. She looked at me like I was from Mars, and Uncle Cliff who was sitting near by laughed out loud. "Your mother doesn't want to be bothered unless there's an emergency," my aunt said, "And you missy, do *not* decide what you need in clothing." I felt foolish, I mean how dumb could I be? I was angry, very angry and I didn't think that my requests were out of line. I stomped back to my room and slammed the door. I thought the next time I see my mother I am going to scream at her until I turn red as a beet.

It was Tuesday night and the next day was school. Peggy and I only saw each other once over the weekend, and we had made plans to meet at the end of my driveway, so we could walk together to school through the glen. Aunt Glady told me to go take a bath and to prepare for school the next day. Will wonders never cease! I was allowed to take a bath! A whole week had not gone by! I think playing in the glen helped me look as clean as I did. I knew that it was not really clean water. I wondered at times if I smelled. I thought that maybe Peggy was too polite to say anything. I listened, and after I took my bath my mother called on the phone. I was all excited. Mommy called and she wanted to speak to me! I ran to the phone and said, "Hi Mommy!" she said hi back. She had called to wish me well for the next day, and she explained that a teacher would be waiting at the front door for me because I was new and not to be afraid. I said okay, and then I told her that I needed more clothes for school and socks too. She agreed and said she would buy me more that weekend. I felt so happy. Mommy was thinking of me and she called to wish me well! We said good night and I hung up. I turned and looked smugly at both my aunt and uncle and went to bed. Not a word was spoken, if anything my uncle had a nasty look on his face. We didn't make eye contact.

The morning had come and I admit that I was a little excited and thankful that a teacher would be waiting to greet me. I had laid out the dress that I chose to wear for day one. It was a cool September morning. I could tell because I felt the window in my room, and it felt cool, so that meant that I needed a sweater too. My Aunt was calling to me to come down and eat before I had to meet Peggy. My cereal was waiting for me and Aunt Glady had made me some hot chocolate too. That was a treat and I thanked her for it. She actually gave me two cups. To me things were looking up. I was given hot chocolate and Mommy promised me more new clothes. Now if only the monster would leave me alone, I could possibly get a little happier until this mess in my life cleared up.

Peggy and I met as planned and we left. The road in the glen was a rather long winding road. There was only one house on this road. The lady who lived there had a nice house, and a big fenced in yard, because she had three large nasty looking guard dogs. As Peggy and I approached her house, we were suddenly greeted by them – all three of them. We screamed and ran as fast as we could. I fell down and scraped my knee. Peggy helped me up and we continued to run. I wasn't able to run as fast as she could because I hurt myself. I heard the lady yelling at her dogs, but it was too late, one had jumped over the fence and was chasing us. "Oh My God!" I screamed. We had never been so far in the glen before. Peggy had just told me that when the time came she would show me the way to school. I turned around as I ran for my life, and not far behind was this ugly black dog that was trying to attack me. Now I was really screaming. I thought, "Now I'm dead, like the bird that just died for no reason in Aunt Gladys house." Lucky for Peggy and me the lady caught the dog at the last moment, as he was getting ready to charge. We were very grateful, but the damage was already done. We both looked like rag dolls. I looked worse because I now had blood on my sock. What do we do? Should we go home or go the rest of the way to school? We chose to go to school, but as far as I was concerned our first day was ruined.

I found the teacher waiting for me at the door and she looked at me with a look of shock on her face. I was dirty from falling, and my knee had bled enough so the blood had run down onto my sock. What a mess. She was very nice and took me to the girls' room and cleaned me up. She asked me what happened and I told her. She wanted to call my mother to discuss with her the need to get in touch with that lady who owned dangerous dogs, so this wouldn't happen again. I had to tell her that I didn't live with my mother; instead I lived with an Aunt and Uncle. She looked at me sadly and said she was sure that when my mother had registered me, she must have given some information. Luckily there was a telephone number and she was called. The problem of the dogs was taken care of immediately. My mother left work early, and she and Aunt Glady went to the lady's house and complained. She was told that Peggy and I would be walking through the glen five days a week all year long, and that this had better not happen again. The lady was not very nice, but agreed that she would keep the dogs in during the times we'd be walking through. The problem was solved. Mommy waited for me to get home from school and we had a pleasant visit. As Mommy was getting ready to leave, Aunt Glady took her aside and again I saw Mommy give her a lot of money. I heard my mother raise her voice a little, but I couldn't understand what was being said. She yelled goodbye to me and left. I felt strange. Maybe I was a burden to everyone. Mommy had to pay a lot of money for me to stay in this house of horrors.

Saturday had come. Peggy and I still went to the glen. The days were pleasantly warm enough, and the water that we waded in was not yet cold. After Peggy and I parted our ways for the day, I was told that Mommy had called and she wasn't going to make it this week. I was so hurt I felt like screaming. How could Mommy do this? I asked if she was sick. Aunt Glady said no, that something had come up and she would see me next week. A whole week is a long time for a little girl who is being abused, and who desperately needs to see her mother. I just wanted to run away, but where would I go? I needed to see my mother and have her reassure me that she still wanted me. Is she going to desert me like Daddy did? He ran away. No one seems to know where he is. Of course when I calmed down I knew that my father was not a person that I should really be missing, I really did feel that way. But it would have been nice to have a daddy who cared about me.

All of a sudden I heard a car pull up, and I thought that Mommy is here after all. Mommy was not here; instead it was my grandmother on my fathers' side, and Aunt Priscilla, and Uncle Jack who was my fathers' brother. We had company and I was happy to see my family again. It had been a long time and we were going to have a good night. These people were truly a lot of fun. I watched as they came into the house and actually forgot about Mommy not coming. When my grandmother walked in she immediately called for me to come and see her. I left the living room window and ran to her to get a big hug. I was never disappointed by her. She always gave me lots of hugs and kisses. My grandmother then looked at me and frowned. "Glady," she said, "I think Carol is a little too thin." Aunt Glady immediately said, "Oh she is a finicky eater." I thought to myself, "No I'm not! What a liar! Mommy pays her a lot of money for me to live here. I'm sure there is plenty of money for my food. Mommy also buys my clothing so what is she talking about?" As they were talking, Aunt Glady brought out a loaf of rye bread that she had gotten from the bakery, and two boxes of soft cheese. She also brought out several bottles of beer. It was sort of a family ritual to eat bread and cheese, and to drink beer when this part of the family gathered. I was always delighted when the joyful trio would show up. Also, I knew that grandma and Aunt Priscilla would encourage me to eat with them. They would have beer, and I would drink coke. I would go to bed happy for once filled up with cheese sandwiches and soda.

I sat around the table and listened to their wild stories of what this one did and that one said. They did a lot of laughing, and this side of the family didn't seem to mind my presence at the table. The more they drank the wilder the stories became. I was very amused and probably shouldn't have heard half of what was being said, but no one cared. Uncle Cliff stayed in by the television most of the time. He was more of a loner. The only time I saw him come to life was when a girl named Pugsly (obviously a knick name) came to visit. Then my uncle would follow her around like a puppy dog.

He all but drooled on her. She seemed to like the attention. That made me sick. Pugsly was in her twenties and kind of nice looking. She was a member of his family, a niece. I had to wonder if he ever touched her the way he touched me. She didn't seem afraid of him, or repelled by him like I did, so my guess was no.

The stories continued and it was getting very late. I felt myself needing to go to bed. Aunt Glady saw me starting to open and close my eyes while sitting at the table, and yelled into the next room for my uncle to take me up and put me to bed. Whoa, that woke me up. I cried out, "No! I can go by myself!" I looked at everyone at the table and noticed a strange look come across my Aunt's face. I lowered my eyes because I didn't want her to see that I was frightened or she would get suspicious. For some reason I felt ashamed, like I was the guilty one. I yelled "Goodnight everyone!" and upstairs I ran. I quickly got my clothes off and put my pajamas on and got under the covers. I thought how stupid of me. I knew that I acted strangely, I didn't even say goodbye to my grandmother, which upset me. I lay in bed and listened to see if anyone was going to come up the steps, but no one did and I fell asleep.

Sunday morning! To Sunday school I went, and Aunt Glady was upstairs in church learning how to be a good person. She used to tell me that my going to Sunday school would make me good, and people who went to church like she did were already good. I asked why Uncle Cliff didn't go to church and she just looked at me and told me to mind my business. She went on to say that Uncle Cliff worked very hard and made life easy for all of us by making a good living. So this made him a good person. I thought she sure has her hand out when Mommy comes around, and if she knew what he did to me when she goes down to fix his breakfast, would she still think that he was a good man? I wasn't a dumb kid. I had a lot of savvy. But I still had to figure out a way to tell on Uncle without getting killed. I had to be very careful.

Sunday came and went. Peggy and I went to school on Monday morning, and the dogs were nowhere to be seen. We hung out together for a while after school, and Peggy was telling me about her experiences. Neither one of us liked school that much, but she did say she had made a couple of new friends. I admit I felt a little threatened. One of my biggest fears outside of Uncle Cliff would be to lose Peggy to another friend. That would make my life completely unbearable. I would have no one. She asked me how I was doing in school and if I had managed to make any new friends. I hung my head and said no. The truth is that I was slowly becoming one of the kids that other kids picked on. A lot of times I think I looked dirty. I'm sure that I could have used more baths and no one really kept up with my hair. In my little girl way I tried to comb my hair, but my hair had a mind of its own, and my dresses needed to be ironed better. I guess Aunt Glady just didn't know how to iron or maybe she just didn't care. I think Peggy could sense my sadness, and she told me that she would always be my friend, and that I shouldn't worry. I felt better, but also a little ashamed that I was so needy. Peggy was a little older than me and certainly we both should be allowed to have other friends. We couldn't see each other as much during the week, but Saturdays and Sundays we did see each other for a few hours each day. I still was invited at times on Sunday for dinner. Peggy's' mother always marveled at how much I could eat and still stay so skinny. Little did they know that I was half starved all week! That's why they saw me eat so much.

CHAPTER 9

Tuesday morning Uncle Cliff came back into my room again. Aunt Glady had gone downstairs as usual to make the monsters breakfast and in he came. He climbed in bed with me, and this time he started out with a warning. "So you thought you were real smart the other night when your family was here, did you? If you ever act like that again when people are around, like you are afraid of me, I will give you something to be afraid of." I lay there frozen with fear. Then all of a sudden he reached over and pinched my left nipple. That hurt me badly and I jumped and made a little sound. He put his hand over my mouth and glared at me. I wanted to pee my pants I was so afraid. He then jumped out of my bed and left the room. I lay there crying and wondered why I had to go through this. What did I do to deserve this poor treatment?

Aunt Glady yelled up the stairs some time later and told me to get dressed for school. I slowly got out of bed and prepared for my day to begin. The truth of the matter was I wasn't looking forward to school either. I was starting to realize that I was having trouble concentrating. My thoughts were on my life and my fears. I was even more afraid of uncle now that he had pinched my nipple so hard. I wondered what he might do next. I had many visions of him torturing me in other ways. It was really starting to affect my life and school. There were many times I wouldn't hear what the teacher was saying. She would call on me and I would either have no answer or give the wrong one. The kids would laugh at me and they now had started to call me grease-ball. My hair had darkened a lot, and I guess because I didn't have enough baths, my hair was pretty bad and was probably greasy looking. The teacher that I had for most of the day was not the same teacher who had met me the first day of school. This one was not as nice. She made no attempts to stop the teasing that I was getting, so needless to say, school was not on my list of favorite things to do.

The school year was going by, Halloween came and went. Peggy and I had dressed as witches. We made out pretty well. Of course Aunt Glady rationed my candy because she said it was bad for my teeth. I was sorry that I hadn't eaten more before I got back home. Thanksgiving was right around the corner, and Uncle Cliff had left me alone for a while. I thought maybe he was afraid he had gone too far last time. Maybe he was waiting to see if I would get the nerve to tell on him. I didn't know, but I was getting too comfortable, because early one Thursday morning in he came again. This time he climbed in my bed and immediately started to feel me all over, only this time he went a little further. He took my hand and put it down by his privates. I felt this long hard thing and pulled my hand away. He took my hand roughly and put it back in place and told me to rub up and down. I again felt myself stiffen and I started to cry. He jumped out of my bed and glared at me, and in a loud whisper said, "Shut-up!" I put my hand over my mouth and he smirked at me and left the room. I didn't go to school that day, I instead told Aunt Glady that I didn't feel well at all. She looked at me and admitted that I looked sick. She called Peggy's house and told her not to bother to come by that day as I was not well. I didn't care if she told Uncle Cliff this time that I had stayed home, and I didn't care what he might say or do to me. I was starting to get a numb feeling that went all over me. I picked up my dolly and started to talk to her. I told her all of my problems and she told me not to worry, that soon something good would happen. Then I picked up my Teddy, and the Teddy told me the same thing. Aunt Glady walked in the room and asked me who I was talking to and I told her, my dolly and Teddy. She shook her head and said they don't really talk to you, but you can hug them. After she left the room, I told my dolly and Teddy what I really thought about her, and they agreed. Talking to my make believe friends became a habit. I found it gave me comfort. I told them everything. We were not having little tea parties. I just had too much to deal with, and I had to express my feelings and fears to someone, or in this case, something. They became real to me. I needed to talk to them to help me cope with life.

Thanksgiving came and went. I had dinner over at Grandma Myers house. Everyone from my mothers' side was there. I saw my cousins whom I hadn't seen since my birthday party. It was quite a gathering. I ate really well that day and played with my cousins. I saw my brother for the first time in months, and he looked at me and remarked that I didn't look too good. I knew that he was right. No one else said anything. After a wonderful dinner and dessert we kids were ordered to go into the other room, it was adult time. Of course this meant they wanted to talk or I should say whisper loudly. At times we kids would go to the kitchen door, which was closed and try to eavesdrop. Sometimes we could hear partial sentences. One time I heard my name mentioned, but couldn't make out what they were saying about me. Too soon it was time to go back. In the car I asked my mother again how long I would be at Aunt Gladys, she just sighed and said, it would be for a while yet and not to ask again because she was doing the best that she could. She did promise that some day she would come and pick me and my brother up for good, and we would live together again. I relished that thought and said a silent prayer that it would happen soon. I had had enough.

Peggy and I had off from school for a couple of days. The big holiday vacation was Christmas. We saw each other at her house and played and had a lot of fun. On Saturday my mother came by to visit. She didn't take me out this time. She had gotten a call right before Thanksgiving from one of the teachers at my school. She would have told us sooner but she didn't want to spoil Thanksgiving. Apparently, I was doing poorly in school. My mother asked me if there was anything wrong. Uncle Cliff was sitting in his chair in the living room and he rose up and came into the dining room where my mother and Aunt Glady and I were sitting. I felt myself freeze. I looked up at him and he had no expression that I could read on his face. He appeared expressionless. I looked down at the table and said that everything was fine, but I admitted that I was having trouble concentrating on my work. She accepted that answer, and said that in time things would be different. She knew I was troubled by all that had happened with the separation and the divorce to be. She asked Aunt Glady if she would mind helping me with my math. That seemed to be the biggest problem. Mommy then got up to leave, and of course the usual money was given for my care. Uncle Cliff went back to the living room and sat down. I swear I heard him chuckle. However, Mommy came back into the house and she was holding a bag. "I almost forgot," she said, "I bought you another new dress and a jacket for school, come try the jacket on." Mommy had kept her promise to me. I really needed two dresses but one was better than none, and it was now cold in the mornings as Peggy and I walked through the road to school. I was very thankful. The jacket fit well and she had bought me new socks too. The kids in school were making fun of me because I didn't have what I needed, so I could go to school on Monday looking better. I thanked her very much and gave her a quick kiss on the cheek. She smiled and got up and left. Neither Aunt Glady nor Uncle Cliff made any comment. I looked at Uncle Cliff and he looked annoyed.

I went to my room and told my Teddy and dolly all about it. I think that my aunt and uncle resented when my mother would buy me things. Maybe they thought that meant less money for them. I sighed, it was only clothing. Aunt Glady could sew well, why didn't she make me a dress, but of course how foolish of me, that would be a nice thing to do. She also played the piano very well, and lately she thought that she might give me lessons. I wasn't sure that I really wanted to do that. I didn't like the piano that much. However, I would try. I was really pretty bored because the weather was getting really bad out and Peggy and I could not see each other as much as we did all summer long and early fall.

One day after school I had lesson number one. I was shocked at how quickly I learned the different notes, and I looked forward to the next lesson. After school days, Aunt Glady and I would go to the piano and I learned more. All of a sudden I was playing real songs. I appreciated that she took the time to teach me, and felt proud of myself that I was able to play piano songs, and I don't mean chop sticks. My aunt was very stern and didn't make learning fun, but secretly I knew that I was doing well and had learned something new. Uncle made no comment except that Aunt Glady should spend her time giving piano lessons for money. After all she wasn't getting paid to teach me. That weekend I showed Mommy and she was very pleased. We went out to eat and I didn't eat quite as much, so I didn't get sick. I had a good weekend with Mommy showing her how I learned to play the piano. I was invited over for Sunday dinner at Peggy's, so that topped off the weekend. I wish every day could be like the days at Peggy's house. Their home was always filled with laughter. It always appeared to be so normal there. It reminded me somewhat of Amy's house.

———

CHAPTER 10

I was having a really hard time in school. I just couldn't concentrate. I didn't like my teacher and the kids were not nice. At lunchtime I ate alone. My lunch was always the same. I either had a bologna sandwich and a couple of graham crackers, or peanut butter and jelly also with a couple of graham crackers. I was allowed to buy milk, but I never had money for ice cream like the other kids did. One day I was looking at a little girl eating a Dixie cup of strawberry ice cream. I felt very envious of her. I was sitting alone as usual and I wanted that ice cream. She caught me watching her and she started to laugh, "Poor Carol, no one to sit with and no ice cream, isn't that a shame?" Everyone at her table laughed. I felt my face start to burn and instead of crying or getting up and running away; I went over and pulled her hair as hard as I could. It was pretty long blonde hair like I used to have. She screamed out in pain. One of the teachers aids came running over and took me to the principal's office. I was in trouble and I knew it. Then one of the people in the office left the room and closed the door so I couldn't hear them talking. My mother was called and she was told to come to the school right away.

I sat quietly for quite a while waiting for my mother to come. I had no idea where she was coming from. I no longer had any idea where she worked or lived. If you think about it, I didn't know much about my mother anymore at all. I suddenly felt very scared. I had her phone number, but that was all I had. As I was thinking about all of this, in she walked. She looked at me and came over to me. "Carol," she said, "You don't usually behave like this. What happened?" I told her the whole problem in the lunchroom, and also how I never had any money for ice cream. I also told her how my sandwiches were always the same and she became mad. She wasn't mad at me, she was mad at Aunt Glady. Mommy took me aside and said, "I give her plenty of money to take care of you. You should be eating better than this." I went on to explain that many times I would leave the dinner table hungry. I didn't tell her that Ginger and I ate dog bones. I was afraid that I had said too much already. I was afraid of what Uncle Cliff might do to me, and maybe to my mother as well. I begged her not to say anything but she was boiling mad. She was going to tell them to feed me more and give me better lunches.

We left the school, but before we left, I was told to keep my hands to myself. For the next two weeks I would be eating in the office, not in the cafeteria. I was actually relieved about not having to eat in there. Now I had bigger problems. It was too early for Uncle Cliff to come home from work. He got home around 5:30 or even 6 p.m. I knew that Mommy wouldn't stay that long, and I wasn't ready to tell her about what Uncle does to me many mornings during the week. When I do that I need to be able to leave there and never go back again! This however was going to be bad enough. We left the school and headed toward Aunt Gladys' house. This was not going to be pleasant. My mother spoke very little to me on the way there. She seemed to be in a total world of her own. I would look at her face at times, but she stared straight ahead. This made me feel worse, I was somehow getting used to it. This is the way that she had become with me. I thought with sadness, does she talk to my brother more than me, or does she seem far away in thought with him as well?

Suddenly we were turning down the road that leads to Aunt Gladys house and I started to feel nauseous from fear. I was however very thankful that Uncle was not home yet. The thought of having to look at him right now was more than I could bear. We pulled into the driveway and got out of the car. I was feeling very frightened now and was very sorry that if I just took my usual taunting at school, none of this would have happened. I mean how much of this conversation was going to be told to Uncle Cliff. I think that's what scared me the most. I could see him coming into my room and pinching me in the breast again to get even with me. We were almost at the door when Aunt Glady opened it for us. She had a puzzled look on her face. We went in the house and my mother said, "Let's all sit down at the dining room table." We sat down and my mother began to speak. "Glady I give you plenty of money to take care of Carol all week long. It's come to my attention that Carol isn't being fed enough, and also, she has the same lunches every day." My Aunt made a funny noise and said, "If Carol is hungry why doesn't she ask for more food?" They both turned and looked at me. I suddenly felt very much on the spot because I knew that there were a few times that I did in fact say something. Was I supposed to say that she was lying? I thought and decided to just shrug. To me this was the safe way out of a situation that could put me in harms way. My mother looked at me and she said that I wasn't to feel shy. If I was still hungry at dinnertime, I was not to leave the table until my tummy felt satisfied. I agreed to this, and that part of the problem seemed to be taken care of. "And another thing," my mother continued to say, "I'm looking at Carol now and she doesn't look to be clean. Is she taking enough baths?" My Aunt said that she asked me to take more baths and I gave her a hard time. I felt like kicking her. Now I was sorry that I didn't just ignore her when she had fallen down the steps! Maybe she would have ended up like the bird that lay dead in its cage and I would be with Mommy! The lady was just simply not being truthful. I felt nothing but contempt for her. My mother felt that enough had been said, and she was expected back at work. My Aunt assured her that these were minor issues and that with a little more communication and cooperation from me there would be no more problems. My mother left and told me she would be back soon to take me out, and this weekend we would go see Grandma Myers. She left the house and now I had to deal with Aunt Glady.

We stood and looked at each other. Mommy didn't tell her about the fight in the lunchroom, and that I had to eat lunch in the principles office for two weeks. I was a little surprised, but maybe she felt that this was something that was between her and me. My Aunt glared at me and she said, "Poor Carol, the little girl who has no home. I think I feed you plenty and you want more baths? You can go up and take one right now! I think I'm going to ask your mother for more money to take care of you very soon. Out of my sight!" she yelled." I ran away from her and ran up to my room. I started to cry and shake. I took my dolly and told her everything! I didn't want to take too long because I was told to take a bath. This was a good thing to do as I needed one, and I was happy that just maybe I would be allowed to take more than one a week now. I may have been only six years old, but I knew that I needed more than that. I went into the bathroom and removed my clothes and took my bath. When I was with my mother she always prepared my bath, but that seemed like a long time ago. I got out of the tub and went back to my room and continued my conversation with my dolly. Teddy had some things to say too.

———

CHAPTER 11

I heard a car pull up. I knew that it was Uncle. It was time for him to come home from work. I could smell something good cooking in the kitchen and I was hungry. Aunt Glady made very good vegetable beef soup. It was not a thick soup but it had a good flavor. I walked out into the hallway just like I did when I lived with my mother, father and silly brother. I had no idea what Aunt Glady was going to tell Uncle Cliff about the days events, so I had no idea about what if anything, was said. I really couldn't hear too much, it appeared that I was worried for nothing this time. Aunt Glady and Uncle Cliff didn't fight, but I could tell they didn't talk to each other that much either. Sometimes at night if I couldn't sleep, I would hear Aunt Glady saying to my uncle, "Please, please," and then I would hear him utter something, but I couldn't make out what he was saying. I knew that things weren't quite right between them, but at least they didn't carry on like my mother and father did.

Aunt Glady was a strange looking lady, not at all like my grandmother, Aunt Ruby, or Aunt Connie. Actually none of them resembled each other that much. I don't remember my Great Grandmother or Great Grandfather, so I couldn't tell who looked like whom. I remember being over at my father's mothers house one day, and I was introduced to my 100-year-old cousin. She was in a wheel chair and was completely wrapped up with ace bandages.

I remembered how she scared the heck out of me. This was a cousin? I play with my cousins! This lady sat in a wheel chair and moaned like a trapped animal. She was 100 and I was 5. I ran out of the room to go and hide. I heard my grandmother call me, and when she figured out that I was hiding because I was afraid, I heard her laugh. I never saw that poor lady again.

It was time for dinner. Aunt Glady came to the bottom of the steps and yelled for me to come down and eat. I felt really strange and scared. I had no clue if Aunt Glady had told uncle anything or not. I went shyly into the dining room not knowing what to expect. I sat down as usual and began to eat my soup. I made no eye contact with either of them. There was the usual silence at the table, and I thought to myself, "If I'm not allowed to speak, how am I going to ask for seconds?" I thought with a sense of amusement that I could do what the mute people do and make hand gestures! I remember the class that I had to attend right after going back to school when I had polio. There was a girl there who was mute, and was being taught how to communicate with her hands and fingers. I would watch her with amazement as she learned how to talk that way. The soup was good and I wanted more. Aunt Glady always gave me such small portions, that I'm sure two portions were really equal to one regular bowl. I cleared my throat, looked at my Aunt Glady, and raised my bowl up with out saying a word. I found a way to ask for seconds without speaking! She glared at me and took my bowl into the kitchen returning with another portion. Uncle cliff looked startled, and then looked from her to me, but said nothing. She hadn't told him about the day's events! I was really happy about that. He stared at me for a second and then continued to eat. Aunt Glady had a cake for dessert too. Wow, I thought, this is turning out well. I didn't ask for seconds of cake, as I was truly full for once. I got up from the table and went back to my room to color. It wasn't very late; I could have watched a little T.V. with them, but I just simply didn't want to be in the same room or even near them. I soon got into my pajamas, and then went to bed. Even though nothing had been said about my mother coming over and complaining, I still didn't feel safe, but then why should I? I had a hard time sleeping that night and desperately missed being with my mother. I continued to have frequent nightmares, which would wake me up and I would cry myself back to sleep.

The week went by quickly. I ate in the office as instructed and had liverwurst sandwiches added to my lunch menu. Aunt Glady also gave me cookies and I had money for milk and ice cream too. I finally had a bigger lunch and felt better, and was given more at dinnertime. My portions became larger so I didn't have to ask for seconds. At breakfast time I was given larger portions as well. I started to feel better, and I thought to myself that maybe I wouldn't have to sneak downstairs at night to drink coke and eat a dog bone with Ginger. I would also get more sleep and not be so tired for school the next day.

My grades didn't improve however. I still had too much on my mind. I thought that my mother was probably doing the best that she could. She claimed she was saving for the divorce and all, but the truth is I felt deserted.

Peggy and I continued to walk to school every day, but we didn't see each other as much afterwards. It was just because of circumstances. Peggy could always make me laugh and I missed her very much. She always assured me that when Christmas vacation came we could see more of each other. It was very cold outside and walking to school was really hard. By the time we got to school our legs were always so cold. We each had hats, gloves and pretty warm coats to wear, but it never seemed like enough. She had heard about the scuffle in the lunchroom and how I had pulled Lisa's hair. She also heard that the kids my age thought that I was weird, but they were scared of me now, because I showed that I couldn't be bullied anymore. I thought, "Good, maybe this too will improve. No more bullying!" The kids now left me alone, but when you're really young, being left too alone is lonely. I was not a happy kid. I felt different, and many times I caught kids looking at me. I thought, "Maybe I should give them something to look at!"

I would sit and entertain myself with funny things that I could do, or scary faces to make them even more afraid of me. That was how I spent my lunchtime.

———

CHAPTER 12

Christmas was right around the corner. I didn't believe in Santa Clause. When my brother and I were still living with our parents, I remember feeling so joyful and being filled with anticipation. Christmas was coming! The streets were all decked out with beautiful decorations, and the town of Westwood was not cheap with their decor. All the stores were decorated too. It was truly a beautiful time of the year and everyone seemed to treat each other nicer, everyone except Mommy and Daddy of course. One night right before Christmas I heard them fighting really bad. Mommy was saying to my father that Christmas was almost here, and she needed to buy gifts for my brother and me. I stood at the top of the steps and thought to myself, "What are they talking about? Santa will bring us our toys so why is Mommy so upset?" We had our tree because Daddy had bought one the day before and we were to decorate it tomorrow. Santa would not be disappointed and we had Christmas cookies to put out for him, so what was the problem? I went into my brother's room and asked him what was going on and he said, "Little sister, I hate to inform you, but there is no such thing as Santa Clause." "What!" I yelled. I thought that he was lying to me. I remember hitting him. He just laughed and told me to ask Mommy tomorrow, if there was a tomorrow. I asked him why he didn't do more to help instead of hiding under the covers. He just said that even though he was a lot older than me, he was still a lot smaller than my father, and he wanted to grow up and grow old. I thought about that remark and knew he was right. I went to bed and I knew in my heart that he wasn't lying about Santa either. I was barely five years old.

The next time I saw my mother she asked me what I wanted for Christmas. I told her I wanted a bike and a new dolly. My dolly was pretty shabby looking because I had it for a couple of years. She said all right, but seemed surprised that I wanted a bicycle. It's snowy outside why would you want that now? I told her that there are some winter days that if I am bundled up well I would be able to ride my new bike, and spring would soon be here. She said that she would surprise me. I asked her what we would do on Christmas day, and she said that we would go to Grandma Meyer's house for Christmas dinner. I was satisfied with that answer. Grandma and grandpa didn't give me much attention, but at least I would see my cousins and other relatives. I wondered if I would see my father's mother too. I loved my other grandmother because she was always so funny and good to me. Since my father and mother separated I didn't see her as much, only when she came to visit at Aunt Gladys. I sure hoped that would happen again soon.

Uncle Cliff surprised us and went out and to buy a small Christmas tree which we decorated. I must say that we did that in silence too, with the exception of asking for certain lights and ornaments. It was almost cordial. I thought, don't these two know anything about joy and kids? Our school had decorations up and down the hallway. We had to make decorations for our classrooms. Everyone was full of joy and excitement. You have to remember that most of the kids my age still believed in Santa Clause. I felt a little sad like I had lost something. My friend Peggy also knew there was no Santa; after all she was two years older than me. We just spoke about what each of us wanted, and what we thought we would get. She came from a larger family than I did, and I'm sure her parents didn't have much money either. Peggy was so blessed in other ways and she didn't even know it, but who was I to tell her? At that time I would have given anything to be her, and to live in her house that seemed to be so filled with love. For their Christmas tree they had decorations made out of glass, but they also made pretty decorations made out of colored paper, and they strung popcorn making the tree very decorative and giving it a real homey look.

Christmas morning was here! Mommy had snuck over in the middle of the night so I would have presents to open. She also brought over Christmas cookies and a Christmas plant for Uncle Cliff and Aunt Glady. I thought that was nice, but I felt funny in front of my aunt and uncle opening up gifts. They of course didn't buy me anything, but after all I was just a business deal, so I wasn't surprised. Mommy came later to pick me up. I had gotten my bike, a new dolly, and a new dress and boots. I was satisfied and happy. Uncle Cliff thought that I had gotten too much of course, and Aunt Glady made no comment either way. She did however knit me a woolen scarf that was pretty. She told me she had done it while I was in school. I thanked her. We hadn't spoken much to each other since the school incident, and she had stopped giving me piano lessons. Mommy had asked her to help me with my schoolwork, which she didn't do either. Oh well! I felt that she secretly hated me and I wasn't fond of her either. This is just a roof over my head and a place to eat. I wondered for how long. Mommy told me not to ask anymore, so I didn't. I was just going to have to wait and see.

After Aunt Glady gave me the scarf, my mother and I left to have fun over at my grandmother's house. Their house was full of cheer, and I got a new sweater from grandma and grandpa. Jimmy, who lived with them, got a lot of clothes and toys that he was interested in. I felt envious of him. I knew that he was being treated far better than me, and then I found out from my cousins that my mother visited him more, just as I suspected. There were lots of times that she saw him twice a week. I was really starting to feel sad because my suspicions were right, but I knew though that these grandparents were her mother and father, and she probably went to visit them as well. I just had to accept things for what they were, and hope that some day this nightmare would come to an end.

Peggy and I had five more days of free time before going back to school, and we planned to make the most of it. Of course I spent most of my time over at her house. We both agreed that it was more fun over at her home than at Aunt Gladys, who was so strict.

We certainly couldn't run or play or speak loudly. All we could do at my house was sit quietly and draw in the sunroom. In those days some houses still had coal furnaces. I would watch my uncle go down the basement and I would hear him shovel the coal into the furnace. The house had an odor of coal, and if Aunt Glady didn't clean well, there would be a film on the furniture. Sometimes in school kids would say that I smelled funny. I was taking more baths now so I didn't understand it. We had five days not to think about yucky school. Of course Uncle Cliff had to ruin things about half way through our vacation. One morning he came into my room again. One could never tell when he would decide to do his ugly thing. I opened my eyes when I heard the doorknob turn. I knew what I was in for. He climbed in bed with me and took my hand which he placed on his private area. I recoiled and told him to stop this. He grabbed me roughly around my wrist and bent it backward. I started to scream, but he put his hand over my mouth. In a rough voice he warned me to not yell, and that I had better do what he wants or I would pay the price for not listening! He touched me all over and then quickly got out of bed. This little stint didn't last quite as long as usual. As he was leaving he whispered loudly "You had better cooperate or else." My wrist hurt and I was very, very mad. I don't think that I have ever been so mad. I knew that I was going to have to tell someone soon or I was going to burst.

After he left, I pulled the covers off of me which had gotten all twisted up from my struggle to get free, and got dressed. I went over to Peggy's house. I felt like confiding in her, just telling her everything and I almost did, but I remember all of his threats and I had to admit that I was very afraid of him. I really had a reason to be afraid of him now, because as the day went by my wrist turned black and blue and swelled up a little. There were no handprints or finger marks on me, just the black and blue. Peggy's mother put ice on my wrist, and asked me what happened. I wanted to tell her so badly, but something told me not to. I told her that I fell and bent my hand back on the icy road outside. She sighed and told me to be more careful when I walk over to her house. Suddenly, Peggy asked if I could stay overnight. Her mother looked at me and said all right, but there wasn't much room. I was so happy that I told her that I would sleep on the floor. She laughed and said that she would put blankets down and we could have an indoor camp out. I was very excited. Peggy's mother called Aunt Glady and asked her if it would be all right, and Aunt Glady said that would be fine. I was thrilled, a day away from the monster and his wife.

I went back to the house to gather a few things for our indoor campout. Aunt Glady saw my wrist and the black and blue marks. She asked me what happened, and I just stood there and looked at her. We stared at each other for a few seconds and I felt tears start to roll down my cheeks. She got a strange look on her face and I quickly said, "I fell earlier outside and hurt myself." I really didn't know if it would do any good to be truthful or not. I just didn't like her or trust her. I ran up to my room and got my pajamas and a change of clothing for the next day. I went downstairs and hardly looked at my aunt. We glanced at each other and I said goodbye. Peggy and I played and played. It was almost like being back in the glen. We were young and imaginative and I was able to put my cares on the back burner for a day.

Our indoor campout went far too fast for me. I didn't want to go back to that house again, but I had no choice. Peggy's mom told me it was time to go back home after lunch. I could understand and thanked her for her generosity. I packed my clothes and went back home.

Aunt Glady was her usual sour self, but told me that my other grandmother and Aunt Priscilla would be coming over to visit that night. I was very happy to hear that. I knew that Uncle Cliff would leave me alone the next morning because sometimes they would stay overnight. They would laugh and have a few too many drinks and once in a while they would stay. They were always such fun that I immediately got back into good humor. I went up to my room and spoke to my dollies and Teddy, and told them everything that had happened starting with yesterday's incident with Uncle Cliff. I said to my one dolly, "You said that things would change soon, dumb dolly!" That dolly was of course my older doll. I then started to draw and wait for the arrival of my aunt and grandmother.

I didn't have a long wait. In they came in high good humor. They both had a present for me. I was so excited! I hadn't been forgotten by my grandmother and aunt. My grandmother had gotten me a beautiful doll and carriage. The doll had a beautiful pink gown on her, something like the gowns the pretty people wore to my grandmothers' parties. I was very happy. My aunt had gotten me a very pretty dress that had a matching sweater. They too were pink. I looked at the dress and almost started to cry because it was so beautiful.

As I was looking at my dress aunt Priscilla noticed my badly bruised wrist. "Hey," she asked, "What happened to your wrist?" I dropped my dress and looked at her with fear and shock. I wanted so badly just to blurt out the whole thing, but now was not the time. One might ask, "When is the right time?" To me the only time to tell would have to be when I could run out the door afterwards and never have to go back. I meekly told her that I had fallen on the ice outside and had bent my wrist backwards. It sounded plausible to me. My aunt Priscilla had a way of looking at me as though she was examining me under a microscope. I couldn't look at her straight in the face because I don't think she believed me for a second. I wasn't sure what she thought and I was not going to ask. I never felt threatened by her because like my grandmother, I knew she loved me very much. She was a very good aunt and she was not stupid.

That night we sat around the table laughing and eating rye bread and cheese. I was drinking my coke, and I looked up and realized that Aunt Priscilla was really examining me. I felt my face get hot because I knew that I was blushing. I hated to blush, so I just looked away. I felt so weird and dirty. I didn't know why I felt that way. After all, I knew that what Uncle Cliff was doing was very wrong, so why did I feel bad? I removed myself from the table and went upstairs to my room. I listened by my door, but no one was outside in the hallway.

Uncle Cliff was downstairs in the living room as usual so I was alone, but this time happy that I was. I started to play with my dollies and talk to them. All of a sudden there was a light knock on the door. I knew that it had to be Aunt Priscilla or grandma because no one else bothered to knock. Auntie came in and sat down next to me. She had brought my new dolly and carriage up, along with my new dress. She looked at me and said, "Carol, you know that you can talk to me any time about anything, right?" I was afraid to look at her in her face so I answered yes with my head facing down. She wanted to know if there was anything that I wanted to talk about. I said no. It just wasn't the right time to spill my guts. What would happen to me? Where would I go? I obviously couldn't go with Mommy yet, and even though grandma had a big house, she was always going to fancy parties in New York with Grandpa. She also had her hands full because he drank like my Daddy did. Aunt Priscilla was not a good choice because she had a very busy life, and she drank way too much as well. My aunt was always the clown. She never hurt people when she drank, but I wouldn't fit into her lifestyle. I was afraid that she would end up not liking me after awhile if I had to stay with her. I was after all, a burden to everyone, wasn't I? Aunt Glady and Uncle Cliff sure acted as though I was. I looked up at her and smiled and said that I knew that she loved me, and she would always be my friend. She accepted that answer and went back to join my grandmother and Aunt Glady. I felt relieved that she left the room; it gave me time to think. My grandmother and Aunt Priscilla did come to visit at times, and I made the decision that when the time was right, Aunt Priscilla would be the one that I would tell about my nightmare existence. I felt sad that I had to actually plot and plan to stay alive, but that was the position I was in.

CHAPTER 13

Winter vacation was over. I didn't see Peggy as much as I would have liked because the weather was really bad. I was afraid that Mommy would not make it either because of icy roads, but she did. We went to the diner and I had a hamburger and fries and hot chocolate. We spoke about school and she said not to worry, that when this was all over she was sure that I would do better. She still had no answer as to how long it would be before she was divorced. She did assure me that she was saving her money, and that as soon as legal issues were taken care of we would be a family again. I wanted to believe her and I wanted this horror to stop. I wanted to tell her what was going on at Aunt Gladys house, but I knew that she was not ready for me to come and live with her yet. She finally told me that she was living in a rented room, but that later things would change. I thought to myself, you bet they will. I knew that I had Aunt Priscilla as an ally and I would be talking plenty when the time was right.

The monster left me alone for over a month. I think that the bruising of my wrist scared him, and he didn't like it that so many people were aware of it. There were times at the dinner table that I caught him looking at it and he would become aware that I was watching him. He didn't smirk at me when this happened, he would look at me with no expression at all, or maybe I just couldn't read him. At times Aunt Glady would make a nervous sounding noise when she knew that we were looking at each other. Now that

I knew that I had an ally I felt a little bolder. I knew that this was going to come to an end someday, somehow, someway.

The winter was coming to an end. In about a months time the weather would really be changing. The days would warm up and the nights would still be cold, but at least there was a light at the end of the tunnel. I could play in the glen again. I had so much fun last year. I was looking forward to spring and being outside away from the house. Peggy and I spoke about the coming spring with joy. She really was a good friend to me. We also spoke about Easter vacation, which was soon to be. We planned on spending as much time together as we could. We each had new bikes, and planned on riding them in the glen. I did notice a change in Peggy's mother. She was a pretty regular looking person, but I suddenly noticed that she was wearing makeup and fixing her hair. I mentioned this to Peggy and she just shrugged, but did admit that she was leaving the house at funny times, and when she came back her mother and father would have fights. This was something new! What had happened to this wonderful family? She went on to say that her mother had to get a full time job soon because there wasn't enough money in their house. I thought to myself, "Are there no really happy people?"

We played as usual at her house. I always had to go to Sunday school to learn how to be a good person, but afterwards I spent my time at Peggy's house to get away from the bad people at mine. The thought of her house becoming a bad house because of fighting, was too much for me to accept. Her mother never really cared that I was there because we each kept the other occupied. One Sunday afternoon, instead of making dinner as usual, Peggy's mother got all dressed up and went out for the day. Peggy's father was to make everyone dinner. Wow! This will be interesting. Interesting it was. He tried to make homemade chicken soup, but he didn't have the faintest idea of how. He just winged it. The soup was not horrible, but it had very little flavor. No one made any bad comments. We didn't want to make him feel sad. We had delicious bread from the bakery to go with it, and a cherry pie for dessert. No one was hungry. I played a little while longer and decided to go home.

On the way home I got a big shock! I looked up the road that led out to another street, and there was Uncle Cliffs' car. Inside the car was Peggy's mom! They were sitting close to each other and the car was parked! I thought, "Oh my God, I can't let them see me, and if someone else comes out of the house, they might be seen by them as well!" I was not sure what they were doing, but I knew in my heart that what I saw didn't look right. I hid behind a tree and just stood there for a few minutes trying to figure out what to do. I don't know why I felt like I was the guilty party; I guess that I felt like I was spying. Actually, I was. Yuck! He just kissed her on the mouth! I thought that I was going to vomit for sure! This was not right, but I thought possibly this is why he's been leaving me alone. It looks like he now likes big people. The thought of that gave me some relief because maybe I would be safe until Mommy could afford me.

I must have been from another planet or something to dare to even think that, because two days later he came into my room and climbed in bed again. I thought, "Boy this guy can't make up his mind, can he?" I felt like yelling at him and saying, "Ha Ha, I saw you and Peggy's mother the other day and I'm going to tell on you!" I knew that he would kill me for sure if I said that, so I just lay there. He said "Good girl, just be quiet and all will be alright." I closed my eyes so I didn't have to look at him and tried to think of other things. He felt me all over and kissed me on the mouth. Oh my God! All I could think about was how I watched him with Peggy's mother. I jumped up and yelled softly and he left the room. I ran around my room and looked for something to throw because I was so mad and disgusted. I grabbed one of my dollies and threw it as hard as I could against the wall. Then I ran into the bathroom and rinsed my mouth out and scrubbed my face as hard as I could! At least I would have a clean face for school today. Aunt Glady only allowed me to have two baths a week now. I hadn't taken one for days at this point. I silently screamed in my head "Oh Mommy! Oh Daddy! Look what you have done! Look at me now! I hate both of you!"

School was a pain in the neck as far as I was concerned. But it was a necessary evil. Easter was right around the corner, and we were making pictures for the hallway. That seemed a little silly to me, but I drew pretty well, and my picture was considered to be one of the best ones that year. It was hung in the hallway in a special place. I admit feeling some pride in myself. Mommy had told me that I might stay at Grandma Myers for a couple of days during vacation, so I made her a picture too. When I got back home I went upstairs and drew some pretty strange pictures of Aunt Glady and Uncle Cliff. I showed my dollies and Teddy, and we all had a good laugh. Then I drew a picture of Uncle Cliff and a lady that looked like Peggy's Mom and laughed some more. It occurred to me that wasn't a good idea, so I threw it out making sure that I tore it into pieces first. I had to be careful or I wouldn't live to see my next birthday. That wasn't far away either. In fact it was in May, which was next month. I decided to make some Easter pictures instead.

I made one for my mother and wasn't sure if she would like it or not. I never heard her speak about God. One time Aunt Glady tried to get me baptized at our church. My mother found out about it and had a fit. Someone brought my brother over to our church, and we were both to be baptized, and as the minister was almost finished with his ceremony in stormed my mother! She was furious because Aunt Glady had gone behind her back. Some how my baptismal paper got torn up and my brothers did not. My mother has it in her dresser drawer to this day. I suppose it was wrong of Aunt Glady, but I always believed in God, even at that age.

———

CHAPTER 14

aster was here. Aunt Glady and I went to church. They had a special service and I attended church instead of Sunday school. I sat and listened to what the preacher had to say. He seemed like a nice man, and I liked his sermon. I never minded church or Sunday school. I found it to be interesting. However, I didn't understand how people like Uncle Cliff could go on and on doing bad things and seem to get away with so much. I'm quite sure that he would go to hell when he died, because God didn't like it when his children were bad. That is what I was told, and that is what I believed.

Mommy came and picked me up. I had on the dress that Aunt Priscilla had given me at Christmas time. It was early spring and still pretty chilly out so the dress was fine, and I loved the color of it. My mother had to admit that it was very pretty too. I went to grandma and grandpa's house with a little overnight bag, because I was to stay for a couple of days as planned. I was happy to see my cousins again, and even my brother, although we didn't have too much to say. We had a wonderful dinner as usual, and soon after dinner my mother left and so did everyone else. This was the first time that I had ever spent time alone with my grandparent's without my mother being present. I felt a little self-conscious. Grandma actually tried to be nice to me. She asked me how I was doing at Aunt Gladys's house, and if I was happy. I told her that I was all right, but that I was not happy at all being there. She asked me why. I certainly wasn't going to tell her the truth because I knew that it would be stupid to do so. She had to take care of my brother already, and she favored him. Everyone knew it, even the cousins. I think we were all secretly jealous of Jimmy. Jimmy always had new clothes and toys far beyond anything that the rest of us had. He was a real smarty-pants now. He knew that he had it made and acted like it. None of us liked him very much. He was really different acting to me. He had a different life than I did at this point, and was much older than me. I wasn't quite seven yet. We had nothing in common then, and it remained that way. The visit went all right because there were a couple of kids on the block I played with that were about my age. That helped and I had a good time.

My mother came back to pick me up and take me back to the house of horrors. I would be able to see Peggy again and that made me happy. I didn't tell anyone how I had seen her mother with Uncle Cliff. I kept that to myself. I somehow knew that there would be trouble, and I didn't want to be the one to start it. Big people sure do strange things. I still had not totally forgiven Mommy for sending me and my brother over to the dog ladies house. That seemed like a lifetime ago. I sure got an eyeful that day!

Peggy and I played together the next day and had a good time. Her mother stayed home which I was very happy about. The following day was very warm. That was a pleasant surprise. Peggy and I took our bikes into the glen and had a lot of fun. In fact, the next few days were warmish, and we had good times before the weekend was over. Then back to yucky school for us.

The next few weeks were uneventful. Aunt Glady had given me a few more piano lessons, and one day after the lesson I played the song without the sheet music much to my Aunts' surprise. In fact, I played quite a few songs without the music book. She came to the conclusion that I was able to play by ear. She was right. I felt a certain sense of pride knowing that I could do something well. It set well with me as the saying goes. It's actually better to play by note though, because you can become limited in song selections. I couldn't play every song that I heard. If I played solely by note I would have been able to. I still felt proud though, because I played with feeling. That was a good thing.

── Chapter 14 ──

My seventh birthday was right around the corner. It seemed like a long time ago that my brother and I lived in Westwood. Sometimes I thought of Amy and wondered how she was doing. So much had happened since I saw her, and I wouldn't be proud to tell her anything. So I put her out of my mind. My mother promised that I would have a good time for my birthday, and that something nice would happen. Like all little kids my age I was full of anticipation. It turned out that there was going to be another party at Aunt Gladys for me. I wasn't too excited about that, however I didn't let on. She meant well and everyone was there, except my father, who I was starting to forget about. He made no effort to see or contact me. I over heard while eavesdropping at the kitchen door at Grandma Myers that Daddy had a girlfriend, and moved out west to California. I wondered if the girlfriend was the dog lady.

The only other person who wasn't there on my birthday was Peggy's father. He was still home, and Peggy's mother told me to run over and get him. So run over I did. I didn't think to knock because she said to go right in. I ran in and called to him. His name was Carl and he didn't answer. I went from room to room. I finally went to his bedroom and there he was lying on the bed. There was this huge naked man! I remember that I screamed and ran out of the room. He jumped out of bed naked as a jay bird and came running into the living room where I was, and asked me what I was doing. I yelled at him, and told him to put some clothes on, and said that he looked funny. He ordered me out of the house, and told me it was his house and he would do what he wanted! Of course that part was right, it was his house. I ran out as fast as my feet would take me, and suddenly I started to laugh hysterically. To me he looked like a big fat whale. Then I stopped and got serious, what was I going to tell everyone when I got to the house and what would he say when he arrived? God I wondered, are all big people crazy? My party had not yet really started, and already I was beginning to have problems. I didn't really know what to do or say, so I just walked up the driveway, and onto the grassy area, and started to do cart wheels like I used to. That to me made just as much sense as anything or anyone else.

All of a sudden I saw Carl talking to Peggy's mom and they were looking at me. I didn't know what to do and I felt strange. Uncle Cliff was standing close to them and I know that he heard what they were saying. He was listening to their conversation, but not offering any comments. I thought to myself that I'm in trouble with two of the most important people to me. I considered their house as a safe house, and now they hate me. What should I do? Uncle Cliff had a smirk on his face, and I wanted to hit him with a rock. All of a sudden my party was turning into a disaster. Why was it my fault that Carl was laying in bed naked? Peggy's mom told me to go over and walk right in. That's exactly what I did. I then saw Peggy's mom and dad walk over to my mother. They spoke, and now I had too many eyes looking at me. My mother started to approach me and I felt my heart sink. Uncle Cliff was still smirking. Peggy was playing with my cousins and oblivious to what was going on. Mommy came over to me and she said, "Carol, I have always taught you to knock before entering some ones house." "Yes," I said. I thought that there were some times in my life that it wouldn't have made a difference. Needless to say I was thinking of the dog lady, and I was starting to get mad. My mother told me to apologize to Carl, and to never just walk into some ones house ever again. I hung my head and felt like crying, but didn't. I went over to Carl and said that I was very sorry. He looked at me and asked "Buddies again?" I said yes in a loud voice so my stupid uncle could hear. I thought I'm sure glad this is out of the way. I looked at uncle and he was not smirking. The party continued on. I had turned seven years old, but felt much older.

School was coming to an end. I thought to myself "Thank God!" Peggy and I can go back to playing all day in the glen like we used to. I will be out of the house and away from both of the people that I despised the most. I found it hard to believe that I had been living there for over a year, not that I was having fun. My days and nights were filled with feelings of anger, frustration, fear, total upset, and I had no one to share these feelings with except my dollies and Teddy for right now.

Peggy and I played after school as usual, but since I saw her mother with Uncle Cliff, and her father nude, I had different feelings about them. I still liked them a lot, but I felt bashful and dirty. I saw too much and I knew too much. Her father certainly didn't mean for me to see him without clothing, but that just happened. Now, every time I saw him I felt like laughing, and that made me feel mad at myself. He was really a nice guy and I felt sorry that his wife was too friendly with Uncle Cliff. I was only a little kid, but even I knew that was wrong.

Peggy told me that day her parents were starting to fight more often. We discussed what would happen if her parents broke up like mine did. She said that she would probably have to live with relatives in another state. She would have to stay with people on her mother's side of the family, and her brothers would probably live with her father, not far away from here. They wouldn't keep the house because money was a big problem for them. They were simply poor. What a conversation for kids to be having. We both felt sad and decided to not talk about it again. After all, what could we do about it anyway, we were just kids and the world and all of life problems just seemed too big.

That Sunday after Sunday school I was invited over to Peggy's house for dinner again. I gladly accepted. Peggy's parents raised chickens. They were always getting out of the chicken coup and running around everywhere. We always laughed and chased them. It was a lot of fun. All of a sudden Peggy's mother came outside and caught one, and quick as a flash twisted its neck, actually she swung it around several times and put it down on the ground. The poor animal got up and walked a few feet before dropping dead! I was horrified, as I had never seen anything like that before. I loved animals. She saw the look of horror on my face and asked, "You want dinner don't you?" I thought I was going to vomit. Maybe she and Uncle Cliff did make a good couple! I know that you have to kill animals to eat them, but I didn't think that it was necessary to do it in front of kids. Peggy took me by the hand and told her mother that we were going to go to the glen. I was thankful to get out of there. Peggy said to me, "You have to toughen up or you'll always be upset." Toughen up? Wait until I tell on uncle and then she will see how tough I've been! We played for a while until it was time to eat. I ate my dinner and put out of my head what I had seen. It was a good dinner as usual. I thanked her mother, and after we ate I went back to Aunt Glady's house.

Uncle Cliff was standing in the living room when I walked in. He just stood there and stared at me. All of a sudden he asked, "How was dinner?" He took me off guard because he never spoke to me unless he had something ugly to say. I told him that dinner was very good, and then I went straight to my room. I felt strangely shaken by his question. Maybe he did see me watching him that Sunday. He was acting funny. The last thing I needed was for him to start to threaten me about that too. I thought about him kissing me on the mouth and I wanted to puke!

Peggy and I met to walk to school and we had fun on the way. She was talking about who she thought were funny looking kids in her classes, and I was talking about who I thought was funny looking too, like kids do. Then we spoke about her parents. Peggy admitted that a couple of times during the week her mother would put on make-up and a nice dress and out she would go. Her father would beg her to stay home and she would just ignore him. I thought to myself that during the week uncle goes out as well, and isn't this getting cozy? I couldn't tell her what I saw and what I knew. It would cause trouble, and she would be crushed. Uncle had at times in the past come into my room several times a week and now it had become less. I'm sure that it was because of Peggy's mother. He of course was never going to stop bothering me completely. This I knew in my heart, but I admit I was relieved. Who wouldn't be?

It was only a few days after that talk in the glen that he came into my room again. He got into my bed and took my hand and put it on his private parts. I as usual felt like I wanted to throw up, but was afraid to put up resistance. I was very afraid he would pinch me or hurt my wrist like he did before. He made his usual grunting noises and then suddenly jumped up and left the room. It was becoming old news to me. I knew that it was going to continue to happen and he was going to go gaily on. I hated myself for not telling on him, and yet I knew that I just couldn't. Not just yet! My mother did say that all was going well, and that she had almost enough money together to take care of her legal issues. I wanted desperately to believe her, but so much time had gone by; and I was still there battling for my safety and my sanity.

———

CHAPTER 15

School was out for the summer! We were both told to read books during our vacation, as it would be a good thing for us to do. Yea, right we will, ha! That was the furthest thing from our minds. School had ended in the middle of the week, and we had a long summer to have fun and enjoy life. That's what we were going to do. We were having a ball every day, and on Saturdays Mommy would pick me up, and take me out. We would do the usual thing, which was going to the diner, or once in a while go to Grandma Myers' house. The summer was going well except for the usual pestering from uncle. The 4th of July was right around the corner, and Mommy had managed to get fire crackers and sparklers which she dropped off. She said she wouldn't be around to take me to the fireworks, but she thought that this would make up for it. I was disappointed but accepting. I really didn't have any say in the matter anyway.

On the weekend of the fourth Aunt Glady had a party, and the family on my fathers' side came. It was a good night. Aunt Priscilla had come and I was delighted to see her. I knew that she would drink too much, but I didn't care because she was always so much fun. Everyone was having a glorious time. I had my sparklers and firecrackers, and my father's brother, my other uncle, had brought a lot more. We had our own fireworks display! All of a sudden my Aunt Priscilla came over to me. She said that she wanted to have a talk with me later on. I said all right, but like I said before, she had a way of looking at me that made me feel transparent. She was smart and I knew it.

Finally after a lot of laughs and nonsense, the night started to wind down and people who had too much to drink left, but my Aunt stayed. She took me up to bed and we both lay there looking at each other. Suddenly, I began to cry like I've never cried before. She didn't have to say a thing to me. Somehow in my heart I felt she knew. After I stopped sobbing, I quietly told her everything from beginning to end. She was not shocked. In fact she didn't make much comment at all. Both uncle and Aunt Glady were passed out because they had too much to drink. Aunt Glady hardly ever drank too much, but she did on this particular night. Aunt Priscilla got a wet washcloth and wiped my face off. She then went downstairs and got me a glass of milk. After I had finished the milk, she told me not to worry. She was going to contact my mother in the morning, and I would be out of there immediately. She further went on to say that I was a very brave little girl, and a good little girl, and deserved better than this. She also told me that Uncle Cliff had liked little girls for years, and in fact he didn't care if they were a little bit older than me. She said he had a problem, and needed a good swift kick in the ass. I actually giggled at that and agreed. He just simply was a monster. She told me to try to get a little sleep and not to worry. She assured me that she would handle everything. She would wait for Cliff to go out on one of his rides, and she would call Mommy on the sly and get her over here. I asked, "Where will I live?" She said my mother would have to figure that one out.

I felt so much relief that I now had shared this dirty secret, but I was also very scared of the outcome. I only slept for a short time. Aunt Priscilla passed out drunk. She had brought up two more bottles of beer when she brought me my milk. I got up and crept into the bathroom as I certainly didn't want to disturb uncle. Then I went down stairs and sat by Ginger. I told her that I would never forget her, but that I surely had to go. Even though Aunt Priscilla was very drunk, I knew she had understood everything that I had told her, and that she was good for her word. I actually went back to my room and very quietly pulled my clothes out from the dresser drawers. I started to pack my suitcases that I had brought in the house over a year ago.

Uh oh, I fell asleep! After I packed my bags I had lain down and I fell asleep. Where is Aunt Priscilla? What time was it? I looked at my suitcases and they were still packed, so no one had touched them. I felt very frightened. I opened up the door to see if I could hear anything from downstairs. There were no voices and no movement. What did this all mean? I had bared my soul to Aunt Priscilla the night before, and I didn't want to be sorry that I did. I felt like I had entrusted her with my life.

Suddenly I heard someone coming up the stairs and I ran back to my room and closed the door. I started to run wildly around my room out of fear. My heart started to pound and my mind was racing. I must have looked like a trapped animal in a cage, and that was the way that I felt. I picked up Teddy and clung on to him for dear life. I looked at the door and watched the doorknob start to turn, and in walked my mother. I thought that I was going to pass out. I must have been holding my breath. Neither one of us spoke at first. My mother broke the silence. "I had no idea what was going on here." She said, "Why didn't you tell me?" I stood there and had no answer. My mind felt blank. As I stood there it suddenly occurred to me that I didn't know how to tell her. I never knew how to tell her. I felt very sad because the truth of the matter is; I felt that Mommy and I were not really that close. I had come to feel like I was Mommy's burden, not just her little girl. I needed her to come over to me and hug me, but she didn't. I needed her to tell me that everything was going to be all right, but she didn't. I needed her to say that we were all going to be a family, and that this nightmare was over! Mommy went and picked up my suitcases and told me to get my dollies and whatever else I needed, and to follow her. I did as I was told. I had not gotten dressed yet, and I felt funny going down stairs not knowing who was there. As it turned out the only person who was there was Aunt Glady. Aunt Glady looked at me with hate. I remember I looked back at her with pleading eyes and a pleading heart. She started to speak to me and she called me a liar. She had said that I had never liked

Uncle Cliff, and that I was making this all up! My mother then spoke and she said" "My daughter *does not* lie! She would *never ever* lie about a thing like this!" I felt very relieved and grateful for that comment.

Suddenly my Aunt did a very strange thing; she went over to the windows in the dining room and started to take down the curtains! My mother said to her that she might as well not do that because she had nowhere to go. My aunt yelled, "Neither does your daughter!" My mother said, "Yes she does, she'll be staying with my brother George and her cousins for the duration of the time that I need to get my divorce." My aunt yelled, "Good! Get her the hell out of here this minute!" We opened the door and out we stomped! I could hear her yelling and crying as we walked to the car. We walked in silence. It was an uncomfortable silence. Even my dollies and Teddy couldn't make me feel good. We got into the car and drove away. I felt numb.

I looked at Peggy's house and felt really sad. I knew that I probably would never see her again. Then I realized that maybe it was better because after all, Peggy's mother and Uncle Cliff liked each other too much, and some day all of that mess would come out. I thought, "Poor Peggy," now it's my turn to feel sorry for *her*! As we passed their house, I saw Peggy's mother outside and she had a lot of red lipstick on. I wondered, "Where is Uncle Cliff?" And then I silently laughed and said to myself, "Who cares, I AM FREE!!"

———

CHAPTER 16

Uncle George lived nearby, and before we knew it we were at his house. My cousins ran out to meet and greet us. All of a sudden I felt a huge weight had been lifted from my life. I got out of the car and took a deep breath, and looked at my new home. I said to my cousins, "Where on earth am I going to sleep?" We all laughed and ran in circles like a bunch of carefree children. That's what they were, and that's what I desperately wanted to be. My mother got my suitcases and went inside. My mother, Aunt Jane, and Uncle George spoke for a long time. Uncle Georges' house was very small, and because I had to move in, they decided that my cousin Katie would have to move into their bedroom, and sleep on a single cot. I felt bad about that, but my cousin said not to worry. My Uncle had three daughters and only a two-bedroom house. He didn't need to have me there. The three girls had the largest bedroom and had to share it, and because of me one had to leave. I really felt out of place. Mommy assured me that it wouldn't be for much longer. We all ate an early dinner together, and Mommy was getting ready to leave. Before she left she took me aside and asked me a few questions. "Carol" she asked, "How many times did your uncle touch you?" I felt very uncomfortable, but I told her that I had lost count a long time ago. She looked shocked. She said that I would never have to see that pig again. She told me that she and Aunt Priscilla had a long talk that morning, so Mommy knew most of what I had told my Aunt Priscilla. She also said that she was very sorry that I had to endure so much pain, but now I was safe, and that I should put all of the bad memories out of my head. What is she kidding? I may have been a little kid, but I knew that I had a lot to get over. I also knew that it was going to take a *very* long time.

Aunt Jane and Uncle George were very nice people and quite good to me. I liked Uncle George a little better because he went out of his way to make me feel welcome. Aunt Jane was more of the disciplinarian as far as I could see, but still she was very nice. Uncle George always made us laugh, and he joked around a lot. They both assured me that I was welcome. We kids were all of different ages. Katie was the youngest, and then came me, and then Donna and Karen. Karen was quite a bit older than all of us. My brother was almost five years my senior, and Karen was two years older than he. We kids for the most part got along. My stay there, though it was very cramped to say the least, was pretty good. We had the usual squabbles that kids have, but nothing ever lasting. I still went to the same school as before and still had problems learning and concentrating. Aunt Jane used to try and help me with my math, but I was pretty hopeless when it came to that. Again my mother told me not to worry. When things become normal everything would fall into place. We kids played all day long, and at dinner we always had a very good meal to look forward to. Aunt Jane was a very good cook, and I went from being very skinny to normal in size pretty fast. My mother came to visit me as usual, but we hardly went out because she felt comfortable at her brother's house. I don't know if my mother had to pay for my care or not. That matter was never discussed in front of me or in hearing distance, but I thought to myself that they could probably use it.

The months went by. I was living a pretty normal life at my uncles' house, until one day on the way home from school I looked across the street while I was walking, and there was Uncle Cliff! He was parked in his car looking at me! I was alone, because it was okay for me to walk home by myself. I was actually a little closer to the school from Uncle Georges' house. I felt myself freeze! I stood there, looked at him, and could see his face very well even though he was across the street. We stared at each other. Suddenly all the old feelings of fear and panic came back and I thought, Run Run Run!!! I started to run as fast as I could down a side street. My heart was pounding! I looked behind me and he was following me! He was going to run me down! "Oh My God" I screamed! I ran faster and faster, and every time I looked behind me, there he was. I thought to myself, "I have to get out of his sight so he can't follow me." I didn't think he knew where I was living, and I didn't want to show him! I ran down another side street and tried to run through people's back yards hoping to get home that way. He realized what I was doing, and drove ahead of me. At one point I didn't see him, but then I realized that all he had to do was keep driving, because he was driving parallel to how I was running. I stopped running for a minute and decided to run back to the drug store on Main Street. As I ran through another yard trying to back track, I heard dogs barking like crazy, but I didn't care. I was running for my life! Uncle cliff warned me that if I told on him he would kill me, and I knew that he meant it. I never doubted that for a minute. I ran right into what seemed like barbed wire and screamed out in pain. I heard someone from a house yell at me as I pulled myself free. My legs were badly scratched and bleeding, but I started running again. I worked myself back down to Main Street and stopped for a moment. I tried to straighten my dress out a little, but that was not possible. My dress had torn in two places, and my legs were a bloody mess. Uncle Cliff had turned his car around and he saw me enter the drug store. I looked at him from the doorway and he sped quickly away.

People in the store looked at me and gave me strange looks. I looked like a dirty little girl who was covered with dirt and blood. No one offered to help me, or even took the time to ask me what had happened. I knew that I had to kill some time before I left the store again. I wanted Uncle Cliff to be afraid that I was going to tell on him, and then maybe he would leave me alone for good. I had no money on me because I had spent my lunch money in school. I decided to look at the comic books to stall for some time. As I stood there looking at the comic books, I was trying so hard to act normal. I don't see how that could be possible after what I'd just been through. I looked up at one point and caught a man looking at me. He was looking at me with disgust and shaking his head. I thought, "Oh yea, I really want to look like this!" What a moron.

I finally went to the doorway of the store and peeked out. I looked left and right over and over again, and Uncle Cliff was nowhere in sight. I left the store, and suddenly I heard someone call my name. I looked behind me, and there was my cousin Karen who had stayed late after school. I never was so happy to see her before. Karen took one look at me and asked, "What the heck happened to you?" I told her that I had seen Uncle Cliff, and I had to run away from him because he was chasing me with his car. Her eyes grew big as I told her how I ran through people's yards, and how I got caught in the barbed wire. She said that I should call my mother and tell her, and maybe Uncle George would give him a call.

We walked the rest of the way in silence. I could feel how badly my legs were stinging. I also realized that I lost my books and Karen told me not to worry about it, so I didn't. By the time we got home I was feeling a little less shaky. I went into the bathroom and wet a washcloth and put soap on it. I knew that I had to clean my cuts or they would get infected. As I cleaned my legs and tried to clean my cuts off, I started to cry. Not only was I in pain, but I thought to myself this nightmare is real, and it will never go away.

That evening my mother came over. We all sat around the kitchen table and spoke about what had happened. My mother was furious and said that she wanted to call Cliff right away. My Uncle George said, "No Way!" *He* was going to call him. My uncle went into their bedroom and made the call. When he came out it was hard to read the expression on his face. I heard him say to my mother that Uncle Cliff denied everything, and that came as no surprise to anyone. It didn't make me feel any better that the call was made, because I knew that at any time he could chase me again. My mother did say that she felt that the phone call would put a stop to him bothering me, and that I should try to forget everything that had happened. I thought to myself that she is trying to make me feel better, but I doubted that I could just forget. How does one forget a whole year, and then some, of horror?

I found that in the coming weeks I began to look over my shoulder no matter where I walked. I also developed a fear that people were looking at me. If I caught anyone staring at me I would feel myself turn red. I felt embarrassed and different. I also started to have constant nightmares. I don't believe that I ever screamed, because someone certainly would have heard me. I remember waking up in a sweat and feeling frightened. I would look around the room, and sometimes end up laughing because my eldest cousin snored very loudly. My box of clothes stood in the hallway. I would get out of bed and go stand by them and wonder, "Am I ever really going to have a home again?"

———

CHAPTER 17

School vacations came and went and time went by. What I didn't realize was my mother was planning to gather up brother and me and make a complete move. She was waiting for the school year to end. Plans were being made behind closed doors. My mother had met a nice man and they planned to get married. I had no idea, and nothing was ever discussed. My mother had gotten her divorce and had not told my brother or me. I have no idea about when she met my step-father to be, and my brother and I were never told. I admit that I didn't think about my real father because I saw too much violence at the Westwood house, and I knew that it was wrong. My father never called, or came to visit brother or me in all this time.

As time went by, it appeared that Uncle Cliff was going to stay away from the school and leave me alone. I continued to look over my shoulder and have nightmares. I needed to move far away and have my own house, my own room, my own space, and my mother. My eighth birthday came and went. We had a quiet little party at Uncle Georges' house. I missed Peggy, but I knew I would never see her again, as she was too close to the enemy.

One day my mother came over, and my brother was with her. We hadn't seen each other in a while and as usual we didn't have too much to say. I did notice that he was dressed much nicer than I was. In fact, he was dressed nicer than any of us were. We all stood and kind of looked at him. It was no secret that my brother was my Grandparents favorite. Truth be told, they hardly gave me any attention at all. As far as my other grandmother on my fathers' side and Aunt Priscilla were concerned, it would be years before I would see them again. I missed them so much because they were always good to me. My grandfather who was well known for his famous flower growing, and of course his circle of friends, had passed away a while ago due to excessive drinking, and a bad heart. I remember that in the past when I would go over to my fathers' parents' house, both of those grandparents always treated my brother and me well. There was no favoritism. We both felt loved and special, and that is what made this grandmother so loved by me. She truly had a free spirit, but with the divorce, relationships amongst the adults were strained to say the least.

My mother took my brother and me into the living room. She announced that in a few weeks we would be together again as a family, and I would have a new Daddy. I didn't know how to feel about that. My old Daddy was bad, so how do I know that this Daddy would be any better? School was almost over and we were going to move to a place called Staten Island, New York. My mother then told my brother and me to go and play with our cousins because it was adult time. I didn't feel like eavesdropping this time, it no longer seemed like a fun thing to do. All I really wanted to do was to sit quietly by myself, so that is what I did. So much had happened in my life that I just felt tired at the ripe old age of eight.

The day had come! Mommy came to the house and informed me that today was moving day! I thought "Wow!" she could have warned me or something. I felt a sense of excitement and also a little fearful. I thought wasn't this what I had been waiting for a very long time? What was my new house going to look like, and would I like my new school any better? When would I see my cousins again, and most of all, a new Daddy? What would he be like? Would he like me? I asked Mommy some of these questions and she told me not to fret, that everything would fall into place one step at a time, and that I had to trust her. I thought trust? Do I trust anyone? Every time I trusted someone something bad happened, so this was going to take a little work. I didn't really have much to gather, only my clothes, my dollies, and Teddy. I hadn't spoken to them in quite a while, and I wondered if they felt neglected? I thought "Silly Carol, they're not real." A long time ago one of my cousins had caught me talking to Teddy and she started to giggle at me. Then she went and told Aunt Jane, who said maybe they were real to me and not to make fun. I became self-conscious about using them as sounding boards and stopped talking to them. I did however miss it, most of the time they didn't talk back! My brother was waiting out in the car so I said thank you to my aunt and uncle for their kindness, and I gave my cousins each a hug goodbye and off we went!

Mommy told my brother and me that we would be taking the ferry over. I asked her what that meant, and she explained that in order to get to where we were going we would drive our car right onto a big boat. Then we would get out and find a seat, and that the boat would take us to Manhattan. Mommy had to go to the city first and pick up some important papers. Then she explained that we would get a bite to eat in the big city, and go back to the ferry, which would take us back to Staten Island. It all sounded strange, but exciting to my brother and me. We were filled with wonder and anticipation, and sure enough that's what we did.

The ferry ride was quite an experience, and I remember that we sat across from a very old and dirty looking man. He looked at us and smiled though. When the ride was over and the boat docked there we were in a large city that had huge buildings and lots of cars and noise. It was so noisy Mommy had to yell when she spoke. She held brother and me firmly by the hand as we walked! We had quite a walk ahead of us to get to where my mother needed to go, but I was so fascinated with all the people that I didn't even care. We walked into a huge building. Mommy went over to a large desk to get her paperwork, and then we left. I looked at Mommy and said that I was hungry. She laughed and took us into a small diner type of building. She said it was called a café. We sat down and ordered sandwiches and drinks.

I really liked the city. I had been there once before with Aunt Connie when we met Billy Graham, but I was only five at that time, and we had not taken the ferry over. We then went to the ferry to go back to Staten Island. Mommy told my brother and me that we would be shocked with our new home. It was very big and we each had two bedrooms. Neither my brother nor I could picture that. She went on to say that the house was every bit as grand as my fathers' mothers' house. I found that hard to believe. I asked her if it too had a chandelier. She had to admit that it did not, but told me that it had a refrigerator that covered a whole wall, and a fireplace that went from the floor to the ceiling. It also had an elevator that was operated by hand! I asked her why it had an elevator, and she informed me that one of the people that had lived there was crippled, and someone had installed it for them. Wow! This place sounds great! She warned us that the grounds needed a lot of work, clean up and such and maybe we would like to help her and our new Daddy. Suddenly I felt very shy. I had never met him and I didn't even know what he looked like. Mommy told both of us not to be afraid, because she just knew that we would like him.

CHAPTER 18

We pulled down a very long driveway and got the first view of our new home. It was very impressive. This house even had an area where you could walk on one of the roofs. As we drove to the other side of the house we realized that there were other buildings, and that we were in a courtyard that had stables! No horses though. The courtyard was made out of cobblestone. It was all littered up just like Mommy said. I didn't care because this was home, and I was ready to get out and do anything she asked me to do, and I said so. Mommy laughed and said, "Go inside and see the house first." Jimmy was acting kind of strange. I guess he wasn't as happy as I was, or maybe he didn't like what he saw. I think the idea of work made him sick! He never had any chores at Grandma Myers house, and I thought this is going to be interesting. I had chores at Uncle Georges' house, but I never did mind. To me this would be fun, and maybe my new step-father would like me because I was good little worker.

I did as Mommy said and walked over to the back door. As I entered the house, on the right side of the back entrance way was indeed an elevator. Wow! An elevator in my own house! How great was that! I walked into an open hallway, which was large in size, and ran all the way down to the front of the house. As I was running, I noticed that there were rooms off to both sides of the long hallway. At the end of the hall was a spiral wooden staircase that had many steps leading up to the second floor. I ran up the steps and there was another large hallway that had bedrooms off to both sides. I ran into one of the rooms, and saw a large beautiful bed that had a wine colored shiny blanket and two beautiful pillows on it. I also saw that there was a large twisted cord that hung by the bed. I was told that it was used to call the maids. I left that beautiful room and went into the other bedrooms. There were four more in all. My two bedrooms had a sink in one of the rooms with running water. My brother's rooms were the same as mine. This house had at one time been a six-bedroom home. My mother's room had been made into a huge one-bed room. And huge it was. My brothers' rooms and mine were not nearly as fancy, but still quite nice. We each had a nice bed and dresser drawers. The bedrooms had very large closets. I didn't have the faintest idea of what to put in my closet. I had been living out of a cardboard box at Uncle Georges' house. Even though I had a dresser at Uncle Cliffs' house, I didn't have much to put in a closet of this size.

I suddenly realized that I wasn't alone. My mother was standing behind me, and it was as though she had read my mind. She said, "I'll get you more clothes than what you have now." I felt really relieved to hear that because I never had enough. My mother went on to say that it was almost time to meet my step- daddy. I suddenly felt very nervous and said so. I told her that I felt bashful. She just smiled and said that he probably did too. She admitted that he never had any kids of his own. That didn't make me feel any better. I was wondering what my brother was doing and thinking. I know how he had been treated at grandma and grandpas house, so he was probably scared too.

I was eight years old, he was almost thirteen, and neither one of us had a normal life. He may have been treated well at Grandmas' house, but my cousins and I knew that they went overboard showering him with gifts, and they even called him by a different name! They said that his real name was too much like my real fathers, so that was why they changed it. My grandparents were weird people. It's like they only had one grandchild. My cousins felt that way too.

My brother and I were told to go into the living room and wait for our new step-daddy. We both listened and went into a beautiful living room. It had a beautiful fireplace that started from the floor and went all the way up to the ceiling. Mommy told no lies about this house, it was grand. My brother and I waited with anticipation as we knew that any minute we would meet our new father, and in he came. I almost started to giggle because he was not very tall, had long blonde hair, but he did however have a pleasant smile on his face. In his hands he had a very nice jewelry box that had a pretty ballerina doll inside it that danced when you wound it up. It also played a very pretty song. I looked at him and thanked him, but thought as he handed it to me "What am I supposed to use it for?" I surely had no jewelry to put inside of it. I then thought maybe Mommy has something for me, like an old necklace or something. He gave Jimmy some new comic books and a special knife that had several blades and a bottle opener. Jimmy barely thanked him and seemed very ungrateful. After our presents were given to us we were told to go out and play until dinner, but not to go to either end of the driveway.

The driveway was very long. In fact, each end of the driveway had a road at the end of it. These roads had town traffic. I thought, this is quite a place! I overheard Mommy say to my Uncle George that our new home had many acres. We each roamed around looking at everything there was to see, and finally my brother told me to sit down on the grass and we would talk. He said, "Sis, Mommy met our step-father at the greenhouses that our grandparents had owned." I could clearly see that Jimmy wasn't happy. I looked at him and asked "So?" He seemed annoyed that his remark didn't mean that much to me. I then asked him what else he knew. He admitted that he didn't know much more, but that he was going to find out. My brother wasn't a happy boy, and I could tell that he wanted to start trouble. I just wanted to be happy and be with my mother. Had he forgotten all of those terrible nights that he and I heard all of the fighting? I remembered that I wasn't the one to pull the blankets over my head! I actually hid in the upstairs hallway feeling horror with all that took place. I thought what's wrong with him? Why is he acting like this? He made it very clear that he wanted to stay with my mother's parents instead of living here. I felt sad because all I could think of was how I always wanted to be with Mommy. I felt that she secretly cared for my brother more than for me, because he always got what he wanted, and Mommy also gave him more attention than me. I also knew just from hearing adult conversations while we were all living separately, that my mother visited my brother more. I never told her that I knew this, but I did. I said, "Bad Jimmy! Do you know what I've been through these last years?" He said that he had heard a few things, but it had nothing to do with him. I thought to myself, "You snot! I know from where you came, and I know from where I came, and you *are* a brat!"

I kept these thoughts to myself and left him to sit and sulk. I walked around the property alone to discover that there were greenhouses on the property too. There were a lot of greenhouses. Who would ever think that one place could have so much. I really liked what I saw. The house was beautiful, and the property needed a lot of work, but I decided right then and there that I would do everything I could to help out. I wanted to stay here forever.

I heard Mommy call us in for dinner and we went inside. Jimmy came into the kitchen after me, and gave our new step-father a dirty look. I told Mommy that I loved our new home and she looked pleased. I couldn't look at my new Daddy's face quite yet because I still felt bashful. I would try to steal a quick look at him from time to time, but nothing more than that. I did notice that he had quite an accent. Mommy told us he was from Denmark, which was a country very far away. She had told us in the car on the way to the house that he was very different from our real father, and that he was a very kind and gentle man. Every time I looked at him I wanted to giggle. I wondered if all men from Denmark wore their hair down to their shoulders, but was afraid to ask. Sometimes he wore shoes made out of wood! I felt shocked the first time I saw them, and wondered how they could be comfortable.

Chapter 18

I looked over at my brother and he had a sour look on his face. I really had to wonder what was wrong with him, and why my mother cared so much about what he thought about things. He clearly didn't like anything he saw here, and didn't make any conversation during dinner. We finished our dinner, and we all went outside to look around. Mommy and John (our step-father) spoke with much enthusiasm as they talked about all the changes that they would make to the property, and I yelled, "I'll help too!" My brother looked at me with disgust. I thought to myself "What an idiot he is!" I was also very disappointed in him because over the last years we had barely seen each other at all, and I was hoping to have a nicer acting brother. Oh well. I had learned at an early age that life is full of surprises, and too many of the surprises were not pleasant. I ran around the property like I had just been given a huge gift. I was full of hope for the first time in a long time. I felt, Happy! Happy! Happy!

The next morning I woke up with a start. Where am I? At first I felt strange and lost. I forgot where I was for a minute. I had no nightmares. I jumped out of bed, and ran down the stairs to the huge kitchen. There was Mommy and Jimmy. Jimmy was giving Mommy a hard time. My step-father was already outside working. Mommy was pleading with my brother to please try and act nice and not be so surly. My brother looked at me and stomped out of the house. I asked her what was wrong and she told me that Jimmy wanted more toys, and that a few comic books were not good enough. I mentioned to her that he already had a lot of toys. Grandma and Grandpa Myers had gotten him so many, but she said he wanted more. I thought "What a brat!" Mommy made me breakfast, and then said that I could go out and play. She also mentioned that there was a little girl who lived at the end of our driveway on the Victory Boulevard side, and that she had spoken to her mother a week ago. Mommy explained that we were the new owners of the property, and had a little girl too. I was delighted to hear that, and I would meet with her in a few days. I first had to get settled in our new home. I thought things are really looking up, a great new home with Mommy, and a step-father too. Wow! This is how normal people live. What could go wrong in my life now?

That afternoon I was watching my step-daddy work on the cobblestone area. It was full of trash. There were a lot of cans and papers and broken bottles everywhere. I felt sorry that he had so much work to do alone. I walked over to him feeling very shy, and asked if I could help out. He looked at me and smiled and said that there was too much broken glass in this area, but I could go over by the stables and pick up cans there. He gave me a plastic bag and thanked me for whatever help I could give. I decided that I would give it my best shot. Jimmy was off at a distance giving me dirty looks. I thought that he was just acting awful. He should at least try to get along.

I worked for what seemed like hours, and then Mommy called us in for dinner. I was pretty dirty, but Mommy gave me a big hug and thanked me for all of my help. I went into the downstairs bathroom that was located off of the kitchen, and washed up. We all sat down for dinner. My mother announced at the dinner table that the next day a big truck would be coming down the driveway, and there would be a surprise on it for my brother and me. We couldn't imagine what that could be. It turned out that Mommy had bought a beautiful piano for my brother and me to play on. She had heard me play, and she was told that I had talent, even though I played by ear. Jimmy had been given lessons at one time from Aunt Glady as well. I was really happy to have the piano. Jimmy was not that impressed. No matter what my mother tried to do for us, it was never good enough for him. Jimmy was clearly a problem, and soon the gentle pleading from my mother was no longer effective. Our step-father and Jimmy now had real issues with each other. I knew that in time, these issues would cause problems.

One day the two of them were really fighting, and I watched as John grabbed my brother by the ear and told him he had better start to act differently or else! I thought or else what? My brother was acting out terribly, and he wasn't trying at all to get along or cooperate. I could tell that my mother was heartbroken. In my heart I knew my brother would win the argument because he always did, and would just get what he wanted. I was angry. My brother continued to sulk around for days and I decided to just ignore him. I tried to be as helpful as possible, and at night-time, I would go up stairs and play in my room. I still talked to my dollies and Teddy, but at this point I had good things to say. I told them that I would go and meet my new friend the next day.

──────

CHAPTER 19

Morning came and I went downstairs and had breakfast. Arrangements had been made for me to walk up to the end of the driveway to meet Jenny. Mommy warned me to go directly from our driveway onto Jenny's property, as the street that she lived on was very dangerous. There were a lot of cars, buses and trucks, and they were almost on her front yard as they drove down the street. I did as I was told and very bashfully knocked on my new friends' door. Jenny was one of three children, and her little sister who was only four, opened the door and said in a loud voice "Come on in!" I immediately felt welcome. In I walked, and there was a girl about my age who was a little shorter than me who had long red hair. We eyeballed each other and we both started to laugh. I knew that I was going to like this girl. Jenny's mother seemed pleased, and we went outside to play in the back yard. It had a pool and everything. The pool wasn't very deep, but it was deep enough for a couple of little girls to have fun. We had a glorious day and we spoke about the upcoming school year. Things would be different for me because unlike any other place I had lived; you had to take a city bus to school. Mommy would have to buy tokens for me to hand to the driver so I could ride the bus. I was told that the school was very large, and kids from kindergarten to eighth grade were taught there. The school had three floors and was very old. Jenny told me that very poor people went there too, and they had a soup line at lunchtime for the kids who didn't have lunch or milk money. I immediately felt sorry for these kids because of course; I knew what it was like to go to bed hungry.

The day came to an end. Jenny was allowed to come over to my house as soon as we finished cleaning the property a little better. The place was coming along, but the greenhouses still needed a lot of work; and in that area there was a lot of broken glass, so for days Jenny and I played at her house.

The arguing between my brother and step-father John continued. It was actually becoming rather frightening. One day they were both upstairs in Jimmy's room. Our bedrooms led out onto the area of roof where you could walk. I thought that was pretty great, however Mommy told me not to use the roof because the fencing around that area wasn't that good. It needed to be done over. Well, they both went out onto the roof anyway. They were swinging at each other! I was standing outside looking up in horror! I screamed for my mother to come and watch too. She had been out by the greenhouses and she heard me yell. In a minutes time she was standing at my side looking up with fear. She yelled for them to stop, but they didn't hear her or they ignored her. My mother ran into the house and I followed. We were both afraid that one of them would fall over the railing and get badly injured or worse. We ran into the house as fast as we both could go and into Jimmy's room. My mother told me to stay put, and that she would handle this. I looked out the small doorway that led outside to the roof, and all three of them started to swing at each other! My mother however, was able to grab my brother's arm and pull him away from my step-father. My brother yelled at John and said, "Next time it'll be over the roof with you!" I stood there in total shock. I wondered if life would ever be good. This was a major problem, and what was my mother going to do about this one?

Jimmy stayed in his room as the three of us went downstairs. I went into the living room and sat on our new couch. The living room wasn't far from the kitchen area that we ate in, so I could hear what was being said. I admit that I was very sad and wanted to cry. I could see our whole world falling apart again, and I just couldn't stand for that anymore. I heard my mother talk in a voice that sounded like she was crying, or about to, and I felt sorry for her. I heard her say, "I know Jimmy is a terrible problem and I warned you of this." He said that he understood and not to worry so much, but Jimmy had to realize that he has to behave and treat him with respect. My mother agreed with John and said, "I know that children shouldn't be rewarded for bad behavior, but maybe if he had the car that he wanted, he could work on it and drive it up and down our driveway. That would keep him occupied. I thought, "A car?" That's why my brother was acting out so badly? Because he wanted a real car of his own? How could he, and how could they give in? My brother wasn't even quite thirteen yet! So, I guess if you act out really bad you get BIG presents! I was furious! I actually felt like throwing a tantrum! I had never had one, but I knew what they were because Jenny's' youngest sister, who was two years old, had them. The fact is she too always got what she wanted. Her mother would give her something just to shut her up! I didn't have tantrums. It wasn't my nature.

I went over to the piano that I used from time to time and played a song Aunt Glady taught me. I used the piano a lot of times when I was feeling sad, it somehow helped me to feel better. I would play happy songs, sad songs and even make up songs. I was told that I played well. I really should have learned to read music though. I didn't really have the interest to do so.

Two days later I heard a car come down the driveway from the Signs Road side, which was the other end of our property. The car stopped at our house and a man got out and came to the door. He was driving what I thought was a strange looking car called a Kaiser. A minute later another car came down the driveway. Both men approached the house and knocked on the door. My mother and step-father went outside to speak to them. My brother had won! The Kaiser was for him! I watched as my step-father took out his wallet and gave the man who drove the Kaiser a wad of money, and he wrote out a receipt which he handed to my step-father. A few more words were spoken and they left. I felt a little jealous and mad.

After dinner Jimmy sat in his new car with a big grin on his face! I was told to stand by the driver's side door and Mommy took a picture of us. I thought to myself, "Why was I a part of this?" Jimmy acts like a monster and gets a reward?

The time had come when Jenny was allowed to come over to play at our house. I admit that I was very proud to show her around. I heard her say "Wow!" a couple of times, and that made me feel good. Mommy had given me quite a bit of old jewelry that she didn't wear anymore, and that she thought I would like. I put it all in my jewelry box, and it almost filled it up. My friend Jenny looked with envy at the pretty jewelry box and all of its contents. I felt some sense of pride that I had some things that were nice, and not the usual hand me downs. The jewelry box was new, and even if the contents were Mommy's castaways, they were pretty to me. Jenny looked at my jewelry as though it was one of the prettiest things in the world, and I suddenly felt sorry for her. It reminded me of when I didn't have enough clothing, and my friend Peggy had so much more of everything than me. I took out one of the pretty necklaces that was in the jewelry box and gave it to her. She looked up at me with a look of shock and asked, "Are you sure that you really want me to have this?" I assured her that it was all right and she thanked me profusely. I was sure that my mother wouldn't mind. We went outside and my new friend put her necklace on, and we ran around the yard like wild little Indians. Her yard was so small and we had acres. For once in my life I had more than others. It didn't make me forget how little I had at one time. Nothing would take that away, or the horrors that I had suffered.

During the first months of living in our new home, most of my mothers' time was spent with my step-father working on the property. John was getting the greenhouses back in order so that he could use them. He too was a florist and did a magnificent job of growing flowers. No one grew flowers like my step-father, not when it came to chrysanthemums and the different varieties of them. He actually became known for his expert abilities. He didn't have the glitz and style like my grandfather had, but he was in the newspaper from time to time. When the greenhouses were in better shape he started to plant, and was trying very hard to have a fall crop. He started to work on the greenhouses before my brother and I moved out there, so he had a head start. He did well and worked seven days a week.

———

CHAPTER 20

The summer was over and time for Jimmy and I to go to school. I was a little scared and Jenny and I had different teachers, so she and I would see each other off and on during the day. We had the same lunch period though. I was thankful for that. No more sitting alone. At recess, if the weather was nice we went outside like all kids do, but when it was nasty out we had to stay in a gymnasium that was the size of, or seemed to be the size of a football field. On days outside we would play hopscotch, and we were allowed to leave the school grounds to walk down to the candy store. I did that a lot.

One day when I was walking alone back to the school yard, I saw a group of kids that were much older than me standing on the outside of the fence. There was a car that had pulled up, and I saw an exchange of money as kids were given little bags. I later learned that day that the person in the car was a drug dealer, and he was handing out pills for money. The kids looked tough and very skinny. I realized that there were a lot of kids on drugs in my school. Jenny told me that this was nothing new, and I might as well get used to it because it was not going to go away.

Jenny and I played after school on most days, and I noticed that there were a lot of cars coming and going on our property. Mommy explained that people came in to buy my step-father's flowers and plants. One day I thought that I saw my father drive through. I told Mommy and she said that was impossible because he was in California. Sure enough, that evening my father called, and demanded that he see my brother and me on Sundays! He said that he had that right. My mother got off the phone and told me that I was quite right that I had seen my father. She was very upset and I felt uneasy. I hadn't seen my father since I was five or six, so why would I want to see him now? He wasn't good to us. I still had a lot of bad memories. I wondered how my brother felt about this.

After dinner Mommy called my brother and me into the living room. She told us that by law my father had the right to see us if he chose to. He said that he would be over this Sunday at two pm to pick us up. He had remarried as well, and it was time that we got to know our step-mother, whose name was Virginia. My brother seemed a little leery, but not really that upset. I was scared. I thought maybe he thinks he can get more stuff from our father, and perhaps there could be something in it for him! I was not a happy little girl and didn't want to go. My mother had to coax me. I finally agreed, not that I had any choice.

Sunday came, and Mommy put a pretty dress on me and made sure that Jimmy had on nice clothes as well. I felt my heart beat a little faster when I saw my father come down the driveway. He had a nasty look on his face as he got out of the car and looked around the place. His wife Virginia stayed in the car. I said to Mommy, "I'm scared and I don't want to go." She told me that I just simply had to. My brother stood with a rather pleasant look on his face and said "Hi Dad." My father turned around and looked at both of us and said, "Let's go." My mother reminded him that we were to be back by six because we had school the next day. He just gave her a nasty look. When we got into the car I felt like I wanted to vomit. This is the man that I saw drink too much, this is the man that I saw hit my mother, this is the man that didn't visit us, this is the man who was not there when I needed him. Why were we here now? I think my brother was upset because he wanted to show off his new car to Daddy, but didn't get the chance.

My father introduced us to Virginia as we drove away. She turned around in her seat and faced us. She had a pleasant smile. She told us that we were going to go to a fancy restaurant for Sunday dinner. My father had nothing pleasant to say, instead he said "I bet that stupid guy from Denmark isn't treating you well." My brother told him that they fight a lot. He was probably trying to get on my fathers good side. I thought, "How can he talk like this when John really tries so hard to be his friend?" From what I had seen, my step-father was a hard working man, and probably one of the nicest guys I had ever known. It's true that he and I never spoke that much. I think it was because we were both shy towards each other. All he wanted to do was work and be left alone. I just kept silent because I was scared to stick up for John because of my father's terrible temper. If he knew that I approved of my step-father he would give me a very hard time. I knew that John was a good man and if there were times that I could be helpful I was, because I did want to please him.

My father didn't talk nicely to Virginia either. They didn't really fight, but he spoke roughly to her. I actually felt sorry for her. I could tell that she became embarrassed when he yelled at her, and I thought, "Lady, you don't know the half of it!" We arrived at the restaurant. It was pretty fancy and we all had a good meal. It was quite a ways from home, so after eating we left right away, and were home a little before six. My mother came out of the house. My father said to her in a nasty voice, "Have them ready next week at one." He then left, and my mother took us in the living room and asked how everything went. Jimmy said it went well and I felt like hitting him. My father hadn't changed, he was still nasty, and anyone could see that. Sundays were going to be bad days from now on.

Jenny and I played as usual after school and things around our house were all right for a change. I didn't like my school, but that was not unusual as I never did. We had this teacher who was very cruel. On nasty days we were not allowed to play outside, we had to stay in the gym and were told to form a circle and stand there. This made no sense to me. If you asked to sit down, this nasty teacher would walk quickly over to you with a belt in her hand and threaten to hit you! One little girl was so afraid of her, that at times she would pee her panties. The witchy lady would look at her and laugh, and take her out of the circle and make fun of her in front of everyone. This would make the little girl cry. I vowed to myself that she would never make me cry or intimidate me!

One day she decided that it was my turn. She stood there and glared at me, and I glared right back. She then came over real close to me and said, "You think that you're smart don't you?" I answered with a pounding heart, "Yes!" This infuriated her. She went to raise the belt to hit me in the legs and I said "If you hit me, I will call the cops on you." She dropped the belt and got even closer to me. As she was speaking I realized that she smelled like Daddy! She was drunk! I ran from the gym and hid in a hallway until the bell rang. When I got home I told Mommy everything. She kept me home the next day, and she called Jenny's mother and told her everything that I had said. Jenny stayed home too. Both mothers went to the school the next day and had a talk with the principal. The teacher was called down to the office, and when she started to try and defend herself, the principal smelled booze on her breath. She was dismissed immediately! I was told the next day by the principal, that a bottle of booze had been found in the ex-teachers desk, and that I had done a good thing by making them aware of the teacher's drinking. The little girl who peed in her panties was real happy too. The news spread quickly that the teacher had been fired, and what I had done. I felt proud of myself because I had done a good thing!

———

CHAPTER 21

For me, Sundays came too quickly. Daddy was never really nice and he started to pick us up late. I don't know why he bothered because he was never really happy to see us. I felt like he was trying to pump us for information about my step-father and our home. With the exception of one time, we always went to eat. That one time, we went to Coney Island and had fun that day, but that was the only time. On Sundays, just to pass time, I would walk up and down the road waiting for the inevitable to happen. That of course was Daddy's arrival. One Sunday I went further than usual down the driveway so I could look up and down Signs Road to spot him coming. He was so late this time. As I stood there looking for him, a light blue car pulled up at the end of my driveway. I had never seen this car before or the man in it. I stood there looking at him, and all of a sudden he bent over and rolled down the passenger side window. I was about ten to twelve feet away from his car when he started to speak to me. I couldn't hear what he was saying so I got closer, and still couldn't hear. I stood dumbfounded not knowing what he wanted. He moved over closer to the passenger side of the vehicle, and still spoke so I couldn't hear him. Quick as a flash he opened the door and pulled me in! I yelled, "What are you doing!" He said, "Don't be afraid I just need you to help me with my radio because it isn't working right." I said, "I don't know anything about radios, how can I help?" He had already sped away and we were going down the street. There was no one else on the road so he was able to drive fast. Signs Road had no traffic lights and hardly any houses or people at all. I knew that I was in trouble. None of this made sense to me.

I looked over at him and noticed that he was about my stepfather's age. He had short blonde hair and when he looked at me I noticed blue eyes. I also saw a pretty good size scar on his face. It was sort of half moon shape. He gave me a smile and told me that we were going for a long ride! I told him that my Daddy was at the house waiting for me, and I had to get back home. He made no comment. I was holding a coffee can that had one hundred pennies in it, and I said to him, "I'll give you all of these pennies if you take me back home." He looked at me and laughed and said that he didn't want them, he wanted something else. I had a very bad feeling, a feeling from the past that I used to have with Uncle Cliff. I started to pray and I said, "Lord if I get back home alive I promise I will never be so stupid again." I looked at the man, and noticed that he wore a ring on his pinky that had a huge diamond in it. He saw me looking at it. He told me that it was very valuable, and maybe someday if I made men very happy, I would have one too.

After a while he asked me what I meant when I said that my Daddy was waiting for me at the house. I told him that my parents were divorced, and he said that happens at times. I looked out at the road and I realized that I no longer had any idea where I was, and my heart started to beat faster. I knew that the worst thing that I could do was panic. I had to somehow stay calm so I could think and not make him mad. If I yelled no one would hear me anyway. No one was on the street. I had been reading Mommy's detective magazines that spoke about murder and stories like this, and I thought that I am now one of those stories. It dawned on me that if I got back alive, I would have to talk to the police, and I would need to give them as much information as I could. Mommy didn't know that I was reading her magazines, and would have been mad if she did know. On the other hand I was now happy that I remembered some of what I read. One thing other than music that I knew I was good at was reading, and I did read quite a bit. I thought to myself that I know what he looks like, and the dashboard said the word Plymouth, and I knew that the seat covers were plaid. I also knew that the car was pretty new, if not new. I had seen advertisements in the magazines that I read and had seen cars like this. I also knew that he smoked. The windows were up and the car was pretty smoky. I thought well, I have a pretty good description of him. We drove and drove. I kept trying to find landmarks. He looked at me and laughed and said, "You'll never find your way back here again."

I felt myself start to cry and he said "If you are a good girl, a very good girl and do everything that I say, you'll be alright." I still couldn't hold back my tears because some how I knew that this was going to be another Uncle Cliff thing. However, unlike Uncle Cliff, he seemed mild mannered and not cruel acting. He didn't make ugly faces like Uncle Cliff did, nor did he speak roughly to me. This was a new situation to me. I did know that I was in big bad trouble. This man had kidnapped me!

Suddenly we turned down a long driveway that was somewhat like mine, and at the end of the driveway was a house. It appeared to be empty. He stopped about twenty feet away and turned off the engine. I felt my heart pounding. He pulled me out of the car and put me in the back seat. He said "We wouldn't want to get such a pretty dress dirty now would we?" I didn't answer. It never occurred to me to run away. Where would I run to? The house was empty and no one was around. In fact there were very few cars during the whole ride. I had a pretty dress on with matching socks, but at the time I didn't care if I got dirty or not. All I wanted to do was get out of this nightmare alive.

He pushed me down on the seat and pulled my dress up, and then pulled my panties down. I started to yell. He put a hand over my mouth and for the first time spoke roughly to me. "Look little girl" he said, "I told you to behave." I kept my mouth shut and he removed his hand. He then opened his belt and pulled his tan pants down. I watched as he began to pull down his underwear.

He now had a different look on his face that was not so kind. He completely pulled down his underwear and I closed my eyes. I suddenly felt a sharp pain in between my legs, and I cried out in shock. He told me in a very nasty threatening voice that I had better be quiet, and to hold still and not to move. I felt myself stiffen just like I did with Uncle Cliff, only this time this man was doing something to me that was very painful in my privates. This was not touchy feely and grinding against me. I yelled again and he got really mad at me. He took both of my arms and held them above my head, and pinned them down so hard that I couldn't move. He did his dirty deed, but wasn't quite able to enter me completely, as I was too small. He hurt me badly in the process of trying, and I felt like passing out. I was so dizzy. I lay there crying and he got up and out of the car. He ordered me to do the same. I got up and felt a sharp pain in my stomach area and down lower. I noticed that I was covered with sticky stuff and a little blood. He yelled at me to get dressed. I did as I was told. I bent over and pulled my panties up all the time feeling a lot of pain in different parts of my little body. He told me to get back in the car and we drove away.

We didn't speak. I felt myself go limp. I could hardly hold myself up. I was very sore to say the least and my mind was just blank. We drove and drove just like we had done on the way there, and suddenly we came to a stop. He said to me roughly, "Get Out!" I looked out the window and realized that I was at the Victory Blvd. side of our driveway! He was not going to kill me! I opened the door and found a new strength come over me. I got out of the car and watched it speed away. I knew that it was blue, but didn't think to look at the plate numbers. I knew everything else though. As I started to walk down the driveway I didn't look at Jenny's' house. I felt dirty, and did *not* want to be seen. I walked very slowly because I was hurting all over, and quite frankly, I felt very ugly.

I walked down the long driveway, the house came into view and I saw a lot of cars there. I saw Daddy's car and also two police cars. I didn't yell, I didn't cry and I could not run. My father said to me. "Where were you, you idiot? We've been going nuts here not knowing where you were!" He didn't ask me what happened. My mother took one look at me and took me aside. I told her everything. She told the police what I said. I wasn't prepared for what happened next; my father looked at me with disgust on his face and asked,

"What did you do to that man to make him act that way? Did you lead him on?" I was so shocked and hurt that I gasped! I couldn't speak. One of the officers became so mad at him that he came over to my father with open handcuffs and cuffed one of my father's hands to the steering wheel of his own car! The officer said, "You're a moron and how dare you treat your daughter like that after what she's been through? In all of my years as an officer I have *never* seen anything like this before!" My father stood there with a look of shock as he looked at his cuffed hand. I thought, "Good!" He's an animal too for talking to me like that!

My mother took me to the side, away from the police officers, and she pulled my panties down. She said in a disgusted voice, "That pig!" And then she told me that the man who raped me would pay for this. She told me to go into the house right away, take my clothes off and take a shower. No one mentioned the hospital or anything else. I went in and took a shower as Mommy said to do. I remember that I was very sore and only patted my vaginal area with soap and water, and I remember that it burned like a cut. It felt the same way as when my legs had gotten caught in the barbed wire fence so long ago.

Mommy was standing outside of the bathroom and she gave me fresh clothes to put on. She also told me that the police wanted to talk to me and that they were now downstairs in the living room. I asked her where Daddy was, and she told me that he left and said he wouldn't be back. I had disgraced him. I thought "Great!" whatever that means. The police asked me what the car looked like and what he looked like, and I was able to answer all of their questions. They were pretty shocked that I could tell them so much. I thought "Well, I pretty much have been here before, haven't I?"

I stayed home from school for a few days because I just simply couldn't face people, and not to mention how sore I was. Mommy gave me Vaseline to pat on my injured areas, and aspirin for pain. I was also very frightened that he might come back. I couldn't sleep at night and jumped at any strange noise. I knew that the news had gotten out about what had happened to me. It was in the paper too. They didn't mention my name, but Mommy had told Jenny's mother and she told so and so and on it goes. Mommy said that people have to be warned about this man, and that it was good that I was able to describe him and the car so well. I knew that what she said was true, but it didn't make me feel any better. I felt embarrassed and dirty. I wanted to scream, but nothing would come out.

Several days later there was a knock on the front door and there stood two men. These men were detectives. They had brought two big wide books with them. I was asked to look at pictures of men who were sex offenders, and who hurt little girls and boys like me. Boys, I thought! I never thought about that before. I thought that only little girls got hurt that way. It was explained to me by the two detectives that it could be either. They asked me to please look at the pictures and see if I recognized the man who had raped me. I felt sick as page after page I looked at these monsters. Some of them were young, some were old, some big and some small, but none of them looked like the man who hurt me. I felt disappointed that I couldn't pick out the picture, but he just simply wasn't there, not in these books. The detectives thanked me and said to my mother in the hallway that there were more books for me to look through. My mother asked if they could wait a couple of days because I was clearly upset. They said that they could, but to remember that he is out there, and must be caught.

I hadn't spoken to Jenny since this happened. No one called or came over. In a way it was probably better, but I felt like I could have used some support. I felt like I was a very different type of kid, and I felt like there was something wrong with me. I felt lonely even though Mommy was there. My father's words kept going through my head. I knew that he was wrong to treat me the way he did, and I didn't quite understand what he meant when he asked, "Did you lead him on?" He acted like it was my fault, and he felt like I disgraced him? I thought how about the way that I feel? Does anyone ever think about the way the victims feel? Do they really know? I thought he could just stay away forever!

The days that I stayed home from school I hardly left my room. I just wanted to be alone for the most part. I simply didn't feel safe.

At times I would sit and cry, and at other times I actually found myself laughing, and then wondering if I was starting to go crazy. What was there to laugh about? How could all of these things happen to me? I dreaded the thought of going back to school. All eyes would be on me and I knew it. People would forget how I got the bad teacher fired, and that was a good thing. They would now look at me with different thoughts. Instead of being the little girl who had the bad teacher fired, I now was the little girl who had gotten kidnapped and raped. I thought that Jenny should have at least called to see if I was all right. She didn't have to come over, and I didn't even think that I could play with her. I just needed to hear a friend's voice. I had all kinds of mixed feelings. My mother didn't speak about it, in fact no one did. This kind of conversation was a no-no. I was to forget that it happened. How do I do that? Does that mean that the ugly man forgets what he does? Does he ever feel shame or regret?

———

CHAPTER 22

The day had come to go back to school. I saw Jenny waiting at the end of the driveway. I tried to read her face to see if she was going to be friendly to me. When I got closer I saw she had a sad look, and she ran over and gave me a hug. We stood there clinging to each other and I started to cry. She took out a hankie and gave it to me, and said she was so sorry about what had happened. She further went on to say that she didn't know if I wanted company or not, so she stayed away. She had not forgotten me, but she admitted that she didn't want to hear about it, because it would make her very mad. It also scared the hell out of her! "Wow," I said "You said the H word." She then giggled and admitted she heard her Mommy and Daddy talking about all that had happened, and she kind of learned a new word. We both giggled, and I said she had better keep that one to herself! I promised that I would keep all the gory details to myself, and our friendship was re-established.

The bus came to take us to school. As I walked through the hallways I did see kids look at me at times. They really had no expression on their faces that I could describe. The story had been in the paper, and it mentioned that this was happening to a lot of eight-year old girls in the general area. I heard Mommy mention this to my step-father John. Nothing however was ever directly said to me. I guess my mother had an idea if you didn't speak about it, the nasty would go away. I felt very self-conscious, and quite frankly I had all kinds of fears coming back now. I started to look over my shoulder, and began to have nightmares again. I felt very threatened. I would go to class and sit alone, and I really didn't want to talk to other kids. I was afraid that there would be some who would want to know the gory details.

One day a detective walked into the classroom. I was mortified! I knew that he wanted to speak to me! The teacher looked annoyed and pointed to where I was sitting. I had to go downtown to look at mug shots! He took me right out in front of my classmates and I wanted to die, I was so embarrassed. I went with the detective and not a word was spoken all the way to the police department. I got out of the car and followed him into the building. He sat me down, and gave me a big glass of milk and a jelly donut. I admit that it made me feel better, because unfortunately, food always did. After I drank my milk, and ate my jelly donut, it was back to the mug shots. I looked and looked, and after a time I had to admit that I just hadn't found a picture that looked like him. They seemed disappointed and took me back to school. I had done the best that I could to help, but his picture was just not in these books.

Two days later they came back into my classroom. I heard a few kids talk under their breath and I wanted to run. This was very stressful to me to have the law come in and drag me out of the school in front of my classmates. I said nothing, gathered my books, and away we went again. I didn't see any man that looked like the man who raped me in the books that were shown to me. One detective sighed, and said "Take her home." I told my mother that night that if the police or the detectives want to speak to me, tell them to come to the house! I had enough. I felt dirty and different and even though I knew in my heart that I did nothing wrong, this whole procedure of the police or detectives coming to school just made me feel guilty, like it was my fault.

The next day my mother called the station. She told the detectives how I felt about them coming into school, and taking me out in front of my classmates. They came to my house in the evenings instead. I could deal with that, and I knew this awful man had to get caught. I went through many books but failed to see his picture.

One Saturday the detectives handling the case came to the house and asked me if I thought that I could take them to where the crime happened. I said that I thought so, and I did. They were shocked that I could remember the way, and were very pleased as well. Then, something weird happened to me after that day. I realized a few weeks later I was having a hard time finding places that I knew. I had told my mother about a restaurant that my father had taken Jimmy and me to, and that I thought that it would be nice for all of us to go. My mother spoke to my step-father, and we decided to go out for a nice family dinner. My mother said, "Carol knows where it is" and try as I might, I could not find it. Finally my brother remembered the way and made fun of me. I realized as time went by, that after showing the police where I got raped, I lost my sense of direction utterly and completely. I thought "Great! That's something else to have to deal with!"

One day the police came to the door and said they wanted to speak to me. My mother let them in, and moments later the detectives who had been handling the case showed up too. They caught the man who had raped me! The same man had raped many little girls my age. Because I had given such a good description of the car, and the man himself, a teenage boy saw him pull another little girl into his car, and recognized him. He was able to get his license plate number and called the police. The man was found and arrested. I stood there in a state of shock, but also felt a sense of great relief. I suddenly loved the police and told them so. They all laughed and went on to say that when the criminal goes before the judge for sentencing , all the little girls that he so brutally raped, were to come to the courthouse and watch. I suddenly felt frightened because I didn't want to be so near him again. I was assured that by watching the sentencing, it would help me have closure. I would feel safe again in knowing that he was behind bars. I asked how long he would be behind bars for, and they said that it was up to the judge to decide.

After the police left we all went out to the diner to celebrate. We had hot fudge Sundays, and my mother praised me for being so observant, and that I should feel proud of myself for helping the police and all little girls my age. I told her that her detective magazine helped a lot! She looked at me with a strange look and asked me what I meant by that. I confessed that I had read a lot of them. She said that they were not meant for little kids to read. I said, "Look how they helped!" No argument there, even Jimmy had to agree! We all had a good laugh.

Monday morning had come and that meant that I was going to have to go to school. All weekend I had felt light as a feather after being told the big news on Friday. Let's face it; I was no regular little girl. I had been kidnapped, raped, and not to mention all the before this "uglies." I didn't know if I was going to be stared at, or spoken to, or just plain ignored. I preferred the latter. I met Jenny up at the end of the driveway and she said she had heard the news. It was all over the Sunday paper. I didn't see the paper nor did I want to, because I had lived it and survived it, and that was enough for now! My mother said that the next weekend we would all go to Coney Island because my brother and I had liked it so much. It would be like a celebration event to celebrate the capture of the man who was wanted for years, and now was in jail.

The bus came and we went to school. We didn't speak about the capture or anything related to it. I think she could sense that I didn't want to. We just spoke about little girl things and the fact that Christmas was almost here. It was very cold out and there was a possibility of snow. I thought pretty soon I'm going to have to get new leggings, my legs are cold. I noticed that Jenny already had hers on. The bus arrived at the school and we went our separate ways promising to meet for lunch. This meant that I had to walk the hallways alone and face the kids and stares or whatever. I started to walk down one hallway and stare a lot of them did. There were some that smiled at me in a good way, and then there were a few that snickered. I felt like hitting them. I know who those brats are; those are the kids that live near the dumps. I thought Yuk- no wonder they are so nasty. I knew that it wasn't their fault they were poor, and maybe their Mommy and Daddy didn't teach them how or when to be nice. I then thought, I never really had any real do's and don't taught to me, maybe it's just something you should know. I know right from wrong and their snickering is wrong.

There was one little girl that I recognized from the group of brats who were not being kind. I had seen her standing in the soup line that the poor kids stood in. The soup was actually not that bad, and maybe for some of those kids, along with a piece of bread and a container of milk, was all that they pretty much had to eat that day. The little girl saw me staring at her and she gave me a friendly smile. I decided that after this day is over and things calm down, I will try to be her friend.

I went through the morning trying not to look at any more faces, because then I wouldn't have to see their eyes looking at me. I had become very sensitive to people looking at me. I actually at times couldn't handle it. I would feel my heart start to beat faster and I would blush. Sometimes it would be so bad that I would start to sweat and feel like running. I didn't tell anyone about this because I was afraid they would think that I was crazy. I also started to realize that even though I was a very good reader, I couldn't stand reading out loud because I knew that everyone was looking at me. I would then go into immediate melt down. I would actually feel myself tremble. All I could think about was escaping. I hated myself for all of these feelings. I already felt that I was different, and this just added to the problems that I already had trying to cope with life and people.

I made it through the day, and was very happy that it was over. I couldn't wait to get back to the comfort and privacy of my home and bedroom. I played with Jenny a few times a week, but having school, and now some homework, made it difficult. It was a good relationship that we had, but not quite as close as what I had with Amy and Peggy. It was comfortable. If Jenny found another friend other than me, we could all play together, and the same goes for me if I found one. The rest of the week went well. I was stared at only for a couple of days, and then as kids do, they move on to new topics of interest. I was quite relieved.

That weekend Mommy was true to her word. We went to Coney Island and had a very good time. My brother and I ate hot dogs and cotton candy and we went and sat on rides that were closed down for the winter. We all liked walking on the boardwalk and we played games that were open in the inside game rooms. It was finally time to go home, but Mommy promised that in the spring we would come back. It was cold out and a lot of things were just plain closed down for the winter. It was still good to get out and feel the cold air hit my face and blow my hair all around. I looked up at the sky and it was a clear one that was now turning dark. I thought somehow, I feel refreshed and ready to start over again.

That night when we got home we were in for a shock! Someone had broken in and where Mommy had kept all of her important papers she realized that a lot were missing. Someone had also over-turned chairs and broken a few pictures that were on the wall, and a beautiful vase had been broken as well. I ran up to my bedroom to see if anything was disturbed, but as far as I could see everything was all right. Jimmy went to his room as well and couldn't find anything missing. We called the police and were instructed not to touch anything, because they wanted to see everything just the way it was. Neither my brother nor I had so much that we couldn't see at a quick glance if anything was disturbed or missing. Anyway, our dresser drawers were not touched, and I could look at my dollies that were all lined up, and they were in place. The police said it was a strange break-in because only paperwork was taken. In my mothers bedroom the pull cord for the maid was cut down, and the blankets were torn in areas. No ones clothing was disturbed and both Mommy and John had some nice clothes. Nothing made any sense. The police looked around and after a lot of thought, they decided it was a hate crime, and warned us to lock our doors and try to figure out who was mad at us. What a way to ruin a wonderful day.

John went out to the greenhouses to work. He now had lights out there and I felt sorry for Mommy and him for the problems that have been happening. I didn't think that this whole ordeal had anything to do with my brother and me. I was quite right, because in a few days Mommy realized that the break in was Daddy re-lated. He was furious at her because she wanted a new life and had made one. She never asked him for child support, even though she certainly deserved it. He had taken all of Johns' papers from Denmark like his passport, the divorce papers, birth certificates and more. He just wanted to make a stink. He was probably still mad at me because the police cuffed him to his own steering wheel — tough I thought. I didn't feel sorry for my father and I didn't want to see him again, not for a long time, maybe never.

Christmas came and Mommy and John bought us very nice gifts. I had gotten more clothes and another type of doll. Jimmy got new clothes and other things of interest to him. I'm surprised he didn't ask for another car! We had a quiet Christmas and a very nice Christmas dinner. We also had beautiful Christmas decorations, and a great tree that almost hit the ceiling in our huge living room. With the fireplace lit at night, and all of the overhead lights out, everything looked like what you would see in a storybook. All was well.

School started again. Yuk, I would never like it, that's for sure! I saw the little girl who lived near the dumps standing in the soup line. She usually ate alone. I had met Jenny for lunch as usual, and she saw me watching her. Jenny told me her name was Kimberly, and she said that she was really a nice kid, but that her older brother and sisters were mean. I told her that I figured that one out. We both laughed. I said, "I'm going to invite her to sit with us." I did, and she seemed so pleased to have someone to talk to. We three immediately became friends.

During the week I decided that I would ask Mommy if Kimberly could come over to our house to play with me. I explained where she was from, and that I felt sorry for her, but I wanted to become her friend. She agreed and said that if it was all right with her parents, she could come over after school one day, and my mother would take her home afterwards. Kimberly's parents could write a note to our bus driver, and Mommy would pay for her to ride the bus this one time. If all went well, maybe she could come over on weekends once in a while. This made me happy and I couldn't wait to tell her.

The next day at school Jenny and I looked for Kimberly at lunchtime and she was nowhere to be found. In fact she didn't come to school until the end of the week. I noticed that on Thursday she showed up with a black eye. I thought to myself "What a shame," and I had to wonder if her weird acting sister or rude brother had done that. I remembered how they snickered at me when I walked in after everyone knew what happened to me. They were just mean and anyone with a brain could see that. Jenny and I waited for lunchtime to see if she stood in the soup line as usual. Kimberly walked in and I approached her. The minute that she saw me coming near her she lowered her head, and I could see that she felt uncomfortable. I still went over to her. I thought if ever she needed a friend it would be now.

I remembered how I felt with all of the things that I had to face, and to me, the more friends the better. I didn't have many friends during those horrible days, but to have none would have been too much to bear. "Kimberly" I said, she looked up at me and smiled. I told her that both Jenny and I had been waiting for her. She seemed very pleased, and said that she would be with us as soon as she got her food. I went back to the table and both Jenny and I agreed that we wouldn't ask her about her eye. If she wanted to speak about it fine, and if not, we didn't want to scare her away with questions. She came over to the table and sat down and we all started to talk. We made no mention of her eye and I didn't ask her if she wanted to come over to my house yet. I didn't think it was the right time. I wanted her to feel more comfortable with us. I wondered if she got anything for Christmas. I didn't dare to ask. I silently thought that if I get her to come to my house, I would ask Mommy if I could give her a toy or something. She was smaller than me, so I had clothes that I could give her. I thought "Wow, look at me now, I am certainly in a different position than I was some time ago." I have to admit that it felt good. I liked giving to people if I had anything they could use. I knew this, and my mother always encouraged such, now that we had a little more.

———

CHAPTER 23

The time had come! The sentencing of the man who had raped so many little girls was here! The detectives had come to our house, and told my mother that I was to go the courthouse the following week, and watch along with the other victims as he was being sentenced. It's very hard for me to describe how I felt. I didn't feel elation, for some reason I felt fear instead. I asked if I had to do this, and I was told that it would help show the public, and the man himself, that this crime doesn't go unpunished. This information still didn't make me feel better. I can't say why. I think because it did happen, and I did suffer from all kinds of new complexes and bad feelings about myself. I just wanted it all to go away. I didn't want people to look at me at any time, and especially not now. I was told that only one little girl would testify, and that the rest of us would be far back in the courtroom. All we had to do was listen and watch as he got sentenced. I was filled with fear, even though I knew that he couldn't touch me. I just didn't want to see him. I started to cry uncontrollably after the detectives left and no one in my family could understand the feelings I was experiencing. This infuriated me. I thought that none of them had to go through what I did at Uncle Cliffs, and not with what happened here either. I felt that they just didn't understand. They had no idea that I was having so many feelings of self-hatred, and feelings of being dirty and different. They didn't know that I would blush horribly and my heart would race if I thought that I was being stared at. They didn't know about all of the many nights I woke up in a sweat from horrible dreams. I felt like seeing him again would only make matters worse. No one understood this. I was afraid to tell anyone about these feelings, and who would I tell anyway? Who would understand or care? This problem was even too big and weird for Aunt Priscilla. I hadn't seen auntie in a long time. I felt like having these problems weren't normal, and maybe I was a little crazy. None of my friends ever mentioned having problems like these, and I wasn't about to tell them.

The days went by and the big day was almost here. I told Jenny what I had to do. She was shocked, but then said, "Maybe it's good to let people know that he's going to jail, and then if there are any other weirdoes like him out there, they would think twice!" I knew that she was right. I just didn't want to face it.

The day had come and we went to court. We were ushered into the courthouse and I noticed that there were a lot of people around. There were also a few people with cameras and I was told that they were newspaper people. I said, "Oh No, they're not going to take a picture of me!" I was assured that wouldn't happen. I felt my heart start to pound and I felt dizzy. We were taken into a small area off of the courtroom and then I realized that my mother, brother, and step-father John were not beside me. It was a dark area that I stood in, and once my eyes adjusted to the darkness, I could see that there were a lot of little girls just like me standing there. I stood next to approximately fifteen of them. I tried to see their faces, but most of the kids held their heads down looking at the floor. I thought, "They must feel like me."

I could hardly hear what was being said, and I couldn't see that well. At one point I saw a little dark haired girl sitting up by the judge, and a man was asking her questions. At times, I would see her shake her head and say no and other times yes. She was braver than me, I thought. I wanted to run. I could see that she had a hanky and she was crying. Then I saw her get escorted back to the chair that she was sitting in, and a few moments later there was the man that had raped all of us. I felt my heart start to pound again, and I hated myself for feeling like this. I just wanted to run. I heard several little girls next to me crying, and I felt myself stiffen. He was going to be sentenced right now. He stood in handcuffs before the judge, and even though I couldn't really hear what was being said, I suddenly saw the judge point back in our direction, and I knew that he was talking about all of us.

After being wanted for rape for years, he only received a few years in prison. I heard a gasping noise go through the courtroom, and someone yelled "He should get life!" I heard nothing else. My mind went blank for a few seconds. Suddenly I thought that I wouldn't be very old at all when he got out. I was a mess, and I felt like I wanted to throw up. One of the little girls had peed on the floor. I almost slipped and fell in it. I thought," Oh yes, this helped me a lot." I guess that I should have been relieved, but I just wasn't. I knew that he would get out, not in ten years or twenty, but a lot sooner. I thought, "Not good enough. He *knows* where I live!"

I was glad the weekend was here. I didn't go to school on Friday, as I didn't want to have people looking at me, and I only missed one day of school. Jenny came down to my house to see how I was doing, and we played in my room for a while. She asked me how I felt about court and what had taken place. I just said that it was awful; in fact I told her it was shitty, and we both rolled on the floor with laughter. I would of course never say that word around an adult, but I heard one say it! At the days end I thanked her for coming over to see me, and we spoke about going to school on Monday. I said, "If anyone says anything to me or looks at me weird, I'm going to punch them." She said that she would help me and then left for home. My mother told me that I should feel a lot better now that the man was in jail, and to try and put the whole thing out of my head. I thought "Okee-dokee!"

Monday came and Jenny and I went to school as usual. The moment I walked in, a lot of kids began looking at me. Jenny had to go to her classes, and I had to go to mine. My brother who never walks with me because he was a big guy, and to walk with his little sister would be a disgrace, decided to walk behind me in case weird things happened. I was actually a little touched that he showed he cared. We never had much to say to each other, so this was a nice gesture on his part. After he left to go to his class, a few kids did look at me funny. I thought, "So what, I'm getting used to this, yea right!" I'll just walk with my head held down and then I won't see anything. I won't see if I'm being stared or laughed at.

As the weeks went by the season started to change. We all looked forward to spring and then summer. Jimmy continued to cause grief for my mother and John, and it seemed like it was a never-ending battle. I didn't understand it, because even though my step-father never spoke to us often, at least there is peace in the house. Mommy and John *never* fought. They disagreed, but quietly.

My brother made friends with kids who lived over by the dumps, and he always wanted a ride to go see them. He was particularly fond of a girl who lived there. I was shocked to hear that she lived right next to my friend Kimberly. I decided to go with brother and see her, if it was all right with all adults concerned. It was agreed upon, and my mother drove us over. I watched as my brother went into Joanie's house, and I went a couple of houses down to Kimberly, who lived in a really shabby home. To some kids that doesn't mean anything. I noticed that it wasn't clean like mine. I met her mother, and in walked one of the snickering brats that knew what happened to me. I felt so embarrassed and ashamed. Kimberly put her head down and told her sister to shut up and leave us alone. Kimberly's mother stood there not knowing what was going on, and big sister told her that I was the girl from the paper. I knew that I didn't do anything bad, but I felt very self-conscious. The lady said that she was so sorry to hear what had happened to me, and told her older daughter to butt out. I thought these people talk funny. Kimberly took me by the hand and we went into her bedroom that was located at the back of the house. I smelled a really bad odor. Kimberly apologized, and explained that the dumps have a really bad smell, and on really hot summer days, she slept on the couch out front. I felt very sorry for her, and told myself that I would have her over to my house really soon and we would play there.

We played and the day came to an end. Mommy came and picked up brother and me. Kimberly was one of five children and pretty poor. She said that they always had enough to eat at home even though she ate soup line lunches, but admitted clothing was a problem. She got a lot of hand me downs that didn't always fit. Kimberly was second from the youngest and I'm sure that it was bratty sister who gave her the black eye. When I got home I called Jenny up and told her about our friend Kimberly. We both decided that we would do our best to have her over to our houses. I don't think there were any really bad things happening in Kimberly's house, she just came from a family who had too many kids and not enough money. If Kimberly's parents fought a lot, she never mentioned it.

One day Mommy received a phone call from Aunt Priscilla. She called to see how everything was going, and also to tell us the news. Uncle Cliff had gotten caught with Peggy's mother and he was beaten up by Peggy's father! Not only was Peggy's mother going out with the nasty Uncle, but after I left he tried to touch Peggy too. I felt terribly bad about that. I never did get all of the information, or the whole story, but I know that he gave Peggy's mother money. I didn't feel sorry for Aunt Glady, because she wasn't nice enough to me. Also, I was told that they were going to move far away to a place called Florida, so that would be the true end of Uncle Cliff. I actually laughed when my mother told me the story. I thought of my uncle getting a beating and it made me feel really good. I wanted him to hurt, and the man who kidnapped and raped me; I wanted him to hurt really bad too. It was almost like getting a birthday present.

I had a quiet birthday that year. A lot had happened, but I did have a little satisfaction with the news of Uncle Cliff. I felt that a little justice had been served, and he would be gone forever!

School was coming to an end. My brother and I had been promoted, and I was quite relieved because I always had a problem with math. It seemed like that was a subject that I always passed by the skin of my teeth. I always thought that as long as I can add, subtract and divide, leave me alone. I wasn't going to be a scholar and I knew it, and further more I didn't care. Perhaps that was a bad attitude to have, but I just didn't like school, and I had gotten off to a bad start. A lot of bad things had happened to me since day one of school, which seemed like a long time ago. I had three subjects that I liked — English, music and gym. Even though I had polio as a child, and had a few problems with speech, and balance when I walked for a short time, I became very good in sports and I loved to run. I felt a certain sense of freedom when I ran. It helped to relieve pent up anxiety from all of life's problems, and God knows I had plenty of them. I was fortunate to live on a property that I could go out and run on until I felt like I wanted to drop. Then I could go into the house, sit down, relax, and color or whatever.

School ended and Jenny and I were busy making plans for summer vacation. I knew that neither one of us were going to go anywhere because her parents didn't have money, and my parents were too busy in the greenhouses to even think of a vacation. That is just the way it was. Sometimes teachers are so dumb. When vacation is over they expect you to come back and write about your summer experiences. They never take into consideration that a lot of kids just don't go anywhere. When I had to write about my summer experiences, I kept my made up stories simple, so that what I wrote would be believable. What a position to be put in! I'm sure that a lot of kids were in the same spot. Then you have those kids who appeared like they came from wonderful homes, had beautiful clothes, and hung out with only certain people. They would look at you and give you a sad but encouraging look, and you know that you just wanted to slap them. Jenny and I would talk a lot about these types of kids. They even walked differently, and someone like poor Kimberly, sure got lots of looks from the "chosen." We didn't talk to her about that though.

That summer my mother picked Kimberly up quite a few times, and the three of us played together. She walked around my house as though it was a castle. It's true that at one time my house was owned by people, who were very rich, and they had maids and all, but that was not us. I gave her a few blouses that I had outgrown and a piece of jewelry from my jewelry box. She was delighted. We ran and played like little girls do and I was starting to feel more lighthearted again. At times we played in Jenny's small pool, and then one day Jenny asked me if I would like to go to the big pool some distance away. I didn't know what she meant. She didn't ask Kimberly because you had to pay and take the city bus. I was a little bit nervous about this. After my mother took Kimberly home, Mommy and I stopped in at Jenny's house and inquired about this public pool. Jenny's mother told us that it would be a lot of fun, and we would be safe. I felt very apprehensive about this, and after we were back home I told my mother so. Mommy said to try it once and see how I felt. I was beginning to realize that I suffered from a lot of fears. Everything that was new became frightening to me, and if I left the property for too long, or if I was in any unfamiliar setting, I would feel fearful. I shared none of these feelings with anyone. I felt different, and I didn't want people to see this. I felt bad enough about myself already. Right now I was putting on an act like I was fine and the same as everyone else, but this is not how I felt. I decided that I would do like Mommy said, "Try and see if you like it." I didn't want to appear like a chicken to Jenny.

The day finally came for us to go. I put my bathing suit in a little carry bag with a towel, and was told that we would change once we were there. I met Jenny outside of her house and her mother stayed with us until the city bus came and picked us up. Jenny went on first and said to the bus driver, "City Pool please." He smiled and took her money. Then it was my turn and I said the same. We sat down. We talked all the way there and I was feeling very jittery about all of this. I certainly wasn't the same little girl who ran the streets when I was living in Westwood. I was brave then, and even though I had already seen things that kids should never see, I had a good feeling about myself and a sense of hope in those days. All I was doing now was play-acting. I had really turned into a very scared little girl who still looked over her shoulder. The bus pulled into the pool parking lot and we got out. There were quite a few people on the bus who were going swimming too. I could swim, but I was not the strongest swimmer in the world. Jenny's mother had assured my mother that there were lifeguards there, and it was safe. Jenny on the other hand could swim quite well.

We went into a dressing room and took off our street clothes and put on our bathing suits. Then we went out to the pool and went into the area roped off for kids. We had a ball, and for a while I was able to forget and relax. At three pm we have to go back home. Jenny had an old watch that her mother gave her, and we would check it periodically. At two thirty we went into the dressing room to get back into street clothes, and we went out to wait for the bus.

Suddenly I saw a man looking at me and I froze. I don't know why I was afraid of him. I just was. He stood across from us and he kept looking at me. I felt myself start to sweat, and my heart started to pound until I felt like it was going to jump out of my chest. My legs felt weak and rubbery. Jenny looked at me and she could see that there was something wrong. I told her I felt sick, and needed to go home. I didn't tell her that I needed to go home to feel safe!

The bus came and we got on. On the way home we spoke very little, but I told her that I had a really good time at the pool. When the bus dropped us off we parted our ways. I got into my house and Mommy was not in from working in the greenhouses. I went to my room and sat down on my bed, and started to cry. A perfectly good day ruined by me, me and my strange feelings that I didn't understand. I hope Jenny doesn't think that I'm too weird. I hope she believed me when I told her that I wasn't feeling well. I would hate to lose her as a friend because I look strange when I have those fits. Fits are what I called them for lack of better wording.

Two days later we had a surprise visit from the Child Protection Services of Richmond County. Someone had made a call concerning the welfare of my brother and me. The lady who came by was not allowed to tell us who had called the office, it was confidential. I remember the look on my mothers face. She looked shocked, and then angry. How could anyone do this? The fact that I had been left unsupervised at the end of the driveway was why I was able to be pulled into the car. That was a cause for concern. My mother explained that I had been warned never to go past the willow tree, and the small brook that was on our property, and if I had obeyed her, that incident probably wouldn't have occurred.

I felt very ashamed because it's true that Mommy told me not to go past a certain point. The lady then pointed out that children who are more supervised would have been observed doing wrong, and that would have saved me from the awful crime that took place. I wondered if she had gone to all of the little girl's houses, and put the parents on the spot. I thought too, if Daddy was on time like he should have been, I wouldn't have wandered so far away. I wondered who is to blame. I couldn't help thinking though that it was me. I didn't listen. As the lady spoke I continued to weigh the sides, and I was starting to get very upset. This became apparent to all as we stood in the living room. The lady took me aside to ask me questions. I asked, "What about my brother? Don't you want to talk to him?" She told me not to worry, that he would have his turn too. I suddenly felt afraid of her. I was afraid that I would say something wrong, and I would be taken away like those little boys and girls you hear about that have no home, and live in some big old house. They don't have enough to eat, or enough clothes to wear, and if they don't listen to what they are told, they get hit! Wow! I thought it was like that at Uncle Cliff's! I have to be careful!

Oh No! Now I really got scared and started to tremble. The lady told me not to be afraid. She just needed to get to the bottom of the complaint, and all would be well. I felt all mixed up because I felt that everything was fine, and now this happens! I felt like she put me under a microscope like the little girl in court who was being cross-examined. Some of us were treated more roughly than others by that monster, and the truth of possible neglect had to be determined at my house. I felt like I was up on the witness stand.

The lady asked me about our house and my relationship with Mommy and John. Then she asked about my brother and how we got along. She then said that she wanted to see my room. So far everything was going all right, because I said that everything was fine. When she saw that my brother and I had two bedrooms she was quite impressed. I could see it in her face. She looked in my closets and my drawers and she decided that I had enough clothes, not a huge amount, but enough. She did think that I could use another pair of shoes. She then sat me down and she told me that what happened with that horrible man was not my fault, and at no time should I ever think that it was. She also told me that she hoped that someday I would be able to get that crime out of my head, and not let it effect me for the rest of my life. She said that he is bad and is in jail. I thought, "Yes, but for how long?" I already knew the answer to that, and I knew that if I told her about all the strange fits I had been having, that she might think that I was crazy too, and not just abused. I kept my mouth shut. If this lady knew the whole story of my life, boy would her tongue wag! She gave me a quick once over exam with my mother present to see if I had any unusual bruises, and then asked to speak to Jimmy. All Jimmy wanted to do was show her his car! Ha, ha, ha!!! I actually laughed out loud. She made a funny noise and then said that she would write up a report, and as far as she could see that there would be only one follow up visit. She wouldn't tell us when that would be. She warned my mother to keep a closer watch on me, and then she left.

For hours after she left, my mother and John sat down in the sunroom, and mulled over all the people who could possibly be responsible for this ladies visit. Who could have made the call? I was very sorry that I hadn't listened to my mother about going so far away from the house, but also a thought had occurred to me. The monster who raped me, knew where to pick me up and drop me off so I could get back home. No one mentioned this at anytime. To me it meant that he drove in and out just like the people who wanted to buy flowers and plants did. That thought made me feel uncomfortable again. I could tell that Mommy was a little annoyed with me for a couple of days, because she barely spoke to me. That made me feel really bad again, and I could feel the self hatred start. I went up to my room, and even though I hadn't spoken to my dollies and Teddy in a long time, I did that night, and for a few days more.

About a week after the incident had happened, we got a surprise visit from Aunt Priscilla. I was delighted. I hadn't seen her in a very long time. She drove herself and didn't appear to be drunk. We had a great visit and she let us in on all of the new gossip. Aunt

Glady and Uncle Cliff were not doing so well down in Florida, because they were always fighting. I had lots of ideas why!

My father had a child with his new wife, and I didn't even know that she was expecting. I was told that Jimmy and I had a half sister. I had to be told what that meant. In this case we all have the same father. She didn't have any pictures yet, but when she did she would send them. I didn't know how to feel about this news. I wondered if he would be nicer to our new sister than he was to us. Then I felt a little jealous because maybe he would. I came back to reality and remembered the last time I saw him, how he was cuffed to the steering wheel, and why. The jealousy only lasted for a moment. I'm sure that they were in for a hard time too. I then felt sorry for the baby. "Boy, that's who Child Protective Services should see!" I thought. She told us that our Grandmother was going to move permanently to the cabin that my grandfather had purchased so long ago. She was going to sell the big grand house on the hill with the beautiful chandelier, and move there. She also went on to say that when she was settled, we could all go and visit her. My father was out in California, was going to stay there, so he wouldn't be in the way. My grandmother wanted to see her grandchildren from time to time. I felt my eyes fill up with tears because she had not forgotten us, and she had always been kind to my brother and me. My mother said she would keep it in mind, as she knew that we kids would like to see her. It would be a future event. Before she left, my mother told her about the Child Protective Services visit. My Aunt hung her head and said she couldn't be totally sure, but she thought that my father had called. He was in California, and wasn't around at the time of the incident. Phone calls can be made from anywhere. I thought of course, he broke into our house, so why not go further yet? It now started to make sense to me. My Aunt then left, and told us to keep the cabin in mind. When all was settled, which could take a little time, we were welcome to come and visit. I watched as she went up the driveway, and felt like I had just gotten a gift. I had always cared for her so. I didn't even care that she drank too much, because to me, she was my protector.

Jenny came by a couple of days later and apologized for not calling or coming sooner. She had been away with her parents to visit relatives. She and her cousins ended up fighting, and she mimicked how all of them sounded. She was very funny, and we rolled with laughter on my bedroom floor. She asked me how I was feeling and then said something very kind to me. I have been thinking about when we went to the pool and all of a sudden you became sick. I think something scared you and you didn't want to tell me, because you had a look of fear on your face. As I listened my heart sank, because just as I feared, you can see my "fits." She then went on to say, that after all I had been through; she would be more surprised if I didn't have fears of some kind. She said if it had happened to her, she would probably sleep with a knife or a baseball bat. We both laughed and hugged each other. She said not to feel bad about anything, and that she would always be my friend. After she left, I thought she is so smart, and she understands me. She is smarter than the adults. We stayed away from the pool for the rest of the summer, or I should say I never went again. We played at her house or mine for the rest of the summer vacation. Mommy did take us to Coney Island again, and Jenny came too. That was my way of saying thank you for being such a good friend.

———

CHAPTER 24

Summer was over and school was starting in a week. I thought that this year would be better than last. I had decided that I would make an effort to be a better student. Probably nothing would make me ever really like school, but I knew that if I applied myself I could do a lot better. After all, I was no longer in first grade. I was starting to feel a little more grown up at the ripe old age of nine. Mommy had gotten Jimmy and me some new clothes, and he and I had an idea of how we wanted to dress, much to Mommy's surprise. I saw and noticed how the popular girls dressed. I wanted to have at least one outfit like theirs. Jimmy had similar ideas. He was in the big league now, and would go to another school the following year. Mommy and John were doing well with their business, and were making some decent money. I had overheard them talking and they were very proud of themselves. I thought they should be, because John worked seven days a week and never really took off any full days, not even on Christmas. It was a hard life for a florist, and I had seen that in the past with my grandfather, because he too worked all of the time, except when he would go to his fancy flower shows. At times I would try to figure out what I wanted to be when I grew up, and believe me, it was not a florist! I called Jenny up. We made plans to see each other the next day to discuss which teachers we were going to have. We hadn't seen too much of poor Kimberly because she never had a ride to our house, and Mommy didn't have the time to pick her up and take her back home.

This made my brother mad because he couldn't see Joanie. I silently laughed to myself and thought, "Why doesn't he drive over? He has a car!" I never said anything to Mommy about this because I knew that it was a poor way to shut brother up. I was a kid and even I knew this. He sure knew how to get his way!

School is here! I thought another year. Jenny and I walked into our school and we actually had a class together this year. We had the same English class. We were happy to have at least one. Jenny and I wore our new outfits, and she too had managed to get one of the popular girl outfits. We were both proud. We didn't think of what we would wear after that day. It would be back to the usual. We both giggled and I said, "I wonder if we're walking any differently?" Just as I said that, we saw the popular girls standing as they always did together, looking everyone up and down, and making their snide remarks. I pointed them out to Jenny and I said, "I wonder what they are going to say about us?" One of the "popular" girls saw us and immediately she started to laugh. The others looked to see what she was laughing at and they laughed too. They were laughing at us! "Look" one said, "They're trying to be like us and that'll never happen." Jenny got so mad that she said secretly to me, "Watch, I'll get even!" I had no idea what she meant, and she wasn't about to tell me. We had to go our separate ways until lunchtime. We had English class after lunch. The rest of the morning, until lunchtime, went all right. After all it was only day one, what could happen?

Jenny and I met for lunch as usual and I looked to see if Kimberly was in the soup line like last year. I didn't see her at all. Jenny and I sat down to eat, and the popular girls came in and walked right by us, making their usual lousy remarks about some people being poor, and clucking their tongues. Suddenly without warning, Jenny stood up and made like she had tripped spilling her milk all over one of the girl's new blouse. Oh my God! What a scream! You'd think that she had gotten hit or something. The girl yelled at Jenny saying, "You lousy waif, you did that on purpose!" Jenny acted as though she was terribly sorry and tried to help her clean her pretty blue blouse off. A teacher came over and the girl was screaming in a shrill voice that Jenny had started this, and she did it on purpose. She of course had. I thought, "Wow! I never dreamed she would ever do that!" The teacher looked at Jenny and Jenny apologized and said that it was an accident and she was very sorry. The teacher just simply believed her, and told the other girl to get control, or she would have to go the office. I wanted to laugh and shout with joy because these bullies were almost as bad as the bullies from the dumps. Jenny had just plain had enough, and so had a lot of other kids, because most everyone seemed to approve of what had just taken place. I think most of us had enough. What a great first day!

When the day was over, I met Jenny at the bus and noticed that she had gained respect from some of the kids because of her actions in the lunchroom. I must admit that I was pretty impressed myself. Kids that we never spoke to gave her nods or said hello. I felt like I was with a celebrity or something. I didn't care if what she did was right or wrong, because she had shown those snobby girls that the way they looked down on others was wrong. She was my celebrity too and I told her so. The rest of the week went well until Friday. Every year you get more books. We were instructed to take our new books home and cover them. All we had to use were paper bags, and I felt a little embarrassed, but I noticed the next day that a lot of kids did the same thing. In English class we were given an in-class assignment to do. We had to write a report telling what we did this summer, of course. I thought about my summer vacation and quite frankly I didn't know what to say. Jenny sat on the other side of the room. I looked at her and she shrugged too. I mean neither one of us went to Europe or anything. I didn't want to use the city pool because that was where I had a fit, and I only went once. What on earth could I write about? The pool was where the poor kids went, the kids who had nowhere else to go, so it was nothing to brag about. I looked around the room and there were a couple of "popular girls" in our class, and they were busy writing away. I'm sure they had plenty to write about. I finally decided to make up a story that would sound somewhat impressive. I said that I went away on vacation with my family to relatives who lived in a cabin, and the cabin was right next to a lake. I also said that we went swimming every day, and there were woods nearby, where we went on many picnics. We also did some hiking in the woods. I thought I was covered. I pulled it off, and actually I wasn't lying too much because my grandmother did own a cabin, there was a lake nearby, but she just wasn't living there yet. Once she's living in the cabin, that is what I will do, and then I won't have to lie anymore. I sat there and was really mad at the teacher, because I looked around the room and most of the kids came from poor homes. That part of Staten Island was poor.

After a while, the teacher looked around the room and made kids come up to the front one by one to read out loud what they had written. I suddenly started to feel strange like I had before. I thought, "What is wrong with me?" I feel like I had written enough and that it was probably well done. Suddenly it was Jenny's turn and boy what a storyteller she was! I almost laughed out loud. I could hardly control myself. Jenny went to California and had a wonderful time swimming in the ocean, and she had to be very careful of the waves so she wouldn't be swept away. She also went on the boardwalks and played games, and went on many rides. At nighttime, her family would collect shells and she and her mother were going to make jewelry out of the smaller ones as a project! "Wow" I thought, that makes my report a little slim. As the teacher praised her for her writing and speaking abilities, she sat down with a smirk on her face. Next it was my turn. I stood up, and as I was going up to the front of the room, I felt like I was going to pass out from dizziness. I also felt my heart start to pound and then I started to sweat. Here we go again, I thought! Why is this happening? I felt like there were a hundred eyes looking at me, and I knew that I couldn't function. I heard a couple of snickers in the class, and even without looking I could tell that it was coming from the "Popular" ones. There was no way that I could speak, I opened my mouth to start reading and nothing came out! I started to feel even worse like I was all out of breath. My mind was reeling and I just wanted to run away. The teacher could tell that I was having a problem and she asked, "Are you alright?" I thought "You idiot, you

can see that I'm not, so why do you ask!?" It's because you make us
do these dumb oral reports, and then there is some one like me,
who has a problem, and I don't even know why.

I couldn't bear to look up at my classmates, not even Jenny.
I was too embarrassed. I just simply left the room. Not only did
I leave the room I went right down to the nurse's office and said
that I wasn't well, and needed to go home. I needed to go home
right now! The nurse looked at me and she could tell that I was
very upset and on the verge of tears. She didn't question me any
further; she just made the call to my house. My mother didn't answer and I thought great, she's probably in the greenhouses and
can't hear the phone. The nurse asked if there was anyone else
that I could call and there just wasn't. She told me to lie down on
the cot she had in her office, and maybe I would feel better in a
little while. I laid there and just simply hated myself, and I could
feel tears roll down my cheeks. I tasted the salty taste of tears as
they continued to fall. The nurse didn't see this because she was
busy standing in the hallway talking to my English teacher. I was
glad in a way, because I was so embarrassed and didn't know what
was wrong with me. I didn't want to see her. Maybe I *am* crazy?
That was one of my biggest fears. I could hear them say my name
as they spoke, and every once in a while I would hear one of them
cluck there tongue and say, "My, my." I wanted them to stop talking about me, so I made believe that I was having a coughing fit.
The nurse came back over to me and the teacher left. The nurse
saw that I had been crying, and she said she would call my mother
again. This time Mommy answered and the nurse told her that I
wasn't well, but she wasn't sure what was wrong, and she thought
that I should go home. Mommy came to the school and picked
me up from the nurse's office and had a brief conversation with
the nurse.

On the way home Mommy asked me what was wrong and I
couldn't tell her. What was I going to say? I feel like everyone is
looking at me because I'm different? I just told her that my tummy
was sick and left it at that. That wasn't really a lie because I did
seem to have a lot of stomach problems. I wonder why?

I was very happy that it was Friday and the weekend was here. Jenny didn't call that afternoon, and I felt a little nervous that she would all of a sudden not like me. She had seen the fit that summer, but that only took place at a pool, this was school and that made it different. I knew in my heart, to have this problem in school was too much, because this is where everyone sees you and knows you. I was just weird and I knew it. I didn't know exactly why. When I was younger I seemed to be able to shake bad things off, but as time went by I was changing, and I knew it.

The whole weekend went by and Jenny didn't call or come over. I thought, well, there goes another friend. We never did see Kimberly again, so I couldn't call her up. I felt very alone. We had heard last week that her mother and father split up and moved away. I felt very sorry for her, and was glad that at least for a little while she did have Jenny and me as friends. I wished her well. Right now, I was feeling pretty sorry for myself, because I figured that maybe Jenny decided that I had too many problems. Perhaps she was just too embarrassed to hang out with me any longer.

Monday came, and as usual Jenny was at the end of the driveway. As I approached her she smiled, and I felt uplifted. I was happy to see my friend. She was friendly, but a little cool to me, and then I felt my heart sink. She wasn't acting the same. She kept looking down at the ground and finally she said, "After you left, the whole class broke out in laughter and said some pretty nasty things about you." She couldn't find any words to defend me, because my behavior was pretty strange. "You're going to have to get over your fits somehow." I thought, Boy, she has changed from the little girl who said not that long ago, you have been through so much it is no wonder that you have some problems. But I must say in her defense, I had no real answer for her. We didn't speak much before the bus came, and when we got on we sat together, but we didn't speak at all. At lunchtime she didn't meet me as usual. When I went into the lunchroom, there she was sitting with some other girls. I felt a lump in my throat and sat alone.

I finished out the day, and when I got home I told my mother what had happened. I told her that I knew that Jenny didn't like me anymore and about the fits that I was having. My mother didn't offer much help. She just told me that I was having growing pains and that I would go through many friends in my life. My mother simply didn't understand the magnitude of my problem. I went to Jimmy's room like I did when we were both much younger, and tried to get him to understand my dilemma. All he said was that I would get over it in time, and if I felt like people were looking at me, just walk away. He was no help either. No one seemed to understand how much impact this problem had on my life, and there was no one to talk to about it. I suddenly started to really hate my life again and myself. I admit that I couldn't blame people for not liking me. After all, I didn't like me either.

The next day Jenny was waiting at the end of the driveway. That didn't mean anything because we both had to stand at the same place to catch the bus. She had her head down and barely greeted me when she saw me, and I just chose not to speak. It was very uncomfortable, and when the bus came we sat in different seats. Our friendship was over. I was alone and that was the way it was. I thought to myself okay, I can handle it, worse things have happened. I continued to struggle in school and sit alone in the lunchroom. No one bothered me or called me names; they just didn't speak to me. I felt like a freak.

Halloween came and went. I stayed home and no one came to the door for treats. We were so far back from the street that I didn't consider that to be unusual. Then Thanksgiving came, and we had a quiet dinner at home. There were the usual arguments between my brother and step-father that made absolutely no sense to me. One night after dinner my step-father told Jimmy to help him for a minute in the greenhouses, and Jimmy said "No!" What a battle ensued! There they go again! If they ever got physical, I really don't know who would win, because they were about the same size. Jimmy was now a little taller than my step-father, but my step-father was very strong, stronger than Jimmy. They would go nose to nose but never quite hit each other. Sometimes they would take a swing at each other, but never really try too hard to hit. In a way it was becoming comical. Of course my mother was very upset.

She so much wanted them to get along well, but Jimmy wouldn't help with even the littlest thing. My brother was used to getting his own way, and I think Grandma and Grandpa Myers had a lot to do with that. I wondered why they didn't come to visit or call.

———

CHAPTER 25

One night something horrible happened! This would completely change our lives. It was a very cold night, and snow was in the forecast. In the greenhouses there was an alarm system that was hooked up to the house. The purpose for the alarm was a safeguard in case the temperatures dropped below a certain degree. If this happened, a loud alarm would go off in the house and my step-father would know that there was a major problem in the greenhouses. This meant that he had to go out to the greenhouses and see what the problem was. The alarms system alert, to warn that the temperature inside the greenhouses were dangerously low, had failed. If flowers are too cold they just simply freeze and die. On this particular night the alarm didn't go off, and all of the flowers that my step-father grew were ruined!! My step-father got up as usual and went into the greenhouses to start his day. He returned very quickly and I could tell that something was very wrong. I heard him speaking very loudly and frantically to my mother, and I knew that it had something to do with the business. I heard my mother say, "Oh no, we're ruined!" She was crying, and I could tell in my step-father's voice that he too was on the verge of doing the same. What were we going to do? I heard him mention the bank and possibly a loan, but we had lost a whole crop and what were we going to live on? I came out of my bedrooms and Mommy said to no one in particular, that we had better start thinking about moving again, because this wasn't something that we could just bounce back from. I felt so bad for them, because I knew how hard they had worked. What a thing to happen! I went downstairs and walked from room to room of our very pretty house, and had a feeling of despair. In a way, because of all the terrible things that had happened to me in Staten Island, a part of me thought maybe a new start somewhere else would be good, but another part of me thought "Who am I kidding, I am who I am."

That afternoon John went to the bank and they all expressed their sympathy for the situation, but couldn't offer much financial support. My step-father got a lead on a new flower place that was located in New Jersey, and the bank said that they would help us re-locate. The president of the bank knew people in New Jersey, and would make the necessary inquiries. My step-father had proven himself to be a wonderful flower grower, and he had people willing to help. So it was decided, and another move to come was on the immediate horizon.

I continued to go to school, but my mind was not there. I knew that we were going to leave as soon as all legal issues could be resolved. I told Jenny, and I could tell that she couldn't care less. I thought to myself, I won't miss this friend, she's changed, and even though I have problems, I knew that I deserved better treatment than what she was offering. Every day after school we all packed whatever was needed to be moved, and Jimmy was so upset because where was he going to drive his car? "Ha!" I thought, where indeed!

Moving day had arrived! It was time to leave and I was ready. Pretty house it was to leave, but that no longer was of much importance to me. As long as we were a family, that's all that mattered.

It was cold out and Christmas had come and gone. Even though it had been a hard Christmas, we knew that we still had a lot to be thankful for. We had a new home to look forward to, and maybe a better life. I was really trying to be hopeful. I knew that what my mother now called "my complexes" were still a major problem. I guess that I was hoping that they would just go away. I thought to myself, how long can they last? Will I always feel like I want to run when people are looking at me, and all the other unpleasant feelings that go with it? I had to face the facts. To me those facts were that I had more problems than other kids, and somehow had to find a way to work around that. I saw too much, and learned about how brutal life can be at a very young age. How does one share this with their peers? How does one fit in, and how does one forget about all of the ugliness that one has seen, when you are standing in your own way?

My step-father had been taking rides over the past couple of months out to New Jersey. He had seen the new location of the florist business that he wanted to start. This property had a house on it too, and also needed a lot of work. The whole place was in shambles he had to admit, but with a lot of elbow grease as he called it, the house and property could be made presentable. This didn't scare me because I saw what he and my mother had done in our last home. I knew in my heart that they would work very hard, and we would live well again. This gave me a little sense of security, and I'm sure that my brother would have had to admit that he also knew that this horrible situation would be straightened out as well. Unlike my natural father, John was a man with vision and determination.

On moving day, my step-father drove the moving truck to New Jersey. My mother drove the Kaiser. The new place had a long driveway like the other place, much to my brother's relief. I secretly would have been pleased if he had to leave his precious car behind, because how many kids that age own a car? We were all very happy as we were driving along, or maybe it would be better to say very excited. It was a cold but sunny day, and we were all in high spirits anxiously waiting to see our new home. We stopped once to eat and so forth, and not long after that, we were on the road again. My mother had gone out one time to our new home, and was explaining to us not to be shocked at what we saw, because all would be made right. Very shortly after she said that it was time to turn down the long driveway. I noticed that the road leading to our new property was very well kept, and the other houses were not big like the one in Staten Island, but they were very pretty. The whole neighborhood was very pretty.

Suddenly, the moving truck that we were following turned and went down a long driveway. The driveway had a lot of bumps, and off to the left side I saw three greenhouses that had a lot of glass missing. I also noticed a huge and very tall chimney which had a strange name on it. Not long after we continued to drive, we all saw the house. It was not pretty like the other houses on the block. The house was larger than the surrounding houses up on the road that we had passed, but it needed a huge amount of work. I really felt a little shocked, and maybe a bit disappointed. I didn't say anything. The only thing that I could think of was we had all better get to work really fast, and do the very best that we can to get this place looking a lot better. Just like in Staten Island, there was clutter all over the place. There were empty bottles of wine just like Daddy used to drink all over the ground, and empty bottles of soda, and lots of paper and debris scattered everywhere. My brother said, "What a mess!" He was right. I just didn't have the heart to say it. Mommy could tell we were disappointed.

We passed the house and went around the bend of the long driveway. This area was referred to as "down below." It was also the entrance to the greenhouses where all the work would take place. There was a little house attached to one of the long buildings, and we were later told that hired help for the greenhouses would live in there. We all got out and looked around. I walked back up to the house and walked around the yard, which had been neglected for so many years. "Wow!" I thought, this place is going to need a miracle! Mommy and Jimmy appeared and Mommy told us to go into the house and pick out which one of the four bedrooms we wanted to call our own. We raced up the stairs like we were in competition with each other, which we were, and reached the landing. Jimmy was in front of me and eagerly went from room to room. All of the bedrooms were of good size, but I was surprised and pleased that Jimmy chose the smallest one. My room would be directly across from his and was a lot larger. My room also had two windows and both faced the woods in back of the house. Jimmy's faced part of the back yard and the street. We were both satisfied that Mommy had been nice enough to let us choose. The only rooms left upstairs were the other bedrooms, a bathroom and an attic. This house wasn't nearly as big as the house that we had left and not nearly as pretty, but it was home. The living room had a nice fireplace in it, and the kitchen and dining room was smaller than what we had been used to, but it didn't really matter. My mother immediately turned the heat on to get the house warm. My step-father was outside with the truck, and we were ready to unload.

As the days went by we settled into our new home. My mother registered us in school, and we were to start in a week. My brother and I didn't go to the same school this time. They had real school buses here, and we took different ones. Everything was very different. I had a good time setting up my room, and at times I would go outside and help clean the yard. It was pretty embarrassing looking, so I was eager to help. Mommy told us that we only had a few days before starting our new school. A few times she took a couple of hours off from working with our step-father to show us where our schools were, and to look around our new town for the sake of knowing where all the stores were. My school was a small school in a very country area. Jimmy's school was larger and also in a very nice area. The town itself was small and very clean, and there was no litter on the streets like there had been in Staten Island. In fact everything was much cleaner and nicer looking. I was feeling good about this move, and had positive thoughts and high hopes. Maybe with this new move there would be no more "fits" as I so miserably called them, and maybe the nightmares that I so often suffered from would also go away.

The days were going too fast for me as far as I was concerned, because school was coming up on Monday. I admit that I was pretty scared, and hated myself for it. Jimmy on the other hand was always very confident acting around other kids. If he was ever nervous he hid it well. He also did very well in school, and had no problems like I had. I secretly envied him because he never went through the things that I did; also he appeared to adore himself. He made sure that he always looked just so and spent time in front of the mirror admiring what he saw. At times I would catch him standing in front of the mirror that hung in the hallway. He was so self-absorbed that he didn't realize that I was looking at him. I would give him a big whistle and he would get raging mad at me. Then he'd chase me from room to room, catching me, and then tickling me until I almost peed in my pants. I would scream and Mommy would yell, but at times he and I did have fun. I'm afraid that was probably one of the only times that we engaged in any fun type of horseplay. My brother and I were very different and too far apart in age to relate to each other. He also was the favored one, and Mommy considered him to be brilliant. He may have been more academically inclined than I was, but he too had his problems, which developed later on, or maybe they were just hidden. But that's another story.

The day had arrived for my brother and me to start school. I was horrified to say the least. It was a new school, and unlike the other schools that I attended, I hadn't been given time to meet any kids that I would be going on the bus with, or to any of my classes that I would be attending. I had a very bad feeling, but knew that I had to go. I walked up the driveway and crossed the street to wait with the other kids who were waiting for the bus. I tried to walk with head held high and I thought to myself, "If I act like everything is all right, then maybe everything would be all right." I crossed the street and walked over to the crowd of kids who were already looking at me. I felt my heart start to pound, but was determined to ignore the feeling, and not let it get in my way of possibly making new friends. I would settle for even one. I approached them and tried to pick out a friendly face. There actually was one girl who smiled at me, and I immediately went over to her. I introduced myself as the new girl who lived across the street. She said, "Oh you mean that old house that has all of the broken down greenhouses on the property?" I felt really embarrassed and had to admit that was the right place. All of the kids started to laugh and said "Poor you." One of the older kids said that there had been many a party on that property, and the place was sure an eye sore. I felt myself actually get a little mad, and said, "Just watch and see how long it will be in this condition!" I went on to say that my parents were hard workers, and it wouldn't be long and the place would look a lot better. Every one just snickered. I sarcastically said to myself "That really went well."

Just then the bus came and we got on. I went directly to the back. I felt terrible and wanted very badly to get off at the next stop and run away. These kids reminded me of the "Popular" ones, the chosen ones at the school in Staten Island. I wondered if they were all like that. We lived in an area that wasn't poor, and there would be no soup line in this school. I thought to myself "Are all kids who have some money snooty like this?" I knew that I was feeling embarrassed because the place needed so much work, but I also knew that in time my mother and step-father would make it look really good, and then I would have the last laugh. The bus arrived at the school and we all got off. I was to report to the main office. Someone would give me a schedule to follow, and then escort me to my first class. I walked into a school that was immaculate. The floors were so shiny that you could see your face in them! This certainly was different than what I was used to. None of the schools that I went to were like this. I asked a kid where the office was, and he pointed to it, and in a minutes time I was standing inside. I cleared my throat and a lady came over to me and she said, "Oh you must be the new girl!" I said yes, and she smiled at me and told me to follow her to a classroom. As we were walking down the hallways to my class, I felt my heart start to beat faster. I already had a bad day as far as I was concerned, and I knew that I was going to be introduced as the new girl to my classmates. I really hoped that they wouldn't make a big deal out of it and ask me any questions. I didn't feel like being the focal point of any conversations. I really just wanted to hide. I hated myself for the way that I felt, and really wished that I could toughen up and just not give a damn. I would have all kinds of conversations in my head and tell myself how I should be, and how I should behave, but things never really turned out well. I had turned into a little girl who was very frightened of many things, and just didn't know why or how to make them go away.

We walked into the classroom and the lady walked over to the teacher. They engaged in a brief conversation and then she left the room. The teacher looked at me, gave me a smile, and introduced me to the class. I could feel my face start to flush as I looked down at the floor. "Everyone, say hello to Carol," she said. This didn't make me feel any better, but I managed to say hello back, and find a desk in the front of the room so I didn't have to make eye contact with anyone. For the rest of the class the teacher left me alone, which I was forever grateful for. At the end of the class the teacher took me aside and said, "I know you feel strange because you're new, and you didn't have the opportunity to start school in September here, but I promise you that in a short period of time you will feel more at home and better." I thanked her and really hoped that she was right. I didn't hear one word spoken during class, because I just couldn't concentrate. My mind kept wandering, and I would think of the past and all that happened, instead of listening to what the teacher had to say. I knew that this wasn't a smart thing to do, because I had to learn just like everyone else. I somehow had to clear my head and get a grip on myself, or I would never make any friends. In the past my friends were very important to me, almost like my salvation. They helped me get through the day.

Somehow I managed to get through the week. I didn't listen in any classes to anything that was being said. I was given lots of books and had quite a bit of homework. I wasn't used to this. One thing about the New Jersey schools was that they seemed to be more advanced than the one to in Staten Island. This school taught things that I never heard of before in most subjects. I knew that I was good in spelling, and I knew that I wrote well. This school didn't have a gym. Perhaps the reason for that is that it was a small school, only going up to the fourth grade. There was a gym in the bigger school that Jimmy attended. I was a little unhappy about that because I already knew I was good in sports, and that could be something that I could be proud of. I thought of all the times that I would go out and run just to get rid of excess energy, and I discovered that I was a very strong runner. I also played softball and dodge ball well. That I learned in Staten Island.

Saturday came, and Mommy was very busy fixing up the house inside. She was painting and putting up wallpaper. I must say that

I learned a few new curse words, because putting up wallpaper is hard and not at all fun. I went outside to help John clean up the yard. After what those bratty kids said, it was very important to me to help get the place looking really good. My step-father was very happy that I wanted to help out, and told me to get out the wheelbarrow, and pick up anything that needed to be carted away. I was to take a full load of cans and anything else that needed to be removed, and push the wheelbarrow halfway down the driveway, to a designated area in the woods, empting it again and again until the area around the house was clean. He somehow knew better than to ask my brother to do this, because he would just refuse and a fight would break out. I was happy to help for my own personal reasons, but I felt very self-conscious and hoped no one could see me from the road. I thought to myself, "If my brother comes out now and starts to drive his beloved car up and down the driveway, I'll have a fit! I'm working so hard and have blisters on my hands, and he's reading his goofy comic books." I really resented him a lot of the time. He was like one of the chosen ones.

At the day's end, I did have a good feeling because I knew that I had accomplished so much. The big yard that surrounded the house was now clean of debris and looked so much better. I felt proud of myself, and my step-father patted me on the head and said something in Danish. I asked him what it meant and he said "Well done!"I had pleased him, and that was a good feeling. I wasn't afraid of hard work, and felt a sense of pride in doing good things.

The next day I got up and decided that I had better look at my schoolwork. I told my mother that this was a different kind of school and I was far behind. I told her that I really needed a lot to help to catch up, and she said, "I'm so busy, go to your brother and see if he can help you." I did as I was told and Jimmy very reluctantly started to help. I was thankful for anything he could do, and he also admitted that this school system was harder than in New York. He had noticed the difference as well. He however, was doing well of course. My brother had a way of not even study-ing, and somehow he knew the answers. I had to study to get good grades. He did help me a lot that day, and I was very grateful. I gradually noticed that I was having problems retaining any new information. My mind had a way of wandering. I usually would have very unpleasant thoughts and memories. It just simply got in the way of learning, and this problem became an obstacle. I never spoke to anyone about this, because I already felt so different. At times I would look into the mirror and not know who I was looking at. This bothered me because the person that I looked at didn't seem real. I would feel my face, and to me it felt funny. I just didn't have any idea who I was.

———

CHAPTER 26

Monday morning came and I prepared for school. Mommy left out my clothing as usual, and was already out of the house working in the greenhouses with my step-father. On the table were my lunch money and a box of cereal for my breakfast. I opened the box and poured cereal in a bowl, putting lots of milk in it, and lots of sugar on it. I ate silently and said to myself, "Where is everyone?" Jimmy was already gone. He left earlier than I did, and got home at different times, depending on what he was doing. There were no adults there to guide us, or to wish us well for the day. We knew what was expected of us, and that was that. I didn't blame my mother, because I knew how hard she was working. Mommy and John were working really hard to make this new business a success. I was just lonely. I ate, put on my coat, and walked up to the bus stop.

The usual crowd was there, and as I approached them one of the kids said to me, "Hey, I was watching you work over the weekend, when you're done you can come to our house and pull weeds!" I wanted to hit him! Just as I feared, I could be seen from the road. I don't know why that bothered me so. Maybe it's because I didn't know of any other little girl my age that would do what I had done. Maybe I should have felt proud, because I *did* feel proud while I was working! While I stood there pondering this thought, one of the girls who lived down the road came over to me and said, "I think it's great what you people are doing, and I don't think I could ever work as hard as you do." She gave me a big smile and said to me, "My name's Barbara and you're welcome to come over to my house anytime to play." I felt my heart leap for joy. I was making a new friend! I almost felt giddy. I thanked her and said that I would love to very soon, and when our place is more finished, she would be welcome as well! This little fourth grade girl had no idea how happy she had made me. Everyone else was quiet and said nothing. I knew in my heart that in a short time my home would be very nice, and I would feel comfortable if anyone of the "chosen" people came by to snoop, or to say Hi. I thought to myself, "I would never tell anyone about my past." I stood and looked at them one by one, and thought that none of these kids could handle it!

The school week went all right. I saw my new friend Barbara at the bus stop every day. We had different schedules in school, but just like Jenny in Staten Island, we met for lunch and sat together. As time went by we sat with a few other little girls, and had a pretty crowded lunch table. To me, lunchtime was the best because we all enjoyed each other's company. One day at the lunch table Barbara asked if I would like to come over to her house on Saturday afternoon? I felt very happy, and said that I was sure that I could. We exchanged phone numbers, and soon we had to go our separate ways to classes, but for the rest of the day I felt like I was special.

Barbara came from a pretty wealthy family, and lived on a block not too far from our street. She told me where she lived a couple of weeks before. When I was out riding my bike, I had gone by her house and was quite impressed with what I saw. She lived in one of the pretty houses that was nicely painted, and had a picture perfect yard. I thought about our yard, and was a little embarrassed because even though it was cleaned up, it still had to be landscaped, and spring was still a ways off. The days were getting longer and soon my step-father would do his magic, and make everything look a lot better. I knew that I didn't want anyone there until things looked better.

Barbara called our house Friday night, and we spoke about plans for the following day. Both mothers spoke for a while on the phone, and I was to be at Barbara's house at eleven the next morning. I was so pleased and happy that someone wanted to be my friend again, and maybe I wouldn't be so lonely. I thought to myself that I have to be very careful as to what I say. I have to be on my guard, because if anyone knew the truth about me, I was afraid that they wouldn't want to be my friend. I would play act like I had learned to do before. I thought that if I acted like everyone else, people would think that I'm the same as they are, and I'll keep my deep dark dirty secrets to myself.

Saturday was here! I got up and got dressed as fast as I could. I was very excited because I was convinced that today was going to be a good day. I would make sure that it was. Mommy was already out in the greenhouses working with my step-father. Don't those two ever rest? I didn't care, today I was too excited. I got the cereal out, made myself a bowl, and looked at myself in the mirror a dozen times to make sure that I looked alright. Soon it was time to go to my new friend's house, and I went to get Mommy to take me over. I thought that she would want to meet Barbara's mother. Mommy was nowhere to be found! I panicked and thought to myself "She's forgotten." I was mad because she knew how important this was to me. I thought, "All right! I'll just get my bike out, and go by myself." That's exactly what I did.

When I arrived at Barbara's house, her mother seemed a little shocked that I was alone, and that I had come over on my bike. She was also disappointed because she wanted to meet my mother. I was embarrassed, and just told her that she was very busy, but I assured her that she would meet her soon. I was invited in, and what a pretty house it was indeed. No house could measure up to the Staten Island house, or my grandmother's house, because those houses were like mansions, but who would believe me? I've learned that it's more important to be happy, than to live in a mansion. Barbara was very proud of her home and took me on a tour. I thought to myself, "Wow, it's going to be a while before she comes to my house!" After the tour, we began to play in her room, and then we went downstairs to what they called the family room. I had never been in a family room before, but indeed this was very nice. We listened to music, danced silly little girl dances, and before

I knew it, it was time for me to go home. I really didn't want to go. Barbara's mother said that she would like to come over soon, and look at all of the progress that had taken place; she said that the whole neighborhood was talking about it. I felt myself turn red, because even though my parents had worked very hard the place wasn't ready for people to see. I just smiled and told her I would tell my mother.

As I left, I had mixed feelings. I liked Barbara and her mother, but I knew that I was very different than they were. I also knew that there was no way that they could know of my past, because I was sure they would look down on us. They were snobs and I knew it. When I got home my mother apologized because she had to go out, and had not gotten back in time to take me over. I was almost happy in a way at this point. I thought we're so different than the people who live around here, that a gradual acceptance would be a good thing. I knew that I was going to have to be very careful in a lot of ways, if I was ever going to fit in. To a little kid, to fit in means an awful lot. I wasn't sure that I knew how.

———

CHAPTER 27

On Sunday afternoon I was standing outside looking around. I was trying to think what would make this place look really better. I then heard a car coming down the driveway. I looked, and at first I didn't recognize who it was. As the car came closer, it dawned on me that it was Grandma and Grandpa Myers. I was shocked because as far as I knew Mommy hadn't spoken to them since we had moved. Jimmy was outside getting ready to drive his car up and down the driveway. He had a crush on a girl his age that lived on the property across from our driveway. I guess he thought that he could impress her with his car. When he saw our grandparent's coming, he immediately knew who it was, and started to get excited and happy. I didn't really feel the same, and kind of felt sad that I didn't. After all, they hardly ever spoke to me.

When the car came to a stop they got out, walked over to my brother, and gave him a big hug. Jimmy ran to the greenhouses to get Mommy, and I just stood there. I felt awkward in their presence and slowly approached them. I looked at them and said, "Hi" in a shy voice. They quietly said hello, and asked me how I was. I told them that I was doing well. God, it was so cordial that I think we all felt strange. Suddenly Mommy came out and greeted them. She said, "Welcome to our new home!" She seemed really happy to see them. We all walked into the house. Mommy took them into the kitchen and poured them each a cup of coffee. They had brought Danish and donuts, and we all sat at the table. Unknown to me, my mother and John had borrowed a sum of money from them before we moved. When I found this out, it all made sense. Because of the awful pickle we were in due to the freeze up in Staten Island, they had to borrow money to start over again. They obviously had to borrow money from someone, and I guess by their conversation they wanted it back. My brother and I were told to go out and play. This of course meant that it was time for the adults to speak in private. I thought "This is *not* going to be a good visit." I was right.

I went into the greenhouses to tell my step-father John that they were here, and talking about some loan to Mommy. He immediately went into the house. I heard raised voices at times, but nothing too bad. Jimmy wasn't trying to listen this time. He was too busy trying to get the attention of the girl he had a crush on. He would drive his car up to the end of the driveway, and roar his engine, and then back down again, only to do it all over again. Boy, did he look silly. I sat and watched him do it over and over, and I started to laugh. I almost wet my pants. It actually took me away from my eavesdropping. I was so busy watching Jimmy that I failed to hear my grandparent's open the door and leave. I was in their way and they said, "Move!" I jumped to my feet and got out of their way. They didn't say goodbye, and they weren't happy. Jimmy had just come back down our road and he stopped to talk to them. They spoke to him briefly, and grandma moved closer to his car and reached in and gave him a peck on the cheek. She gave me nothing, not even a goodbye. And then I thought, "Oh that's right, I look like the other side." I slowly went back into the house, and as I moved closer to the kitchen I could hear my mother softly crying. John was speaking quietly to her and told her not to worry, that they would figure something out. My step-father was always so quiet and hardly ever got upset. I didn't want to disturb them, so I walked up to my bedroom and closed the door. I got one of my school books and started to study. Today had been a very bad day, and I just wanted it to go away.

Monday had come and that meant school. I prepared myself and went downstairs. I didn't really feel like going. I decided that

I would just stay home. I had a rather bad weekend and knew that school would probably be bad too, so I went back upstairs, put my pajamas back on and went to sleep. All of a sudden, I realized that Mommy was standing over me. She asked, "Did you forget to set your clock?" I didn't want to lie to her, but the only thing that came to my mind was that my stomach was upset. My mother bought my excuse and told me to get some rest. I was thankful, and went back to sleep. I had a terrible nightmare like I used to have in the past. I woke up in a sweat and my heart was pounding so hard I thought it was going to jump out of my chest! I hadn't had one of those lousy nightmares in some time, and thought that I was over them. I guess I should have gone to school. I got out of bed and went into the bathroom and washed my sweaty face. For the rest of the day I tried to study, but that seemed hard to do, because the school in Staten Island was easier than this school. I needed extra help and I knew it. I was far from dumb, but this work was new to me, and no one seemed to care. I again hated school. Wait until Mommy gets my report card. She won't be happy when she sees it.

I went to school the next day and Barbara was her friendly self, which I was pleased to see. She asked me where I was the day before, and I told her that school makes me sick. She laughed and agreed and told me that I was funny. I'm funny all right. That day in English class we had to read out loud. Here we go again, another disaster about to happen! It came to my turn to read, and as usual even before it was my turn, my heart pounded wildly. I felt myself become sweaty, and I wanted to run. I sat there and started to read and some kid in the class came out with a loud fart! Everyone started to laugh including me, and because the focus was now on him, I calmed down. The teacher got order and told me to continue, and I told her I had already read so she passed me by. I thought, "If only that could happen every time, I would never have to read!" I was safe for the day. English was the only class that I had to worry about because of oral reading, so the rest of the day went well. The rest of the week went well, and the weekend was here again. Barbara wanted to come over. Well, I couldn't say "No" forever. If she's going to be my friend, she's going to have to like me for me and not my house! I said all right. I can't compete with her, and I decided that I wouldn't even try.

Saturday morning was here. I felt very nervous because it was almost time for Barbara to arrive. I had slept later than I wanted to and felt rushed. Mommy was out in the greenhouses as usual with John, and Jimmy was still sleeping. I woke him up and told him that I was going to have company. He just said that he didn't care, and went back to sleep. I had to accept that and not worry. I wasn't going to take anyone on any tour, that's for sure. I quickly went out to the greenhouses to remind Mommy that Barbara and her mother were going to be here soon, and she just shrugged. I knew that by her attitude that there was not going to be any chit-chat going on with the adults. I felt bad because I know that if Mommy had not forgotten, or if she had not been delayed when I went to Barbara's house, her mother would have offered Mommy coffee and conversation. I so wanted life to be normal and to fit in with the other kids, but there were always problems. It just seemed like life had too many things wrong with it. I went back to the house feeling alone and rejected by Mommy, and then I heard a car come down the driveway. I looked, and of course it was Barbara and her mother. I thought to myself, "I'll give this situation my best shot, that's all I can do." I could see Barbara waving at me and her mother smiling.

The car came to a stop and they got out to greet me. Barbara came over and gave me a big hug, and her mother asked where my mother was. I told her that she was working in the greenhouses, and to follow me. We walked down the remainder of the driveway and into the working area. There was Mommy full of dirt because she was working so hard. That didn't embarrass me. I knew that my mother and step-father had to work like hell to get the place in order. I was embarrassed because I introduced both mothers and Mommy barely looked at the lady. Barbara's mother started to squirm out of irritation, and maybe even embarrassment. I just wanted to run and hide. Finally the lady loudly cleared her throat and said, "Barbara, I will be back in an hour to pick you up." I stood there feeling like I wanted to cry. My mother was just plain rude and didn't care about my feelings. Barbara took me by the hand and we slowly walked back up to the house in silence. Her mother was ahead of us and already getting into her car. She yelled out of the car window before leaving, "In an hour," she said. I looked at my friend and wondered if she would still be my friend tomorrow.

Suddenly Barbara said to me, "You know at times when my mother wasn't looking, I would sneak down here with other kids on our bikes. I know what this place looked like before you moved in, and I know the place needs more work, but your parents have really done a lot!" I thought to myself "Why is it that sometimes kids are so much smarter than adults?" That remark immediately made me feel much better, and I knew that tomorrow we would still be friends!

Monday came and that meant school. I got up and prepared to get dressed as usual, only this time Mommy was in the house. She told me that she and her parents had a conversation on the phone the other night, and they needed a place to live. She then went on to say that they would be living with us for a while until they re-located. I wasn't a happy kid to hear this because they were never nice to me. I'm sure that Jimmy was delighted. I hung my head and told her that they always ignored me and acted as though they didn't like me at all. She just said that it might be a good thing, because they could help in the house. So much work had to be done outside, and I wouldn't be alone so much of the time if they were there. Under normal circumstances this arrangement could have been beneficial for everyone, but in my heart, I knew better. These people weren't nice and I knew it! I wanted to scream at her and ask, "Is life ever going to be normal? Aren't we ever going to be like other people?" Instead I gathered up my books and started to leave without eating breakfast. I was just too upset and tired of bad things happening. I took my lunch money and said goodbye. I don't think my mother had the faintest idea how badly my grandparent's treated me. There are all kinds of ways to treat people poorly. Ignoring and giving them different treatment is a few of them.

To a little kid who needed love so badly, and encouragement from the people in their lives who are supposed to be there for them, I knew that I was in trouble. Grandparents are supposed to be important people in kids lives, and kids can help enrich their grandparent's lives as well.

I walked slowly up the driveway to the bus stop, and was hoping that today would be a good day. I decided that I have to try to make things good. I really missed the times that I spent with Peggy. She was a true friend. Even though I lived in a nightmare type of existence, I didn't have to work so hard to have a good friend in Peggy. Finding a friend was like pulling teeth. I looked across the street and Barbara was waiting for me. She had a smile on her face, and I felt relieved to see that, even though my mother was so rude to her mother. I really didn't know what to expect. Barbara greeted me and everything seemed fine. We went to school and I had a good day. I actually had a good week.

That weekend turned into a horror show. On Saturday my grandparent's showed up without even a phone call. They just arrived and walked directly into the house right past me, and demanded to see Mommy. I went out to the greenhouses, announced my grandparents arrival, and my mother and step-father went to the house. I was told to stay outside. I wasn't happy about that, because I didn't have a jacket on. I had to sneak in to get one. Jimmy was still in bed and didn't know what was going on. As I was coming back down the stairs from my bedroom, my grandmother saw me and said, "And she looks just like them!" Mommy came out of the kitchen and yelled at me for being in the house. I didn't have a chance to tell her that I came in for my jacket, because grandpa came over to me and grabbed me roughly by the arm and said, "And this one will learn to behave!" I felt like kicking him. He was a mean old man and did everything that grandma wanted him to do. He was like her puppet. I stood there and I started to cry. My mother told me to go and do that outside. My step-father just looked at me and said nothing. I ran outside and I started to run down the driveway as fast as I could. I ran up and down several times until I felt totally drained and couldn't run anymore.

I collapsed on the grassy side of the road and felt numb. I thought, "So this is how it's going to be. Another kind of problem that's just too big for me to handle." Mommy had strange ways about her, because at times she could be nice and other times, which she had shown in the past, she could be very mean. She could also do strange things, like when she sent Jimmy and me to Daddy's girl friend's house in the taxi, which seemed like many years ago. I sure come from a messed up family, and this isn't helpful at all. I'm now going to have to find some way to defend myself from grandma and grandpa. Jimmy is a lucky boy, not only does he get what he needs, he also gets what he wants, and gets a lot more attention. Now he's going to really be spoiled, because they're going to move in very soon.

I slowly walked back to the house. I sat outside on the porch wondering how long it would be before I could go back in. I decided to walk around the back of the house because the kitchen faced the back, and maybe I would be able to overhear some of what was being said. Maybe I could get an idea of how soon it would be before the wicked grandparents moved in. Everyone was at the table talking including my brother. I could smell bacon cooking and I was sure eggs were too. I was standing outside of my own house, and was afraid to go in! I actually didn't feel welcome! I heard my grandmother say, "We can help each other out by living together. I can take care of all of the chores in the house, and you can work in the greenhouses." My mother and step-father liked that idea. I knew that this awful event was going to happen even sooner than I had anticipated. I wanted to go inside and eat like everyone else. I finally decided that this is silly. If I'm going to have to defend myself against the wicked, I would have to get tougher. In I marched and as I approached the kitchen, the conversations stopped. They all looked at me, but said nothing. I looked at my grandparents and they didn't smile or offer any conversation. I went into the front hallway and hung my jacket up and went back to the kitchen. I announced that I wanted to eat too. There was one piece of bacon left and a little pile of scrambled eggs, which was put on a plate, and roughly put down on the table in front of me. I felt myself start to stiffen like I did in the old days when dirty uncle would come near me. I felt scared of these people as well. If Mommy had spoken up and been nicer to me, it would have shown them that it was not all right to be mean. She said nothing, and that's the way it was.

Monday came and I was actually happy to go to school to get away from the house. No one in my family was on my good list right now. School went all right. In English class we were told that we had to write a little story and then read it out loud in the middle of the week. I thought "Oh no, how am I going to get through this?" I knew that I could write a couple of pages and maybe make up a pretty good story, but to read it out loud? All of those eyes looking at me! I felt nauseous. I had a couple of kids that I was somewhat friendly with in English class, but for the most part Barbara was my real friend. I made sure that I didn't tell her anything about my past. It was just easier that way. There was no kid that I knew that could handle or even understand what I was feeling, what I went through, and what it did to me. I always had to play act. I would watch how the other kids behaved, and I would do my best to act the same.

When we lived in Staten Island, I realized that I felt more comfortable around kids who were poor, and who came from homes that were a little questionable, because I didn't feel like I had to prove myself. No one could accept what happened to me as being alright, but at least their lives for the most part, were messed up as well, so I fit in better. I just had to stay away from the "chosen ones." There were only a few of them in the other school. In this school, most of the kids that went there came from "proper homes." I learned to play act a lot, just to try to fit in. God, it was exhausting!

I met Barbara at lunchtime as usual, and we sat down at our table and ate. For the rest of the day, things went well. I told her that my wicked grandparents were going to move in, and I wasn't happy about that. I figured she should know just in case she wanted to come over to play and ride bikes again. I still was mad at Mommy for the way she behaved the day Barbara's mother wanted to meet her. I wasn't invited back to Barbara's house again. I had a lot of things to try and figure out. I decided that the best thing that I could do was to stay out of my grandparent's way no matter what, because I knew that I could never please them. When I came home from school, I made myself a snack and went to my room to think. I was alone as usual, and I really didn't care on this day. I went into the empty bedroom, which was the last of the four. I knew that this was the bedroom that my grandparents would be sleeping in. I felt like burning the house down, and actually entertained the thought of doing it. I knew that it was wrong to think this way, but I was hoping that life would be better with our moving here, and now all hope for that was gone. I didn't know how much money my parents had borrowed from the grandparents, but I knew that they were holding it over my mother's head. I also knew that was the reason why my mother felt like she had to allow for them to move in.

This situation, which was going to be temporary, lasted seven years! How much money did they borrow anyway? The next few years were nothing short of a nightmare. Grandma and grandpa ruled the house and everyone's lives. They never called my brother by his name, because it reminded them of my real father. He was called Tommy. Tommy did nothing around the house and had no chores. My parents had said that his job was to take out the garbage once a week, and even that was considered to be too much. Grandpa did it! I on the other hand had to help with dinner preparations and clean, especially when my brother made a snack. I was ordered to clean up after him! When I came home from school I wasn't allowed to have a snack. In fact, if I was caught trying to make something or take a few cookies up to my room, I was screamed at and told to put them back. Most nights my grandmother, who was a wonderful cook, made very nice meals and a lot of the times she needed potatoes peeled. This job was of course given to me. While I would peel the potatoes grandma would stand on one side of me and grandpa would stand on the other side. Grandma would say.

"Look at the terrible job she's doing!" And grandpa would agree and snicker. I thought to myself, "Why the hell don't they do it themselves?" I wanted to stab them with the knife, but knew that I couldn't. Did these thoughts make me a bad person? I didn't care anymore.

Every day was the same, and as usual Mommy was blind to what was going on. My grandparents hated me, and I felt the same towards them. It wasn't my fault that I looked like my father. I'm glad that he wasn't funny looking because I did very much resemble him, and that side of the family. For this I'm hated? I think that was part of it, but I also believe that my grandmother needed to have a victim, and I was it! She must have been a very unhappy person to behave the way she did.

School was the same for me. I skipped school saying that I was ill when ever I had an oral book report that needed to be done, but when I handed in written book reports, I always received the highest grade, and many times my reports were put out in the hallways for display. This of course made me very proud, but didn't solve my problems, which I now had a real name for. They were no longer "fits" they were phobias. My God, after my uncle's sexual abuse towards me, and then getting kidnapped and raped, it's amazing that I didn't turn into a lunatic. Unfortunately my phobias did get in the way in school, and it did cause me to have lower grades, because I skipped school a lot to avoid the terrible panic attacks that there seemed to be no solution for.

My friends changed quite often over those years from fifth grade through junior high. Some kids thought that I lived in a cool place, and they liked to come over and hang out in the woods that bordered the driveway. Of course, they liked to come over to ride their bikes as well. If I heard kids outside, I would run out as fast as I could before the grandparents would find something else for me to do. I knew that they were bullies, and they didn't want to look bad in front of other people. If I made it outdoors I was safe, and away from their cruelty. I encouraged the kids in the neighborhood to come and ride their bikes anytime they wanted to, and spoke about going out to the boardwalks in the woods to hang out. The boardwalks were constructed because of high-tension wires that were located pretty far out in the woods. We would go and hang out there at times, and some of the older kids smoked. These kids had no idea how they helped me, they were just happy to have a place to hang out.

———

CHAPTER 28

Many times I didn't have enough clothes to wear to school, and some kids started to make terrible fun of me. I remember one year in particular, summer had come and gone, and school was right around the corner. My grandmother told my mother that "Tommy" needed lots of clothes, and because Mommy didn't check his closet and dresser drawers, she believed her. My mother was told that I had plenty of clothes. I knew that I wasn't going to get anything new and had to accept it. I had two skirts that still fit from the year before and one blouse. I told grandma and she went up to the attic and brought down two skirts that had been my mothers from years before! They were in good shape, but out of style. My grandmother laid them on the bed and said, "Here, this will do!" I was horrified and didn't know what to say. I was so scared of my grandmother and had good reason. My brother had gotten shoes and pants and shirts and sweaters. I got one blouse and a pair of shoes and was expected to live with this. I thought, "How could my mother be so blind and uncaring?" It wasn't long before the kids started to make fun of me again, and I came home one day crying my eyes out. I went to the greenhouses and yelled at my mother, "Are you blind!" At first she lunged at me like she was going to hit me, and then she said, "What are you doing with my skirt on?" I looked at her and just shook my head and said in return, "You let grandma rule the house and our lives, and you don't even know that your daughter has nothing to wear!" She asked, "Why didn't you tell me?" I replied, "Why didn't you ask me?" My mother and I stood there in silence, and looked at each other. That night before the stores closed, my mother left the house and bought me four new skirts, and four new blouses and several sweaters. That weekend she bought me another pair of shoes as well. She took me for a ride and told me that her parents would be with us for some time, and I had better find a way to get along with them. I just simply told her that I didn't know how.

My brother was a lot older than me. After I started high school, he was going to graduate in January. He didn't graduate with his class because he refused to do homework; so the school made him attend for several months, and take extra courses to make up for lost work. After he graduated, he and my parents had a very bad fight. Jimmy was always in trouble with them because he would buy cars and get tired of them and buy more. They all came from the junkyard and needed work. He worked at a gas station and grandma would make up plates of food for him at dinner time, and Mommy would take them to him. They would say "Poor Tommy, they made you get a job." I wanted to puke. Mommy told him that he had to get rid of most of the cars, because the place was starting to look like a junkyard. What a fight! My grandparent's of course stood up for him, and for once my parents stood their ground. They had both worked very hard and my step-father had done his magic making our property the best looking one around town. He had planted beautiful flowers and bushes all over, and Mommy of course helped. The greenhouses had beautiful flowers growing in them, and their business was thriving. They had done so well that they hired help to work in the greenhouses. The help lived right on the property in the little house that was down around the bend. Jimmy hardly ever helped with anything, and was protected by the grandparents. The fight was so bad that grandma and grandpa went to Iowa to visit family that I never knew existed. I was so happy, that I started to dance and sing when Mommy told me they were leaving. Jimmy went to his room and slammed the door. I was truly hoping that they would never come back. For three and a half years they had yelled at me, belittled me, ignored me when

I needed attention, and showed such favoritism to Jimmy, that I hated both of them. I felt like a big weight had been lifted from my body when they got into their car, and left for their trip. It was a glorious three weeks for me. For Jimmy there was no way that the damage could be undone from what my grandparent's had done to him. He was spoiled like no other kid I had ever seen, and didn't even know that he was totally unreasonable.

One night I had been over at a friend's house in the neighborhood, and when I came back home I heard yelling in the house. I ran into the house and what a sight to see! Jimmy was sitting on a chair, and Mommy was standing on a step stool right next to him. She was holding a milk bottle in her hand and was about to hit him on the head!! I ran into the room and yelled, "No Mommy! Don't do it!" My step-father was standing nearby, but wasn't trying to stop her. I had to grab her arm with one hand and knock the bottle out of her hand with my other hand, before it landed on his head! I think my mother had just snapped because she had put up with Jimmy's bad behavior and sullen attitude for years.

Jimmy decided to go to one of his friend's house for the night to get away from the situation. For the first time in years my mother and I sat down and had a mother to daughter talk. I told her of all the things that were happening in the house and how grandma and grandpa bullied me. I also told her that any mess that my brother made, I was ordered to clean up. I told her that I feared my grandparents because they had been rough with me the few times I tried to stick up for myself. They had even given me a few bruises on my arms at times. When I tried to stand my ground, they would grab me and order me to go to my room. She of course had no idea of what was going on. I found that kind of hard to believe because she was right there, but she was always out in the greenhouse working and oblivious to my poor treatment by her parents. I think my brother had to really get them to be at their wits end before they would do anything about his behavior, and I must admit that I resented her for that. It made me feel like I wasn't important enough because they had no idea about what was happening in their own house. If you think about it, my brother and I really didn't have any parents because they were never around. We were left in care of the grandparents, and Jimmy made out and I didn't. If I knew where to run away to I would have. I just felt trapped again, but under different circumstances.

The three weeks went by too fast for me. During the time that my grandparents were gone my mother and I talked, played cards at night, and I didn't have to do any housework, or help with dinner. She said I needed a vacation too! For once she asked me about school and I admitted that I still had phobias, which caused me a lot of grief, but she didn't seem to know what to do about them or how to help me. I didn't care. At least we were enjoying each other's company. Then of course the grandparents came back. I felt that at least now Mommy had a better idea of what was going on, and that was helpful. I watched as they pulled their suitcases out of the car and felt like I was going to throw up. They gave me a sour look as they walked quietly into the house. They went directly to their room to put their clothes away. I couldn't watch anymore and decided to take a walk out into the woods. One of the kids who came on our property gave me a cigarette and told me that anytime that I felt up tight to reach for a smoke. It would make me feel better. I lit the cigarette and had no problem smoking it. By this time it was not new to me. I inhaled deeply and thought that I did feel better. It wasn't long before I wanted to smoke every day. I admit that I would take a few smokes from Mommy's packs that were always lying around. I think she figured out that I was taking some, but kept quiet about it. My step-father always made sure that the supply of smokes never went down, and never questioned how many he bought. I guess that he thought Mommy smoked almost three packs a day. Cigarettes in those days were not expensive, and no one thought of them as being dirty or a bad habit.

The next thing that I discovered was alcohol! One day after grandma and grandpa had been really mean to me I went to the liquor cabinet and took a few swallows of vodka. I hated how it tasted, but it did calm me down. I would go to my room and instead of pacing and talking to myself, which I did a lot of, [very quietly of course], I would drink a little booze and it made me feel better.

I knew in my heart that drinking was not a good thing. I could remember how my father behaved when he drank, but I needed something to kill the mental pain that I was having. I didn't believe that he was in mental pain; instead I believed that he gave mental pain to those around him. Of course he did, but as much as I despised him, I knew that he too had issues; I just didn't know what they were.

One day after school Mommy and her parents had a terrible fight! It all came out. My mother had borrowed money and they were demanding that they pay her back, with interest! My mother retaliated by pointing out that they lived here for free. They yelled, "Not good enough!" My mother ran to her room and I could hear her sobbing, and the wicked grandparent's actually chuckled as they went down stairs. I was so mad that I ran down after them and screamed, "You leave her alone you bastards!" The two of them were so startled with my behavior that they didn't know what to say or do. I had a cigarette in my pocket and ran out of the house to have a smoke. They weren't used to the meek me talking like that.

Over the years I had come to realize that there wasn't too much they could do to me except bully me into doing chores, or part of their work in the house. After all they couldn't kill me, right? So what did I have to fear accept a couple of bruises here and there? Uncle Cliff would have killed me if he had caught me that day. He was trying to run me down with his car. He was a molester, and had the potential of being a murderer as well. I was living proof of it.

I had made some friends in high school, and we all became very close. All of my friends came from troubled homes like I did, and we sort of clung to each other for support. We hung out together, cried together, smoked together, and you guessed it, drank together. We always made sure that we had an older friend so we had transportation and booze. We were always there for each other no matter what. One of my friends asked my mother if she could stay with us for a while. She claimed that her life at home was so bad; she just couldn't take it anymore! My mother thought it over and said all right. Mommy told me that she wasn't as dumb as I thought, and she knew that I needed help fighting off grandma and grandpa. She was right.

My grandmother would make scrumptious homemade cakes, and then hide them in the dining room credenza. She did this so I wouldn't know where the cake was. This was so stupid because I watched her put it in there. I would never touch a cake that was meant for dinner and for everyone to eat. It made no sense to me. My friend Helen had a lot of fun with that one. She would wait for my grandparent's to go upstairs and then she would go over to the credenza and slide the doors open making sure that she made a lot of noise. My dumb grandparent's would run down the stairs hoping to catch us holding the cake, and perhaps starting to eat it. We would hide near by and watch. We would laugh so hard that we would almost pee in our pants. The funny part is they always fell for it! "We'll catch them next time Willard," my grandmother would say.

My friends would all come over and hang out in my bedroom, which Helen and I shared. We knew that the grandparents were out in the hallway trying to eavesdrop, just like I had done to them so many years before! It's funny how fate works. I did it to find out what was going to happen to me and our family. They were just hoping to catch us doing something bad to tattle on us. How juvenile is that? At times Helen or one of my other friends would tip toe to the door and pull it open quickly and ask, "Yes?" They would quickly scamper away talking to themselves, and mutter in disgust. If I was outside at times I would look up to the second floor and my friends and I would catch them peeking out at us through the shade. One day one of the guys that we hung out with mooned them!! The tables had clearly turned. I was in my glory.

CHAPTER 29

None of us went to school as much as we should have. I made sure that the school had the phone number for the business instead of the house. One of the hired help who liked me always answered the phone and would say, "Yes, Carol is sick today!" At times I would write my own notes and sign my mother's name. I knew that this was wrong, but I had gotten to a point where I was tired of being neglected. I was tired of my parents not taking control of the wicked grandparents who favored my brother. Most of my friends and I failed ninth grade and didn't care. But Helen who was the oldest, and Alison who was my age, were promoted to the next grade. There were five of us who hung out together, and would at any time die for the other, because we were that close.

One day my other grandmother called on the phone. It was a good thing that I answered when it rang, because if Grandma Myers had answered, she would have either hung up or told my father's mother to go to hell. Grandma told me that she missed me, and had been living at the cabin for some time. She wondered if I would like to come for a summer visit. I explained that I had a friend living with me, and she said, "Bring her too!" I was very happy. Not only would I see my grandmother that I loved, but also I knew that Helen and I would have a really good time. I ran down to the greenhouses and told my mother. She said that she would take Helen and me up to the cabin the following week. I failed to ask Helen if she actually wanted to go. She declined the offer when I later asked, because she had to go back home for a short time to check up on her brothers and sisters. Helen was one of five children. I told her that I would be gone for two weeks, and she said that she would be back in two weeks. Alison begged to go and I was delighted. To me it didn't matter who went, just so long as we got away. There was one problem. I only owned three pairs of shorts and a couple of summer tops from last year. I asked Mommy to buy me some clothes, and to my surprise she said, "No" I was so shocked and hurt. She said she had a couple of tops that she didn't like, and that I could have them and that was good enough. Business was good. I thought, "My God, will I ever have what I need without having to fight for it?"

One of my friends and I decided to go to the nearest clothing store, and we would take care of my problem by getting me what I needed the illegal way. We walked into the store with an empty oversized handbag, and left with it stuffed with summer clothes in my size. A lady who worked in the store suspected that we had just shoplifted, and after we left the store, she followed us with her car. I think she wanted to see if we would pull merchandise out of my bag, which was more like the size of a beach bag. She had no real proof until she saw something. I got scared and was thinking about running, when all of a sudden we saw one of my brother's friends in his supped up Chevy. This car was very fast, and we frantically flagged him down. He stopped, and we quickly got into his car and he drove away. We told him what we had done. He shook his head and offered us a beer. We accepted the beer, and I vowed that I would never shoplift again. The only problem with this friend of my brother's was that if he did anything for you, he expected something in return. He expected sexual favors. I wasn't about to oblige him. I thought "Can't a guy just do a favor with out expecting that in return?" He dropped us off at the end of my driveway and sped away angrily. Too bad I thought!

We were to leave for the cabin in a few days, and Alison and I could hardly wait. We were going to have a couple of weeks of swimming in the lake, and mingling with a New York crowd of kids. I was told they came from Brooklyn every summer. We were going to have a blast! By this time in my life I was drinking and smoking a lot. I found that alcohol helped me cope with my fears and feelings of inadequacy. It also made me feel more grown up. It's very strange that no one in my family realized how much I was drinking. I guess I hid it well. Even the wicked grandparents, who would have given anything to get me in trouble, would have had a ball with that one. Somehow everyone was oblivious to the fact that I was slowly becoming a drunk.

When my friends and I were at a party, I would have a few drinks before we got there, just so I would feel confident about being me. Most of our parties were held over at the house of one of the girls that I hung out with. Her parents knew that we were drinking in their family room, but didn't care as long as we were quiet about it. They also drank too much. I never thought in my wildest dreams I would be a drunk like my father. I never got into trouble or hurt anyone. Instead, I was the clown of all of my friends. Every crowd has to have a clown and I was it. It never occurred to me that I was harming myself, or that I could be an alcoholic. I was just a kid who had developed horrible phobias and complexes from years before, and I had to find something to make me feel better. This was my explanation to myself. People didn't have to be bad to drink. Daddy didn't have phobias, he was just bad, or I should say mean. I didn't drink every day. I just drank a few times a week. No one at home had any idea that I was doing this, because I would chew gum and make sure that I walked straight when I entered the house. I also went home when everyone was already in their bedrooms. I timed it that way.

The day had come. Alison was dropped off by her mother, and my mother told us to put our suitcases in the car because it was time to go. We were very excited. We were going to hang out with the New York crowd, and I was going to see my grandmother, Aunt Priscilla, and Uncle Jack. Two weeks away from the wicked! Thank God! We arrived at my grandmother's cabin, which was a real log cabin. It was very rustic to say the least. I suddenly remembered when I lived in Staten Island how I had made up a little book report on my summer vacation, and how the cabin was my topic.

Wow, it took me a long time getting here! I also remembered sadly how I had my first real panic attack in school, and had to leave the classroom, and lost a friend because of those "fits." I looked at Alison and thought of all of my recent friends, and realized that instead of dumping me as a friend like Jenny had done, they would have tried to help me. I bet if I had a drink before having to do oral reports I would be all right! What am I thinking???

Aunt Priscilla was the first to come outside and greet us. She looked a lot older than what I had remembered, but time had gone by since I last saw her. We gave each other a big hug, and then I introduced my friend. We all went inside. Grandma was walking around the living room singing to herself some strange sounding song and seemed to be happy. I ran over and gave her a big hug as well. I was so happy to be there. The cabin wasn't the neatest, but who cared? Mommy stayed for a few minutes, and I wondered if she felt awkward in the company of my fathers' mother, and so on. The grown-ups were very cordial acting, and maybe a little stiff, but all went well. To my surprise my mother gave me some money and said she would be back in two weeks, and then left. I thought if she had bought me my much needed clothing, I wouldn't have had to shoplift, which I felt very guilty about. Oh Well! If Jimmy wanted clothes he would get plenty, and that's what bothered me.

What a time we had! We stayed in the cabin with my family that evening, and made plans for the next day. We took a short walk and had a smoke, of course. Pine Cliff Lake actually had two beach areas. The smaller of the two beaches was much more private. At the other end was the larger beach, and also the clubhouse, which is where all of the kids hung out. You had to be a member to swim in the lake, or to use any of the rowboats. Grandma had paid her dues, so we had free use of all the facilities. After our smoke we went back to the cabin and made plans for the following day. Aunt Priscilla was drinking pretty heavily, but was her good-natured self. Uncle Jack seemed annoyed that she was drinking so much and would poke fun at her. This didn't cause them to fight though. My grandmother never made any comment about it, and was always just fun to be around. We sat at the dining room table, which was from the big beautiful house on the hill in Westwood, and we played cards until two am. We had no bedtime, and really no rules to follow other than to be in every night by eleven. Aunt Priscilla knew that we were smoking. She laughed and told us to get our own smokes.

The cabin had a fireplace that was made out of rocks, and there was a loft that had a bedroom in it. The steps that went up to the loft were made out of split logs. This was really a cool place and very rustic to say the least. This just added to the charm and excitement of being somewhere different. My grandmother slept on the couch in the living room, so Alison and I would have a bedroom to sleep in. I'm sure that she wasn't very comfortable, but that was just the way she was. She gave up her bed and bedroom for us. It was a two-bedroom cabin. The next day we got up and Aunt Priscilla and Uncle Jack were at work. Grandma was making us some French toast. We ate, and then left to start our adventures. The clubhouse was about a mile away from the cabin. We looked at all of the other cabins we passed along the way. They weren't as rustic looking as grandmas, which in my mind made hers even more special. Finally we saw the clubhouse, and a group of kids were standing outside. I felt my heart start to beat faster and I lit up a cigarette. I looked at Alison and she lit one up too. She didn't smoke or drink as much as I did. She also didn't have phobias or panic attacks either. I was the only one of my group that suffered from those problems. My friends also seemed to like themselves better than I liked myself, but we never spoke about it. There had been times that I considered committing suicide, because I was so miserable. At times we would all sit around and talk about what we thought death was like, and how each one of us would want to die if we had to, but that was just talk right?

The kids heard us approaching them. They didn't look very friendly, but we didn't feel threatened by this. We walked right up to them and introduced ourselves. One of the kids said, "Jersey brats, huh?" But I could tell that he was just joking. I told them that I had lived and gone to school in Staten Island at one time. I told them the name of the school, which was P.S.26, and one of the girls said she had family from that part of New York. That made us fit in better. I could immediately see that, and we started to make friends.

We all went swimming and this part of the lake had a big raft, which was anchored quite far out. I was able to swim, but swimming was not the sport for me. Everyone swam out to the raft and I hesitated. I watched them from the shore as one by one they reached it and climbed aboard. Alison had reached it as well. I saw them yelling at me and motioning for me to come swim out too. I felt scared, but thought I have to do this. I felt like I was swimming forever and my arms felt heavy! I can't panic. This I knew. I just kept swimming, and by the time I reached the raft I knew that I couldn't swim even one more stroke. They all looked at me and knew that I had a hard time. One of the kids said, "Practice makes perfect!" I thought yea, if I live through it! The raft held quite a few kids. Some were jumping off and climbing back on. Alison quietly asked me if I was all right, and said she would swim back with me. I also didn't know how to float. I was so good in other sports. It was strange that swimming was so hard for me.

We had enough. We all swam back, and once on the shore, we lit up cigarettes, and someone had bought beer. We did have to watch out for the adults, and so we moved to a secluded part of the beach. The age range of our new friends was from fourteen to eighteen. That may seem like a big age gap, and it was, but everyone got along famously. The older kids were more like boyfriend and girlfriend to each other, and watched out for the younger ones. Alison and I were fifteen and very much fit in. It's true that these kids from New York were rough, but we were rough too. I think all of us had seen too much in our lives. It's funny how kids just seem to gravitate to their peers, the ones who are most like themselves.

Dinnertime had come and Alison and I were starving. We said our goodbyes and went back to the cabin. Grandma had made hot dogs and beans and a huge salad with watermelon for dessert. Not a gourmet meal, but who cared? We ate heartily and then took a walk to have a smoke. When we got back we played cards again until the wee hours of the morning. We were having a ball.

The next day our friends told us that on Friday nights the club-house stayed open late for teen night. Everyone danced, and hung out and had a good time. We of course planned to be a part of this. Friday came and we put on what we thought were our best outfits and we left. We arrived at the clubhouse. Most of the girls had skirts on, and we only had on our best shorts with what we considered to be our prettiest blouses. We felt a little out of place. We looked around inside the clubhouse for our new found friends, and there they were. None of those girls had dresses or skirts on either, just shorts like we had on. We were both very relieved. They saw us approaching them and they called to us. Our night had begun. I also knew that there was going to be beer, and that made me feel better. I was sure that everyone and his brother were look-ing at me, and I refrained from making eye contact with anyone. It was just too hard to do. Sometimes if I tried to make eye contact with someone, my eyes actually hurt! I needed a beer, or a cigarette or something. I got both right away and was sure that that made me feel better. We all clowned around and had a good time. The clubhouse also had cigarette machines and a snack bar. It was re-ally very nice, and a nice thing to do for the kids who stayed at the lake. There were only a few adults around, and they came and went without supervising us. We were able to drink and smoke. The night went by quickly, and someone had bought gum and potato chips so we wouldn't smell so much from the beer.

We walked back to the cabin and got there by eleven as ordered. Aunt Priscilla was waiting for us, and grandma was sleeping. Uncle Jack had gone to a friend's house. Aunt Priscilla took one look at us and took us back outside to talk, so we wouldn't wake grandma up. She said, "I know that you guys are smoking and drinking, and grandma would be upset if she found out. Just be careful of what you do, and let's not make this visit a mistake." I felt ashamed of myself for the first time in a long time. This was my place of refuge and I didn't want to ruin it. I apologized, and said that I would slow down with the drinking. I said nothing about the smoking. I had to do something! I then thought, "She drinks so much, perhaps she should look at her own self." I wasn't mad though, and never held her drinking against her. She was an adult and didn't hurt anyone, so it was all right. She was just warning us to be careful.

Everyday was a new day filled with a lot of fun. I told my friends that Alison and I got into trouble with the drinking, and that I could only have a couple of beers instead of who knows how many. They didn't want to get into trouble either, because they were supplying it, so they made sure that I only had a couple. One evening the clubhouse boys decided to forget that girls were around and played football instead. The Brooklyn girls were complaining and mad, but the boys just shoved them out of the way and told them to get lost. The girls decided to form their own football teams. We were going to play football too! The clubhouse had baseballs and footballs inside for kids to use, so getting a football was easy enough. Then we had to decide who were going to be the captains. I unfortunately was chosen to be a captain, and a girl from Brooklyn, who was very rough acting, was the other captain. We chose our players and started to play. It wasn't long before it became evident that my team was winning! I might add that I was a darn good player, and of course I ran very fast. The other team members were poor losers and started to play dirty. They hit my team players, pulled our hair, and were really doing their best to hurt us. It turned into a battle! This got the boys attention! They had to come over and break up what had turned into a pretty bad fight. I was punched in the eye and knew that it would turn black and blue. I wasn't happy. One of the boys decided that the captains should fight it out. I have to admit that I was scared to death. The other captain was bigger than me, older, and a lot stronger. I could tell this just by looking at her. I was about to get my ass kicked! I just stood there and the rest of the kids were getting antsy. They wanted to see blood and guts. Whoever won this fight would be winning for the whole team, and that team would win the football game.

All of a sudden, I felt someone come up behind me and push me right into Lucy, who was the other captain. The fight had begun. No matter how hard I tried to hit her, she was faster and stronger. She didn't just pull hair, she meant business. I thought, "Oh My God" I'm going to lose and look bad in front of all of these kids! I'm not going to be respected after this. I decided that I had to find some way to win no matter what! The only thing that came to mind while I was getting pulverized was to pull her clothes off! That'll make her stop! I did just that! I pulled at her blouse and the buttons flew off everywhere, and she immediately screamed and pulled her blouse closed. She had to stop fighting unless she wanted to expose her breasts. No one seemed to care that I had fought dirty, because that's what started the fight to begin with! Dirty fighting! I was declared the winner and so was my team! That worked well.

The night was over early and I was covered with dirt and blood. What a mess. But somehow I felt a sense of power. I think it was because I had never hurt anyone back, who had hurt me, not in this way. I remembered how good I felt when I heard that Uncle Cliff had gotten caught with my friend's mother, and he had gotten a good beating. He deserved that beating and more. I flashed back to pulling the mean girls hair in the school cafeteria because I was made fun of. This girl deserved what she got too, because she had started it all. I felt good. We went home. Justice had been served! I knew that grandma would be upset when she saw me. I was afraid to let her see me. But what could I do?

When we entered the cabin, everyone was home and they took one look at me and started to yell at me. Alison quickly intervened for me as I hung my head, and after she told them everything, they looked at me and said, "Good job," and then we all laughed. My Uncle asked me if I really tore her blouse off, and I assured him that I did, and he had another good laugh. They asked me the name of the girl that I fought with, and grandma said she knew of the family, but said she didn't blame me. I went and got all cleaned up putting different clothes on. We played cards for a while and we went to bed. We were ready to start a new day.

Alison and I got up early and looked at the damage to my face. I had to admit it was pretty bad. We decided to go to the clubhouse and swim for a short time, and make it an early day. I really should have put some ice on it. When we got to the clubhouse everyone greeted us and looked at my war injury. It was like they considered it to be a prestigious thing to have. Everyone nodded at me and acted as though I was someone special. Personally I was amused, and thought that it was pretty silly to be idolized for this. We all went and had some smokes and a can of beer. A few of us decided to go swimming out to the raft. I looked out at the raft and vaguely thought that it looked a little different, but didn't know why. I didn't say anything because I wasn't sure what was wrong. We all got into the water and started to swim towards the raft. I was far behind because I was the weakest swimmer. The lake was very deep and the last thing I needed to do was to be far out in a lake that I couldn't handle. A couple kids made it to the raft and I knew that I was now swimming for my life. No matter how hard I swam, the raft seemed to get further away! My arms had gone from hurting to finally having no feelings at all. They were like dead weight. I looked behind me and no one was around, and I felt myself go down! I popped my head back up gasping for air only to go under again and again. I was preparing to die, when all of a sudden while coming up for my last breath; I felt an arm grab my neck from behind! It's funny how life can bring you up and you can feel like you are on top of the world, and the next minute something pulls the ladder out from under you. I didn't know who was saving my life. I only know that I was very grateful.

When we reached the part of the lake where I could stand up, I turned to see who it was that saved me. To my utter amazement, it was the girl that I fought with the night before! I was shocked! She just smiled and said it was nothing, and that I wore my black eye well. We both laughed and looked out at the raft, and she told me that boats were going to have to go out and pick up the rest of the kids. The anchor that held the raft down had come loose, and the raft was drifting across the lake! So was my friend Alison! The boats reached the raft and brought everyone back. What an experience! I thanked her profusely, and she said that we were even. I had made no marks on her, but she had blown out my eye. Alison came running over to me and asked if I was all right. We decided to make it an early day and just go back to the cabin to rest. We had enough excitement for one day, and because of the incident, I had lost my winning crown. Not only did she give me a black eye, but she also had saved my life! How could I beat that?

The two weeks were almost up, and that meant we had to go back home. We weren't happy. I was almost out of money though and my clothes were a mess. Grandma didn't have a washing machine, and many times she would wash her clothes in the bathroom sink and soak other garments in the tub. I was amazed that she had so much wealth at one time, and now seemed to barely have what she needed. I felt bad. I guess someone had pulled a ladder out from under her too. I did admire her spirit though, because no matter what, she was always singing and happy.

Her idea of cleaning was to take a broom and sweep wildly from side to side, singing her songs and never raising her voice about anything. Sometimes she would put on a bathing suit and take a bar of soap to the little lake. This is where she bathed many a time! She was just different, but a lot of fun; and had an inner strength that I wished I could possess. Nothing ever really bothered her. She just wouldn't let it. She spoke about how we would be welcome to come up the following year, and it only took Alison and me a second to answer that one. We loved the lake and the people, even though there had been a fight. Most importantly, we loved the freedom that we had, and we were made to feel special. We would be back the next year and any other year that we were able to. Now when I had to go back to school this year, look what I could write about! Just don't ask me to read it out loud, Ha! Ha!

We sadly started to prepare to go home, and went to the lake to say goodbye to all of our new friends. We spent the day with them just hanging out and smoking and talking. Each one of us told a little about our lives at home. I was very careful not to say too much about my life. I knew that these kids came from rough backgrounds, but even they didn't have to know everything. I told them about the wicked grandparents and we all sat around and laughed, and thought of ways to tease them, because they had been so mean. A couple of the kids were quite creative. We then parted our ways and promised to meet again next year. I thought perhaps next year we could stay for three weeks.

We went back to the cabin. Grandma told us that Mommy would be up about noon. Our vacation was over. Alison and I went down to the little lake area and sat for a couple of hours and smoked. She had to go back home once we got back to my house, and we wondered if Helen would be there. I knew that Helen couldn't stay at my house forever, because she had to help with her brother and sisters. She was older than us and a lot more daring. Sometimes she did things that we would never dream of doing.

One night Helen was really mad at one of the guys we hung out with. He was older than all of us, and one of our suppliers of beer and smokes. Helen and he had started to date, and seemed to really like each other. Everything was going all right and Mommy didn't care if she had a friend, as long as she got back to the house at a decent time. One night Helen and Frankie got into a major fight. They were parked in one of the neighboring towns and had a really bad disagreement. Helen got out of the car and picked up a big rock and started to hit his car all over. They both ran around and around the car, and every time she had a chance she hit the car, making big dents in it. Finally she got tired and became dizzy. She ran down the street heading towards home, and saw a couple kids that we knew driving down the street. She yelled for them to stop, and she got into their car before Frankie could see where she had run off to.

To a teenage boy, one of his most important possessions is his car and how good it looks. He was furious with what she had done and was shocked too. He knew that she lived with me, and had no job or any money to repair the damage that she caused. This was going to be the end of their relationship for sure. I thought she was lucky that he didn't do damage to her! Helen got dropped off at the end of the driveway and walked to the house. After she told me what she had done, I was a little scared because I didn't know what Frankie would do in return. She said, "He didn't call the cops at the time, or sign a complaint when it happened, so he's screwed." I figured she was probably right.

The next day Frankie drove in after dinner. He went right up to my mother and told her everything. My mother thought that Helen could have found a better way to handle herself that night, and demanded that she get a part-time job to help pay for damages. Mommy stated that since she had been at our house, she could flip us a few dollars as well. Helen hung her head and agreed that what she had done was wrong, and she also admitted to having a terrible anger problem. We had seen her in action when she was mad at someone, and agreed. For days she looked for work, but it's pretty hard for school kids to get a job. She managed to get a job for a short period of time wrapping gifts in one of the departments in Macy's. She flipped Frankie a few dollars, but ended up getting fired in a few weeks anyway. Mommy had enough. Helen started to hang out with a new crowd of kids who were a lot tougher than we were. They were too tough for Mommy's liking. She told Helen to go back home. I panicked, and reminded her about the grand-parents, and how they treated me better, or stayed away from me because I wasn't alone. You might say that if they got out of line, or were abusive to me, I had Helen in my corner. The position I was in at home made me very mad and I felt like I was weak. But, I didn't ask for any of this either. If my grandparents left the next day and I never saw them again, I wouldn't have cared. My mother sighed and said, "All right, she has one more chance." Helen was very thankful. She would have to go back home for a couple of weeks to give the oldest sister a break dealing with the younger kids. Both of her parents worked, and needed help at home be-cause of all the children they had. She was very happy to get away from her responsibilities and stay with us. Her parents had very low paying jobs, and they all ate a lot of pancakes to fill up on. There wasn't any fighting in the house, just poverty. Actually, Helen could have gotten a part time job and helped at home monetarily. We all knew this, but said nothing. We were inseparable, and would never go against each other in any way. That was the beauty of our friendship.

My mother showed up at noon and we had to say our goodbyes to everyone. I felt like I was going to cry, but if I did, I figured I was too old for that, and I would probably make Mommy mad. We left and passed some kids who were on their way to the clubhouse, and they all yelled, "Next year Jersey Brats!" My mother honked the horn at them, and we waved wildly as we drove home. We made some really good friends, and were going to miss them. Mommy asked us about all of our experiences. She was shocked about all of the fighting, and how I almost drowned that time. She wasn't sure that going back next year was such a good idea. I could see her point from a mother's point of view, but assured her that it was the very place that I wanted to be, and I needed a break from the wicked grandparents.

It didn't take us too long to get back to Alison's house. We got out of the car and I helped her take her suitcases in. We said a tearful goodbye, but knew that it wouldn't be long before we saw each other again. It was only minutes before we were pulling down our driveway, and I really felt sad. I knew that nothing had changed in the short time that I was gone. The grandparents would still be mean, and I would still be expected to do chores that should have been divided between three kids. It didn't make sense that Mommy couldn't put her foot down, and insist on me being treated better. Maybe she was afraid of them too! I asked Mommy if she had heard from Helen, and she said that she hadn't. I wondered if she was really going to come back like she promised. We reached the house and I got out of the car. I reached to get my suitcase and there was Helen coming down the driveway! My heart jumped for joy when I saw my friend, and I knew that I wouldn't have to worry about being alone with the wicked. Boy did I have some plans for them!! New York kids gave me some good ideas. We're told to respect our elders, but what if the elders don't respect you? Kids have rights too!

CHAPTER 30

Helen moved back in and things were going pretty well. She didn't know how long she was going to stay with us, but to me, any of my friends were welcome to stay forever. It wasn't long before the five of us were hanging out on the property, and in the woods. We spoke about school, and knew that we had to go back pretty soon. I thought to myself, this year I will make up all of ninth and see if I can take a couple of extra classes towards tenth grade. That is what I was supposed to be in. I didn't like failing school. I was a little embarrassed, because I knew that I wasn't dumb. It was my complexes and phobias that held me back. There didn't seem to be any help for them, and I didn't know what to do about them either. I would rather die than stand up in front of my peers and read out loud. Since I was molested and raped I just couldn't handle having people look at me. That's when those problems started. At times I would get so frustrated with life and people, that I would think that it would be a lot easier if I just didn't exist. Then I would shake those thoughts off and think that I have to be tougher. I have to somehow find a way to live sanely. I was thankful that I had such good friends, and truly believed that they were a good part of my salvation.

I once told Meagan, who was the girl who had most of the parties in her house, that I had trouble reading out loud. She admitted she didn't much like it either, but she did it pretty well. When I told her that I had panic attacks just thinking about it, she told me to picture everyone naked! I had actually heard of that before, so instead of skipping school on one occasion, when I knew that I had to read one of my book reports; I decided to tough it out and take her advice. When it came time for me to stand up and read, my heart was pounding, and I knew that I would sound breathless as usual, but I thought I'm going to do this; I was determined. I looked at the kids sitting there and did my best to picture them naked, and try as I might I couldn't. There was a really heavy boy sitting right in front of me, and I actually started to laugh, because I could picture him naked! It didn't help my cause though because my heart felt like it was going to jump out of my chest; I was doomed. The teacher cleared her throat and told me to read. I looked at her instead and said that I was going to throw up and I needed to go to the ladies room. She told me not until I read. I looked at her and said, "If you don't let me go you're going to have a big bad mess to clean up!" She excused me and the kids thought that I was funny and laughed.

She wasn't dumb however. A few days later, I had been given a note by the teacher to report to the "special" class to see that teacher. I was furious because only the dummies went there, and I knew that if I didn't have such deep-rooted complexes and phobias, that my grades would be well above average. I had to show up though, and the first thing she did was give me a silent reading test which I passed with flying colors. The teacher said, "Oh no, there has to be some error here, because you're reading at college level. You obviously fully comprehend every story that you read, and based on the answers given, English is one of your strong points." Then she asked me to read out loud and she *had* me. No one was in the classroom except us, yet I went right into full panic mode, which actually surprised me! I suffered from panic so badly, that I couldn't even read out loud to one person! I ran out of that room as fast as I could, and ran to the girl's room to light up a smoke! No teacher approached me after that about my problem, and I was left alone for quite some time. Its strange how one's mind can be blown and how it can last and last and last.

Chapter 30

Helen had been hanging out with kids that we had never met before. She had only gone back home for a week, and took off with some kids that she met in Morristown, N.J. They were pretty rough kids to say the least. Some had lived in the city and were on drugs; big time drugs. I had no desire to use or to pop pills, which were really in. The kids really liked Quaaludes and cough medicine at the time. All I wanted to do was drink my beer. I tried cough syrup and had a strange reaction to it. I felt like my throat was going to close up! I had taken two big gulps of it, and while waiting for the big high that I was supposed to get, instead I felt like I couldn't breathe. I thought, "This is great! Oh yea, do this again? I think not!" I was a drinker and was starting to turn into a heavy one at that. I felt like I was superior to people who were "junkies." In those days, that's what most people believed.

One night there was a party, but not at Meagan's house. Instead it was at one of the guys that we hung out with. He wasn't a popular guy, and he came from a family where there had been a lot of personal tragedy. My friends felt sorry for him, but they used him for booze and whatever they thought they needed. That night I drank a combination of booze that didn't agree with me. I had never mixed beer with wine. Wow, did I get sick, and not only that, I guess I drank so much that I also couldn't get sober. Someone took me home and told me to sleep it off. I went into the house and my mother took one look at me and she said, "You're drunk!" I said, "I sure am am amam," or something like that! She got so mad that she went over and picked up her Electrolux vacuum cleaner and was going to hit me with it! I said "Whash the matter with you!" I demanded to know. The more I asked it, the more she wanted to hit me. I attempted to go up the stairs to my bedroom so I could lock the door and lock her out. I may have been drunk, but I knew that Mommy meant business! She wanted to hit me badly. I climbed up the steps on all fours and my brother grabbed my mother and said, "Stop! Can't you see she's drunk out of her mind?" That made my mother even madder, and he tried to hold her back, but she managed to squirm away from him. I made it to my room just in time and slammed the door and closed and locked it. My mother demanded that I open the door and I said "No!" She hit the door with the metal part of the hose time and time again. I was sure happy that I made it into my room.

Finally she stopped. My brother went to the kitchen and made me some tomato soup and brought it to my door. He gently knocked on the door and I let him in. I was very grateful for his help, and drank the soup. It lasted in my stomach for about two minutes and I threw it up all over my bed! He helped me clean up and change my bedding. He said we were even, because I had saved him the night that Mommy was going to hit him so long ago with the glass bottle! It still never dawned on anyone that I needed help. I was very grateful that the wicked were not home to see this. They had gone to stay with my Uncle George and Aunt Jane for a couple of days. I wondered where they slept.

The next day I stayed out of Mommy's way, and it wasn't mentioned again. I told Jeff what had happened, and he said that it was beer for me and only beer. Jeff was a good three years older than me. He was a nice guy who liked me a little too much, but not my type. I wasn't sure yet what my type was, but I knew it wasn't him. One day he came over looking for me and I wasn't home. My brother was there and so was Mommy. The grandparents were out at the store shopping. My brother was fooling around with a gun that had blanks in it. Poor Jeff didn't know that the gun only had blanks. They had invited Jeff into the living room, and I'm sure that all he wanted to do was leave. All of a sudden my brother said, "So what do you think mom, should we make him dance?" My mother said, "Sure son, whatever you want." My brother looked at Jeff who was standing there very startled I'm sure, and my brother ordered him to dance. Jeff evidently said no and my brother aimed and shot at the floor right next to Jeff's feet. The gun made a very loud noise, and poor Jeff started to dance for his life! He kept asking, "Is this enough? Can I stop now?" My brother made him dance for about three to four minutes, and demanded that he dance all different kinds of steps. Finally he said, "I'm gettin' bored so you can stop now." The poor guy ran out of the house and as he was running he yelled, "You people are nuts!" It was a cruel and nasty thing to do, especially to a guy like that. When I got home my mother told me what they had done and I thought that it was funny, but I also knew that they had gone too far. I was really mortified. They didn't know his background and they didn't care. Word had gotten out about the practical joke they played on him, and Jeff of course told people that the gun was loaded. When the whole story got out and back to Jeff, he was so humiliated that he went into seclusion. He refused to leave his house and he definitely didn't want to see me. I was an enemy. He refused to even talk to me on the phone. I was afraid that he would try to commit suicide. He was such an emotional and sad type of guy to begin with. He stayed in his house for about a month, and kids didn't tease him or mention the incident again. It was weeks before he spoke to me, and I apologized profusely for my families' behavior. Eventually, things went back to normal, and if he wasn't having a party at his house then Meagan was having one at hers. I made sure that I never went home drunk again and I would just stay over some ones house if I was too intoxicated.

School was about to start. None of us were happy campers. My mother bought me some new clothes, but not much to brag about. It was enough to start, and I figured as time went on she would buy me a few more things. That is the way it always was. My brother was moving out! There was always too much trouble at the house. He was always making my step-father mad with his cars all over the place. He was older now, and had managed to get a better job. I was delighted because I would never have to clean up after him again. Some of that had stopped when Helen moved in, but still and all I had chores to do, and he never had any. Helen would help out some, but said that I should just refuse. We continued to play tricks on the grandparents, and they continued to try and get us in trouble. It was really very silly and immature, but my grandparent's seemed to thrive on the whole situation. Mommy would take grandma to look at houses to buy in the area, but she always found something wrong with them. My grandparent's simply wanted to live for nothing, rule the house and at times cause fights. What a family I had! I vowed that if I ever had kids I would always treat them with respect, and they would never have to wonder if they were loved. I also vowed that if I were to divorce my husband to be, the children and I would always stay together no matter what. They would never live like I did. They would always have their mother's love.

The day had come. My mother was down in the kitchen singing "School days school days dear old golden rule days." She just did that to bust me. I wasn't mad and I left to go to school. I was going to make this year a good year no matter what it took to do that. If it meant that I had to sip a few shots of whisky before reading a book report, then that's the way it was going to be! I had to get good grades no matter what. When I entered the building I noticed a group of kids hanging around in the hallway. They looked really tough. In those days kids were referred to as either the bookworms or regular kids or hoods. I had a bunch of hoods standing in front of me. I have to admit they looked intimidating. I also noticed that a couple of them were carrying flasks filled with booze. A couple of the girls looked really skinny and sick and had visible bruises on the inside of their arms. The guys wore black leather jackets and slicked back their hair. As I walked past them a couple of the hood boys whistled at me. This made the hood girls mad. I was not a happy camper and wished that they would just go away. I couldn't care less if the boys thought that I was pretty. Clearly, these boys were not my type. I started to get nervous and wanted to find my friends. I decided to go to the ladies room because I figured they would be in there having a smoke before class. I was right and very happy to see them. They took one look at my face and they laughed and said, "You saw the hoods didn't you?" We all then laughed. I said, "I think they have Brooklyn beat!" What kind of kids come to school with flasks of booze and needle marks all over their arms? I thought that this is going to be an interesting year! Helen told us that she knew some of them from hanging out in other towns. I wasn't surprised, because out of the whole group of us she was the toughest one. We also learned that the school principal had stepped down and we had a new one. He was already the target of ridicule because he was openly gay.

As the principal walked down the hallway he had a certain wiggle about him. The hood kids saw this and immediately formed a line behind him, and wiggled while they walked too! In those days to be gay was just not acceptable, and this man was in for quite a school year [if he lasted]. From day one it was obvious that he was never going to be respected, and he simply could *not* keep control. This caused a lot of problems in our school, and as the year went by a lot of kids just simply quit. The hoods were going to run the place! We were sent our schedules in the mail so we all knew where our classes were and none of us had even one class together. We were really disappointed about this. Only Meagan and I had homeroom together. I was determined to do well, and I have to admit that the hood kids did give me an idea about the flask. I thought about it and I knew that booze made me feel more courageous. It helped me put my guard down and relax. This might help me with my problem in English or any other class that required oral reading.

That day, after I got home from school, I called Jeff up and asked him if he had any flasks. He said that he did and would give me one, but wanted to know why. I was too embarrassed to tell him and just begged him for one. He sighed and said "Please don't do anything to get into trouble or I'll get really pissed off." I promised that I would be very careful, and not do anything to get him in trouble for giving it to me. I met him in town, because after the way he was treated at my house he refused to come over ever again. I didn't blame him. I told him that I wasn't treated well either. He gave me the flask and I walked back home. The grandparents were out in the kitchen and Helen was upstairs. I went into the living room and very quickly poured some whiskey into the flask, and then put it into a safe area of my pocket book. I was now ready to address my problem the only way I knew how. I was ashamed of myself and felt very bad, but I had not yet figured out how to conquer this problem that was crippling my life. I felt like a failure.

The school week went well, and there was no need for me to drink. That Saturday we girls were invited to a party. It sounded good to me. This time it was not over Meagan's or Jeff's house. It was held at a kid's house that was a friend of Helen's. It was quite a night, and I met my first love there. His name was Sonny and I fell madly in love. He was a little older, had a car, and lived about fifteen miles away from me. We became inseparable. We would go to Meagan's house and sit for hours, and stare into each other's eyes and make out. We also had lots of beer to drink because Meagan's house was well stocked. I never told him about my past or any of my secret life because I was just too humiliated. He wanted to have sex with me but there was no way that I would let him touch me. For a whole year and a half he was one frustrated young man. I felt like I was too young anyway, and not only that, I had a bad attitude about sex because of what had happened to me. I still had nightmares from time to time, and nothing could wipe away the past. I was constantly trying to find a way to forget about it. How does one forget abuse that continues to rule your life by showing its ugly head? My complexes and phobias were a very real and big part of my life, an ugly part. How do I stop the nightmares? How do I learn to feel good about myself when I know that I'm so different from other kids? I was so screwed up that I needed booze to help me feel normal!

———

CHAPTER 31

As the school year went by there were times that we were assigned oral book reports. Right before it was my turn to get up and read my report, I would ask to go to the ladies room. Once there, I would take out my flask and take a couple swallows of booze. Then I'd take a deep breath and go back into the classroom. When my turn came, I would read and get it over with. I not only got it over with, but because I could write well, I did well. I finally found a solution to my problem and that year I did fine. I had a boyfriend who adored me, and found a way to not only make up ninth grade, but also gained enough credits towards tenth. Just like I said I would do! I was proud of myself even if I had to drink to achieve my goals. My mother was pleased as well. She said, "See, I knew you could do it!" I thought to myself, "If you only knew what I'm going through!" We lived in the same house and my own mother didn't know me.

In those days, it was a big thing to rent a motel room and party. We would drink, play cards, listen to music, etc. One Saturday night that is exactly what we did. Sonny stayed home that night, which made me feel really bad because we hadn't missed a Saturday night since we met. I secretly feared that he was mad at me because I wouldn't give in to him sexually. We had been going out for quite a while. I was hurt and went to the party. There was a guy there that I could tell was attracted to me. We spoke and got along well with each other, but there wasn't going to be any romance as far as I was concerned, because I was stuck on Sonny.

All of a sudden someone said it was time to go for a beer run and I was left alone in the room with this guy. I admit that I had a few beers, but I still had presence of mind. We were sitting on the bed since it was a small room, and there was nowhere else to sit other than the floor. There had been other kids on the bed before the beer run, including us, so we didn't move when they left. Without warning this guy pushed me down on the bed and climbed on top of me. I had a skirt on so he was able to roughly pull my stockings down. The skirt didn't belong to me. I had borrowed it from one of my friends and I could hear it ripping. I tried to get away from him, but he was much stronger than me and I thought, "Hear we go again!" Sure enough, he unbuttoned his pants and pulled his fly down. I was horrified, and before I knew it, he was grinding against me and my underwear was pushed aside. I tried to push him off and was yelling at him to stop, but he wouldn't listen. After a short time he finished his dirty deed. Just as he was finishing, the door flew open and in walked my friends. They knew me well enough to know that I was in trouble and they pulled him off of me. A couple of the guys took him for a ride. This was called street justice. I heard that he was badly beaten and he left town. None of us had any business being in the motel, and none of us had any business drinking like we did, but that particular guy had no business doing what he did either. "No means No!"

My period was late that month, and the next and my friends were afraid that I had gotten pregnant. I started my period at the ripe old age of nine, and believe me I was always on time. I'd been told that if you are emotionally upset it can throw it off. I didn't know what to believe. One of my friends had gotten a hold of some pills and told me to take them, because if I was in fact pregnant, this would cause a miscarriage. I was afraid of the pills and refused to take them. I didn't tell Sonny what had happened, because I knew that he would break up with me for putting myself in that position, and because I didn't give him what he wanted sexually. He was really getting mad at me, and stopped calling me every day. Saying that I wanted to wait until we were married wasn't good enough anymore.

Chapter 31

One day I had a terrible pain in my stomach and lower intestinal area, so I ran upstairs to the bathroom. If I was pregnant it went away! I was very thankful because there was no way that I was ready for that! I quickly glanced in the toilet before I flushed. I could have sworn that I saw something that resembled a fetus, just like the ones that we saw in health class. I was horrified and started to cry and shake. I went into my bedroom and told Helen. We stood there and held each other for a minute until I stopped shaking. I thought, "God! Will my problems ever end?" It's true that I was in the wrong place and I shouldn't have been drinking, but I didn't ask for this to happen. I stayed home for a couple of days and didn't leave my room. I told my mother that I had a bad stomachache and that was true. I never went to the doctors, and hoped that what I thought I saw in the bathroom was something else. That may sound cockeyed, but I love kids. I just wasn't ready to be a Mom. Hell, I didn't even know how to be me!

CHAPTER 32

Hallelujah!! My wicked grandparents had decided that they wanted to leave for good. That was fine with me. They had been with us for seven long years, and had caused so much trouble for all except Jimmy of course. They had actually gone to an attorney to complain about the money that my mother had borrowed so long ago, and my step-father had gotten a lawyer as well. After both sides were heard in an informal meeting, both attorneys agreed that my grandparent's made out well because all of their needs were taken care of. This included medical needs and they paid no rent. In fact, they concluded that if anything, they now owed my parents money for living with us for so long for free! They were told to leave peacefully or there would be trouble. They packed up their belongings and they left! I watched them as they went up the driveway and cheered. I hadn't been that happy for a long time. I was thrilled! My grandparent's had been collecting social security checks and hardly spent any of them, so they had plenty of money and no more excuses. Helen and I ran around and around on the driveway acting like wild Indians. We were so happy that we went out that night and celebrated. You can't blame us.

We met another girl who was in our school. She was to become friend number six in our group of girls. Her name was Kelly. Kelly was a fun loving type of kid who laughed at almost everything. She found humor in things that we didn't quite understand, but we thought that she was all right. Unlike the rest of us, she came from a home that appeared to be "proper," but looks can be deceiving. She was an only child, was spoiled in some ways and terribly neglected in others. Her parents were such cold acting people that the minute you walked into their house, you immediately felt unwelcome. I'm sure that Kelly was a mistake because they didn't like kids, it was clearly that obvious. Kelly lived in a pretty house, in a pretty neighborhood, had clothes that I would kill for, but had nothing else. It's like I said before; we all knew each other without speaking a word. We just would find each other and tried to help one another the best way we knew how, and that was enough. She was a nervous acting kid and kind of strange, but what the heck, we were all strange. She fit in well.

In our girls group there was Alison, Helen, Meagan, Laura, me, and now Kelly. We had a lot of fun together. We all came from dysfunctional families each in our own way and desperately needed to fit into society. I had the worst background to try and deal with; but my friends had issues as well. Abuse is shown in many ways and is always painful. I certainly saw that in myself for years. Think about it, I was threatened, molested, kidnapped, raped, hungry, humiliated, ignored, yelled at and told that I was stupid. I would sometimes think to myself "Am I normal or am I crazy?" I wasn't sure. I knew that I was very troubled, but I didn't know if it was more than that or not. I looked at all the people that I knew and I still felt like I was different. Everyone has problems. It just seems like I had more than anyone that I knew. I had nightmares and trouble looking people in the eyes, or making eye contact unless they were my friends, or I had a few drinks. I knew in my heart that a lot of things that happened to me truly were not my fault, and then there were times that I made poor choices. I did take responsibility when I made mistakes.

Helen had decided to move out. She and my mother didn't get along that well, so she was ready to leave. It was summer again and my mother wanted her to get a part time job to help pay for her stay. My mother was also mad at her because she would leave with friends without telling us, and be gone for days on end. No one knew where she was, and my mother didn't want to be held responsible in case something happened to her. I can't say that I blamed her for that. Helen was the most daring one out of all of us, and could even make us shake our heads with disbelief with her behavior. I was however very grateful for her endless help with the grandparents. I think they were afraid of her! The funny part was she was only about five foot tall and weighed in at ninety-eight pounds at best. She still managed to make a big presence! We said tearful goodbyes and promised to stay in touch with each other.

That summer we hardly saw Helen at all. Our group of six had turned back to five. Another one of my friends was having a hard time at home, and wanted to move in as soon as she heard that Helen had moved out. She had been adopted at a very early age and just didn't get along with her adoptive parents. They were very strict. At times she managed to get out of the house to be with us. She had to sneak out by climbing through her window. When she got caught there would be terrible fights. She really wasn't allowed to have any friends at all. That wasn't right either. She just simply announced one day that she was going to live with us and her adoptive mother, who was tired of fighting with her said, "Go ahead!" Mommy didn't mind because she had to work in the greenhouses and deliver flowers all of the time anyway. She thought she would be good company for me.

This friends name was Laura. Laura arrived in the evening and we were like two little kids. Life at home was getting better because my brother had moved out and my grandparents were gone. For once there was peace. We did have our chores, but they were reasonable and we had no problems with them. It was also time to consider going to the cabin! Grandma called and asked if we wanted to come for a visit. My boyfriend Sonny was keeping his distance and I thought to myself, "Why not?" He obviously didn't care anymore and I was heartbroken. I needed to get away. Laura had a lot of clothes, and she lent me blouses and I had enough shorts, so this year I was in better shape. I didn't want a repeat performance of the year before. I knew that what I did was wrong. I didn't have it in my heart to steal, but did so out of necessity. Mommy should have been more generous and understanding. I didn't understand her at times. Jimmy always had everything that he needed and some of what he wanted. There was never a time that he was made fun of for lack of clothing or anything else. I always had to go without or fight to get what I needed. I did have terrible resentments and felt justified for having them. Jimmy always seemed oblivious to my problems and needs. Or maybe he just didn't care.

The day had come. My mother took us to the cabin. She stayed to say hello for a couple of minutes. She again gave me some money which I appreciated, and I told her so. She said that she appreciated my help over the years when help was needed, and I was always willing to do what I could to be helpful. That was the only time that I felt really appreciated for my efforts. I felt like giving her a hug but refrained. My mother used to say, "I'm from Iowa, and we don't believe in hugs or kisses." I thought, "I'm from New York and New Jersey, and planet earth, and I will never say no to my kids!" I will probably hug them to death! My mother left and we went into the bedroom to unpack. Grandma was her usual happy self. I introduced my new friend. Aunt Priscilla and Uncle Jack were at the store food shopping. We were going to have a wonderful summer. Laura was in for a great experience. She was going to be allowed to have fun and just be a kid. She was very excited to say the least. I had fun just looking at her face. We had dinner and played cards, which is something her parents were against. She couldn't even play cards! They considered it to be evil. What wackiness is that? After we played cards we went out for a smoke. I was another year older and grandma asked me if Mommy knew that I was smoking. My mother knew and she really didn't care, so I no longer had to hide that. We were now allowed to smoke in the house, because grandma didn't want to see me smoking. We all turned in pretty early that night because we made great plans for the next day. Grandma told us that the "Brooklyn Kids" were asking about the "New Jersey Brats!" They hadn't forgotten us and we were prepared to have a ball! Mommy did want us back home in two weeks though, and we were going to make the most of it.

Morning came. We got out of bed and wolfed down some sort of breakfast. Laura and I were like two little kids. We didn't walk to the clubhouse we ran as far as we could and then walked again. It was almost a mile and Laura was not a runner like I was. As we approached the clubhouse, I pulled out the flask and took a gulp. Laura looked at me and laughed and took one too. We saw a group of kids standing outside of the clubhouse by the door. One of the kids saw us and yelled, "Jersey Brats!" We were warmly welcomed! "Hey who is this?" I introduced Laura and the fun began. One of the kids said, "Hey Carol, you're not going to drown again this year are you?" Everyone laughed including me, and we had a great day.

The next day was Friday, which meant Teen Night at the club-house. The kids seemed a little more grown up this year and some of them were driving. We now had cars to go joy riding in. For the most part we behaved well, however we just all drank too much and that night was no exception. We stayed in the clubhouse for a while and of course the beer was flowing. We then decided to pile up in two cars and go out for a ride. There was a road that took us all around to the other side of the lake. This side was not nearly as built up as the side that we lived on. It was easy to find a place to park and party. We did, and drank under the moonlight and had a great time. There were no problems because we all got along so well. We were the misfits, but we were not really bad kids, just confused with life in general, and we did all care about each other. We laughed and joked and suddenly I realized what time it was. It wasn't eleven o'clock, but two o'clock! We were in trouble! We piled into the cars and chewed gum like a maniac, and one by one all the kids were getting dropped off at their houses. When we got dropped off, the outside light went on and Aunt Priscilla came out. She was drunk herself, and the remaining kids in the car laughed at her, but not in a mean way. They thought that she was just cool. She told them to get lost, that tomorrow was another day. She took us aside and said, "You're very lucky because your grandmother fell asleep very early tonight, and I'll cover for you this time." She looked at us and said that we had better slow down. We were very thankful for her understanding attitude and went to bed immediately. We were very careful not to wake up grandma.

Not only would it blow our cover, but the last thing in the world I wanted to do was to disappoint my grandmother. She had been very good to me.

The next day we learned that the two remaining guys in the car we were in decided to continue to party. They were already pretty drunk when we were dropped off, and we could not believe that they continued to drink. They got into a car accident and were hurt badly. One car down! They were hospitalized and both of them had to stay for a week. That slowed everyone down a little bit. We took turns to go and visit, all the time trying to stay out of the way of their parents.

In Greenwood Lake there was a horse farm and we all wanted to go horseback riding. We decided that we needed to get some clean fun under our belt. We had a ball and went there many days. Laura had no idea how to ride a horse and I wasn't much better, but we managed and even met some new kids. A couple of them worked there on the ranch. These kids were not good though and we could tell. They were into drugs and reminded me of the hoods in our school. We loved horseback riding, but Laura and I knew that there was going to be trouble if we hung out there much longer. The guys we were friendly with were getting really mad at these kids, and the feelings were mutual. Tempers were building and Laura and I, and the two other girls that we came with decided that we had better get everyone back into the cars and get out of there. It was too late! A fight between the guys broke out and it was ugly. There were four guys fighting and they meant business. I actually got in between two of them and got hit in the head by mistake! Wow, I didn't try that again! I saw stars and decided that if they were dumb enough to fight, so be it! All of a sudden we heard sirens and knew that some one had called the cops. I wanted out of there and so did the other girls. We started to yell at them and said, "Stop, here come the cops!" They were so busy fighting that they didn't hear us. We girls decided to run and hide. After all, we weren't the ones who were fighting, they were, and so hide we did. The police came and before I knew it they were taken away for disorderly conduct and anything else the cops could think of.

There we were the four of us, alone with two cars to drive and none of us had a driver's license! What were we to do? Well, I ended up driving one car and Laura was scared to death that we would get caught .One of the Brooklyn girls drove the other with her sister as a passenger. They flipped a coin to see who would drive. I, who have no sense of direction, followed them back to the clubhouse. At times I had driven Mommy's car up and down the driveway so I had an idea of how to drive. We were scared to death, but had to get back home. We felt like we couldn't leave the cars there, and after all we had to get back to the lake. This seemed like the right thing to do. I felt like I had an angel watching over me as I drove. I was so stiff from fear, I felt wooden. By the time we got back to the clubhouse there were a group of kids waiting for us. One of the boys had called the clubhouse from the police department and told them what had happened. When they were told that the cars were gone and hadn't been towed, they figured that we had them. All of the kids that we hung out with were very grateful because no one really had any money, and if they were towed it would be some time before they would be able to get them back. Of course, they would also probably have to pay for storage, so we had saved the day. The kids that fought had been given citations, and all except one of the hired ranch boys had been released after a few hours. The one kid had a warrant out on him so he was incarcerated. I thought what a summer this is turning out to be! It wasn't exactly fun, just active. We decided to stay home that night and play cards with the elders. It was safer and anyway my head hurt! We had a good night and made plans for the next day.

We got up bright and early and out we went again. It was a great thing being young, and summer time seemed to hold certain magic to it. Even though there were complications as usual, we were still young and strong and looked at each day with enthusiasm and expectation. The next few days and nights went well. We had fun just hanging out swimming in the daytime, parking and lying down at night in a grassy area, just staring up at the stars. None of us were really romantically involved, we were just good friends. Who needs romance anyway? It just complicates things. Look at Sonny; he sure had let me down.

Our time at the lake was coming to an end. The day before we were to go home, Laura and I took a row boat out on the lake, and we spent a good part of the day just being by ourselves. The lake had a certain magic to it. Just staying there and being in the company of people who really cared about you, was something that both Laura and I were going to miss. We had dinner with my grandmother and went back to the clubhouse for one last hurrah. The night went too quickly and home we went promising to return next year. To me two weeks was not enough time and Laura felt the same, but I couldn't make Mommy mad. These people, who I loved, were after all my father's family, whom she despised. I felt lucky to be able to visit at all. We stayed up late that night just hanging by the lake near the cabin so we would be close by. We didn't go back into the cabin until two am. Mommy came and picked us up at noon just like last year and we went home. My mother told me that Sonny had been calling and I must admit my heart leapt for joy. Ah, young love! Now I wanted to go home. Sonny called that evening and he said that he would be over the next day after work. I was all excited and couldn't wait to see him. He never really verbalized that he loved me, but I hoped that he did.

Laura made plans to see Meagan and some of the other girls to catch up with some gossip. Sonny and I left in his new car to see some of his friends. He told me that there was going to be a big party for one of his family members, and he wanted me to come. He also told me that I had to wear a dress because it was going to be very fancy. He had to wear a tux! I thought to myself, I don't even own a dress, and if it has to be a fancy one it would cost a lot of money. I was too ashamed to tell him that not only did I not own a dress, but I didn't know if Mommy would help me out with this or not. It really irked me in a way because my mother had clothes that were designer names, which she would brag about, and I was always bordering on the line of not having enough. This party was going to be special, and I wanted to look special for myself and for Sonny. I wanted to show him that I could be pretty too, not that I wasn't good looking. I saw the way the boys looked at me and looked at my legs. I was a runner and my legs were strong and shapely. I had no complexes about how I looked physically. My complexes bothered me in other ways that I just could not overcome or understand.

We met with his friends and had a good night and of course the booze was flowing. I didn't know these kids, but as soon as I had a couple of beers it didn't matter because I felt relaxed and enjoyed myself. We laughed, told jokes, and I also told them about the lake and how I had to win a fight last year by pulling the girls clothes off. This went over big and soon it was time to go home. The party was going to be next week and Sonny said, "Remember, you have to get all dressed up and look real pretty for me." We kissed good night and he went home. I had a week to get a dress from somewhere and hopefully my mother would understand how important this was to me. I went upstairs to my bedroom and Laura was sitting there waiting for me. I told her about my date and the upcoming party. She said, "Just ask your mother!" She didn't know that Mommy could be really mean at times. Mommy treated my friends better than she treated me, and that was why they wanted to live with us. It was really kind of freaky.

The next day I told my mother how I had a great night with Sonny and his friends, and explained all excitedly that I had been invited to a fancy party. I told her that I needed to get a pretty dress and his parents whom she had met once before, expected me to be there. His parents had taken the ride to the greenhouses to meet my parents because Sonny and I were spending so much time together. My mother looked at me and said "Absolutely not! I will not buy you a dress!" I was shocked and so hurt because she knew how important this was to me, and she knew that this was going to be a decent and nice affair for me to attend. It could be something that I could have a nice memory of. I thought "God, I don't have many of those do I?" I begged her and I felt myself start to cry. She just told me to stop the dramatics or go outside. I ran to my room and slammed the door.

Laura wasn't home at the time so I grabbed my flask and took several gulps of booze. I calmed down and started to think. Which one of my friends were the closest in size to me? I thought that would be the newest girl to the group, Kelly. I called her and asked if she had anything that I could borrow. She said she did have one really nice dress and she would ask her mother if I could borrow it. She called me back and told me that her mother said no. Kelly was shocked that my mother wouldn't buy me a dress, especially under such important circumstances. She said she only had a few dollars on her, but I was welcome to it. She thought that maybe everyone could chip in, and with a lot of effort on everyone's part, I would gather enough money to buy one. I thanked her profusely and said that I would take it if others were able to do the same.

Later on in the day when Laura came back home I told her what had taken place. She was shocked as well. She said she had a pretty dress at her home and if we got a ride over there she would sneak in the house and get it. She was smaller boned than I was, but maybe Meagan who could sew would help. I thought "All right, this is a plan."

That night we got one of our guy friends to take us over to Laura's house. She knew that her parents went to bed really early and they never locked the windows, so she would be able to get in. She also wanted to get a few things for herself from her closet. We pulled up to the house and in the window she climbed getting the dress she had in mind for me and a few other items. We thanked our friend for the ride, and went back home to our bedroom and looked at the dress. It was very pretty, but I knew that it was *not* going to fit. No way. I was furious and found my flask and took a drink. I tried it on and it was too tight. We looked at the seams to see if there was any material to let out and there just wasn't any. I was screwed. To a kid these times in life are important, and the very fact that I had been invited to this function showed me that they thought enough to invite me. I wanted to please Sonny. What was I going to do, call him up and say that I can't come because I don't have a dress to my name? How about this, "My mother refuses to help me with this problem, so I have to stay home." That is what I should have done! No one had any money to lend me and they decided that maybe "five finger discounts" would be in order.

I vowed that I would never do that again, but look what's happening! If I was Jimmy I would have five dresses in all different colors! I once overheard my mother say to my grandmother on my father's side, "I like boys better than girls." I remember feeling my heart sink and I wanted to cry. That may have been true for whatever reason, but don't say it so I can hear you! I thought about that day and cases like this just proved that she meant it. I was furious and made another vow. I vowed that if I ever had any kids that I would treat them equally and love them to death.

Meagan got a loan from an aunt of hers and bought a car. Off to the store we all went. I looked at the dresses and even tried a couple on. I had no idea how to steal a dress. I felt like an ass. I just didn't know where to put it. My pocket book wasn't big enough, and none of us knew quite what to do. I finally decided that it would be easier to forget the dress and just clip a new pair of pants. If I put on a new pair of pants it would be easier to just walk out! I got caught! I had a few dollars on me, but needed more to purchase the pants. I was taken upstairs to an office and they were going to call my mother. I begged them not to do it, and they asked me why I had done it to begin with. I actually told the lady and the man who worked in security the story of how I had begged my mother for a dress, and why, and they shook their heads. The lady asked, "Then why do you have on a pair of pants?" I told her that at least they would be new ones. She sighed and spoke privately to the other security officer. They came over to me and told me that I could keep the pants, but I had to be back in two days with the full amount or they would tell my mother or call the police. I thanked them profusely and left.

I went downstairs to my friends who were waiting anxiously outside, and told them what happened. "Wow" they said, and we went back to my house. I was back to square one. I approached Mommy, asked her again, and she just said no. I told her how important this was to me and told her I would do extra chores or whatever if she would just help and she still said no. So that was that. I needed five more dollars to satisfy the store and I only had a couple. I walked down the road to a friend of my brothers and told him the story, and he gave me the money I needed for the pants. He drove me to the store and I paid for a pair of pants that were about to cause me doom.

I had come to realize that my mother, who knew how I was suffering over this, was just plain acting mean to me. She was unreasonable and just unkind. Maybe she allowed me to have friends live with us because she didn't want a close mother/daughter relationship. It would save her from dealing with me. Maybe she just thought that I was a freak. Mothers and daughters are supposed to have close bonds aren't they? If I ever wanted to go to a prom for example, I'm sure that a dress would be out of the question, even for that. It was not a matter of money problems for them. They were doing well and my mother could certainly afford to buy her daughter a pretty dress for a special occasion. All of a sudden I felt horrible feelings towards my mother, and felt very very ashamed of myself for having these feelings. My mother was kind when she wanted to be, but she was selective. My friends were shocked because they had now seen the other side of Mommy.

Saturday came and it was time for Sunny to show up. My stomach was in knots because I didn't know what to say to him. He hadn't called all week, but I knew that he was going to show up. I was sitting on the porch outside and I heard a car coming down the driveway. I looked up and it was Sonny. He had a look of shock and disgust on his face. He said, "It's time to go, put a dress on quickly." He stood there in his tux and looked like an Italian God. I wanted to die. I looked at him and said, "Go home and leave me here. I don't have a dress." He looked at me and told me he didn't believe me. We eyeballed each other and he said, "Just get in the car." We drove mostly in silence. I had nothing to say. What was I going to do, start from the very beginning and tell him how my mother refused to buy me one? Perhaps I should tell him how I got caught shoplifting settling for these pants because they were new. Or perhaps I should tell him how my brother's friend saved my ass by giving me the money owed, and how he drove me to the store to square up with security.

We arrived at the place where the party was being held. We got out of his car and some of Sonny's friends approached us. One guy looked at me and said, "Nice dress!" I was numb by this time. I looked around and there were table's set with white linen and crystal glasses and out in the distance there was a pavilion. In the pavilion were three young girls about sixteen years of age who were dressed in beautiful white and pastel colored gowns. Their hair was done up in a beehive, and they had on pretty pearl necklaces and matching earrings. This is who the party was for. They looked like beautiful dolls that hardly seemed real to me. I just stood and looked at them, they appeared to be posing. They would turn one way holding their arms outward, which had a veil type of material draped from their shoulders down across their arms, and then they would turn the other way. I had never seen anything like this before and didn't know what was happening.

Sonny and his friends were talking a short distance away and all I wanted to do was hide or disappear. I felt dizzy and my heart was pounding because I knew that I was out of my league. It was dark out, and lights were strung up around the area of the beautifully covered linen tables. The platform inside of the pavilion was well lit, but other than that it was dark. I decided to take a walk by myself to get away from this and think. I had nowhere to go and I was so out of place that I didn't know what to do. I was simply humiliated beyond words. As I walked away from any people gathering, I felt a hand hit me hard in the back that knocked me to the ground. I was surrounded by three or four young men who started to kick me and roll me around on the dew wet grass. I could hear some of the things that were being said, but it was all really a big blur to me.

Someone said, "How dare you show up here dressed like this!" That I did hear as I was being rolled back and forth and they continued to kick me all over. They didn't kick me like a football, but I felt it. All of a sudden I heard Sonny say, "That's enough." He walked me to the car and pushed me in and said, "Well that's what you get for not wearing a dress." I quietly said, "I told you I didn't have one!" He said nothing all the way back to my house, and as we went down my driveway I looked at him and thought, "He had something to do with this. How could he?" I got out of the car and walked alone to the door of my house, feeling scared and tired. All I wanted to do was curl up into a ball, just like I had done so many times before when horrible things happened in my life.

I went inside the house and quietly climbed the steps to my room where Laura was. She took one look at me and we both started to cry. She went to where I hid my flask and we each took a big gulp. I told her what had happened and she was beside herself with grief for her friend. I was still feeling strange and numb. My hair was full of grass and my pants were full of dirt and stains. I had little cuts on my arms and bruises were becoming evident. I removed my pants and blouse, and we saw red marks starting to turn into bruises on my thighs and a couple by my ribs. I quietly put a robe on, and went in and took a shower. My mother was in her bedroom and I felt nothing for her but anger and disgust. As far as all of the men who raped and molested me and physically abused me I felt feelings of hatred. I knew that if I had a gun at this moment, I probably would have shot each one of them, and have felt perfectly justified in doing so. I went to bed.

The next few weeks flew by and were very uneventful. Laura had been speaking to her adoptive mother. She told her all of her grievances and her mother had done the same in return. I could tell that Laura wanted to go back home and try to work it out. I thought that was all right. The way I looked at it, at least they were both willing to communicate. On the next weekend her mother came by and thanked my mother for all of the good care that had been given to her daughter, and they left to try again.

It wasn't going to be long before school started up, and I was wondering if my mother would at least buy me some good clothes for that. I went to her bedroom one night and just came out and asked her. She assured me that she would get me some, and I was satisfied with that. The house seemed really empty. It was just the three of us now. I thought maybe we could get a little closer. I was hoping for that. Meagan came by a lot and we would go out. Sometimes we would just hang out at her house. I told her the whole story about what Sonny had done, or at least I had believed that he had taken part in. He just wasn't mad enough at the time when I was being assaulted. I thought of all kinds of ways that I could get revenge. For weeks after that incident I was so depressed that I considered suicide. I thought about ways that I would do it. I had enough poor treatment over the years and just didn't want any more. Meagan knew how depressed I was and visited me often. My friends always had a way of helping me get through all of the garbage thrown my way. In return I was always there for them. The next school year was going to be my last, and it was also going to be the last for a lot of people. I didn't plan it that way, it just happened.

September was in the air. Even though it meant school for all of us I always had hope for a good year, sort of like a new beginning. My mother had bought me clothes to start as usual with the promise of more to come. I had lost a few pounds over the summer, which was good. I didn't have to worry about eating more food, and though I was not obese I had needed to drop ten pounds. I was nicknamed "Plumpy," which I hated, and no matter how much I asked my family not to call me that, the name stood. I was not happy. I suppose that I had a little problem with my eating habits because I knew what it felt like to be hungry, and I guess that I went a little overboard at times. So what! Maybe I should throw them a dog bone!

———

CHAPTER 33

School had started. I spoke to the girls the night before, and we made plans to meet before class. We were never assigned the same classes. Meagan and I did have the same study hall together, but that was it. I walked into the school and as usual there were the hoods. This year they had grown in number. I thought, "Oh Boy, this means trouble for the whole school." I was right about that! The principal didn't run the school, the hoods did. What a mess! During the second month, kids who had joined the drama club tried to put on a little play for the school that turned into a disaster. The play was posted and it was to be a Halloween skit. All the kids were encouraged to dress up in a costume for the day. It could have been great fun, but it was ruined. Everyone filed into the auditorium which held a large number of people. There were to be three different shows so the entire school could watch and take part. After the morning show, which went well, disaster struck for the first showing in the afternoon. The hoods allowed for it to start, and then suddenly there was a loud crashing noise that sounded like glass bottles being smashed. That is exactly what had happened, except they were not just smashed in one place, they were being thrown at the players! One kid got hit in the head, and was screaming while blood trickled down his face. Fortunately, he was the only one hurt, but not too badly. Everyone was yelling and ducking, but they continued to throw the bottles until they had none left, and then they started throwing pennies which stung like a bee sting. I know I got hit by one!

Everyone was in a state of panic and shock. The hoods involved managed to get out of the auditorium, and of course weren't caught. To make matters worse they were in costumes! Of course! This is the way it was, and needless to say the school had a very high dropout rate. There were no more plays and no more drama club! That's the way the school handled it. If there were any aspiring young actors or actresses here, they were in the wrong place.

As the year progressed, I continued to skip school if I had to read assignments out loud. My complexes had not gone away. I was tired of asking to go to the ladies room to gulp down booze. One day I decided to tough it out and stay in English class, when the teacher asked students to read out loud. I felt my heart start to pound as usual. I was really getting mad at this, as well being tired of the fact that it was controlling my life. I decided to stay put and not go to the bathroom with my flask. I knew that it was going to be my turn soon, my heart was pounding, and I was sweating and felt dizzy. Great, I thought, here we go again! But the teacher skipped over me! Even though I was very grateful that she forgot that it was my turn or whatever, it showed me that my problem was alive and well. I couldn't *stand* people looking at me. I didn't even like the sound of my own voice. I had it real bad. There was no help for me and all I really wanted to do was run away. I was very frustrated because I knew that I was not a dumb person. I had been through so much in my life and had seen so much, but I had managed to survive it. I did however feel older than my years. I didn't feel like I had a childhood or experienced the pleasant normal life that most kids have.

The next thing that I discovered was that the principal had hired a couple of lesbian teachers. In those times, such behavior was taboo. This caused even more trouble for the school. One of the lesbians was a gym teacher. I became aware of the fact that she was looking at the girls as they prepared for their showers. It was a requirement to take a shower after participating in gym even if it was the last period of the day. My gym class was next to the last.

I saw her looking at the girls in a very inappropriate manner and she became aware of me watching her. I stopped taking showers and received zeros. There was a hostility building up between us, and I wasn't going to give in to her. She knew what she was doing was wrong and so did I. I never told anyone about it, not even the girls. I knew that a couple of them would rebel. They would end up getting into trouble as a result. They knew it was very strange that I would receive a zero for gym when I had won awards for past performances in junior high as an outstanding athlete. In freshman year no one could catch me out on the field, and the fifty-yard dash was mine. I ran circles around everyone. I was a part of the track team and enjoyed it. The next year I didn't care as much, and this year after my little discovery, I didn't care at all. I didn't have enough credits to be a junior, but had more than I needed to be a sophomore. I had planned on taking extra courses like I did the year before, but something happened.

The hood boys thought that I was pretty and a couple of them wanted to date me. I wasn't flattered! Some of the hood boys were good looking, don't get me wrong, but they were trouble and everyone knew it. A couple of the hood girls got really jealous and decided what I needed was a good beating. One day on the way to class the hood girls surrounded me. We were in a desolate part of the hallway and I was in trouble, I was alone. It was after the bell so everyone was in their classrooms. One girl approached me and told me she was going to throw me through a large art room window. I thoroughly believed her as she was a lot bigger than me. Just as she was about to approach me I heard a voice. To me it was like the voice of God, but instead it was my math teacher, Mr. Wilson. He said, "Carol, go to class." A senior was hanging out in the hallway and went for help when he saw me getting surrounded. Who ever you are out there, I thank you from the bottom of my heart! I believe you saved my life. These girls were that bad. I think they put Brooklyn to shame!

Christmas was coming and that meant a nice vacation. I was looking forward to that. It was a nice family gathering at my Aunt Genes house for Christmas dinner. My Aunt Gene was my mothers' sister. She had decided to have Christmas dinner for the past few years for everyone on my mothers' side of the family. We went there and we had a good time. I saw my cousins who kind of made fun of me because I wore makeup. I didn't care; it was all in good fun. I thought that they could use some and told them so. When we got back home, the phone rang and it was my Aunt Priscilla. My biological father was at her house that she had inherited when her mother recently died. I was floored. He wanted to see my brother and me! I felt like saying no, but everyone thought that my brother and I should go. My brother drove and I was not a happy camper. I still remembered his cruel words when I had gotten raped, how does one forget a scene like that? I felt a little queasy when we pulled up to my Aunts house that day after Christmas. My brother and I walked in and there he was. We looked at each other and quite frankly I felt nothing for him. We cordially said hello. My brother felt awkward too. It was not a good reunion to say the least. My grandmother and Aunt Priscilla tried to make things better, and Uncle Jack, who was my fathers' brother, tried to crack jokes to break the ice. I didn't feel like laughing. We sat down to eat dinner, but I didn't feel like breaking bread with my father. My brother and he started to talk and they seemed to get along all right, but I couldn't wait to get out of there. My father and I really didn't speak at all. I could see the upset look on Aunt Priscilla's face. I knew that she felt bad and my grandmother just seemed to ignore the whole thing and just go about her business. It was hard reading her face. I can only say that she was not her jolly self. It was a long ride and we were told that we could stay over night if we wanted to, but I said I felt sick and wanted to go home. I had my usual stomach problems, which wasn't that much of a lie.

My father had two daughters with his second wife, which meant that my brother and I had not just one half sister, but two. I remembered the picture that Aunt Priscilla showed me years ago of his new first born. I was told both were very pretty California girls, but they were strangers to me. I wondered how he treated them. We left, and what is usually a very good visit with that side of the family turned out to be cold and stiff. I didn't know what to think, but thought I'm not sure if I want to go to the cabin this summer. It wasn't their fault that I could not look at my father without wanting to hit him, vomit, or maybe both. He was one of my nightmares that never went away. There were quite a few people that caused me not to sleep many a night.

A couple of days later we were told that my father had gone back to California. I felt relieved that I did not have to see him again. I called the girls up and there was going to be a party at Meagan's house for the New Year. She had made some new friends at school and she wanted the rest of us to meet them. It sounded good to me. And party we did! Her parents were gone and there was no supervision. I have to admit that the house did get somewhat trashed. Nothing got broken, but tables were turned over from the boy's horseplay, and of course no one thought to clean up after themselves. Meagan had a lot of dips, chips, finger sandwiches, a bowl of spiked punch, and a lot of the kids brought their own booze. There were some kids that took showers, although I'm not sure why, unless they got sick and threw up on themselves. They of course left towels and washcloths everywhere. It could have been worse. There were no real fights or holes in the walls. We all watched the ball fall and continued to party until the wee hours of the morning. Kids passed out everywhere from the couches to the floors to the beds. Meagan's parents were not due to come back until noon the next day. By ten in the morning quite a few kids had left, but there were still a number of them passed out on the floors. I was allowed to be there, but I was the only one.

Her parents were home by ten thirty. All I can say is never before had I heard so many curse words in my life. The house was very sloppy and chips were ground into the rugs. Someone had gotten sick and did not make it to the bathroom. Meagan's parents ordered everyone out except me. Boy did we get a tongue-lashing and we also got a slap across the face. Meagan's mother thought nothing of slapping her kids in the face, and on that particular day, I was one of them too. Meagan and I were told to clean the mess up immediately while her parents took a ride for one hour. When they returned the house was to be in order. Meagan's brothers, sisters, and I got real busy. Her parents returned in one hour and even though we all worked our butts off it wasn't to Meagan's mothers liking. She claimed that the upstairs bathroom floor was still a mess, so Meagan went and washed it again and again and her mother was standing over her screaming the whole time until Meagan was crying and shaking. Just when I thought for sure her mother would be satisfied with the floor, her mother took an ashtray that was full and smashed it on the floor almost hitting Meagan in the face! Her mother then yelled at her again and said, "Clean it up!" Meagan cleaned and cleaned and finally her mother told her to go down to the family room. She brought out the ironing board and told her to start ironing the shirts that were there, and to spray starch them as she went along. After Meagan had ironed about seven men's shirts, her mother came down and crumpled them into a ball and told her to do it again! Meagan was not the only one responsible for the party because her older brother and her younger sister had spread the word that there was going to be a party, and yet they didn't have to go through anything like this. I wanted so badly to help my friend, but I didn't know what to do for her. We were wrong in having the party, but what was happening to Meagan was wrong too. I was told to leave at this point but had no way home. I called home and no one answered. Meagan's father decided to take me home and I said all right. I was afraid for my friend and whispered for her to call me later. On the way home her father and I spoke very little and all of a sudden while he was driving he pulled down his fly and exposed himself! I was shocked and horrified beyond belief!! I had gone over to Meagan's house many times and did *not* see this coming. I made like I didn't see it and felt myself stiffen like in the old days, when I would hear Uncle Cliff come into my room. When he saw that I wasn't going to make any comment he suddenly asked me to look at it. I yelled no and told him that I was shocked. He saw that I was visibly upset and put his privates away. Are there no sane men?

We reached my house and I got out and didn't say goodbye. I ran into the house and ran up to my room, took my flask out, and took two big gulps to calm down. I knew that I was going to tell on him for what he had done, but decided to wait a couple of days until things calmed down at Meagan's house. I feared that her mother would find some way to blame Meagan for that too. There are all kinds of abuse and all of them hurt. My mother took a switch to me once during the summer. I was trying to stand up for myself for once, and she considered me to be arrogant. We were out in the back yard and she told me to shut up. I was trying to get a point across which I felt was important, and she went into the woods and snapped a big long switch off and came at me with lightning speed. She proceeded to hit my legs in many places. I had shorts on so it made direct contact with my skin and she drew blood on many areas of my legs. I didn't cry, but the look on her face was the same look that Meagan's mother had when she smashed the ashtray to the floor.

Parents can really make wrong choices when it comes to punishment. I believe that kids should know when they do wrong, but never should there be any corporal punishment involved. There just has to be a better way to get your point across, or what kind of a parent are you, and what kind of a person are you? My mother always bragged about how she was always spoiled when she was a kid and her siblings agreed that it was true. So where did she get her mean streak? She came from a good home and had parents that adored her until they became older and weird. She was favored as a child, and that was one of the reasons that she allowed for them to live with us. What's wrong with some people anyway? To this day people never cease to amaze me, sometimes in a good way, but all too often not.

I called Meagan later to see how things were, and could tell that she was very tired. She had no real life in her voice and sounded monotone. I knew that she didn't want to talk so I said goodbye, and would speak to her at another time. I would see her in school, which was due to start in a two days. I called Alison and told her what had happened to see if I should let the incident of her father just go away. We discussed it at length, and decided that it would be best to tell on him. I decided that I would wait though and see what condition Meagan was in when we went back to school.

We started in the middle of the week and Meagan was nowhere to be found. This bothered me because I hadn't spoken to her since the day after the party, and remembered how bad she sounded on the phone. The day went slowly, and when I got home I called her. I knew that her parents were still at work and she would be able to talk. Meagan answered the phone and she still sounded strange. She asked me if anything had happened on the ride home the other day with her father. I told her exactly what her father had done. At first she seemed shocked, but told me that her father had said I made a pass at him!! I was floored to say the least! The pervert turned it around. Meagan believed me and said that she was very sorry and that she was going to tell her mother. I asked her if she was sure if she wanted to really do that, because her mother might try to put the blame on me, or try somehow to blame Meagan as usual. We talked it over and decided to tell. What he did was wrong and we knew it, and I was ready to stand my ground. Meagan, as my friend, was ready to stand behind me. I didn't tell my mother and I don't know exactly why. I just felt so distant from her that I guess that I didn't think to even bother.

Meagan waited a couple of days to tell. In case there was real trouble, she could come to my house and stay the weekend. She wasn't sure how her mother would take it. On that Friday night she told her mother. At first her mother called me a liar, and she and Meagan went around and around more than a few times. Meagan said that she would have no problem picking me up and we would confront her father directly. When her mother and father saw how determined we were, her father confessed. He did not apologize to me personally, instead he told Meagan to do it for him. What a coward! I let it go at that. I must admit that I didn't know if I could handle ever being in that house the same time that her father was there. After all, now I knew what his character was like and I wasn't happy. My good friend's father was just another asshole! I stayed away from her house for a very long time. But I didn't let this hurt our friendship because she couldn't help how her father was. I know that she was very embarrassed. I didn't talk about it anymore, and told the other girls not to poke fun or say anything either.

The months went by and the situation at school didn't change. I continued to have my panic attack problems. The school continued to have problems with the hoods. One day the gym teacher approached me and told me that I was going to fail for the year because I refused to take showers. We eyeballed each other and I told her that I was just going to have to fail then. She smirked and said "Suit yourself." I got mad and replied," If I am asked by the guidance department why I refused to take showers, I *am* going to tell them why!" She turned red as a beet and got in my face. She looked at me and she said "Meet me out back after school!" I must say that I was very intimidated by her. This woman had been a lady wrestler before she became a gym teacher. She was built like a man, and I'm sure that she worked out every night. I didn't have too much time to think, because I only had one class after gym, and then I go home. If I stayed I could take the late bus home, that is, if I was still in one piece. I didn't hear one word spoken in the last class of the day, which was history. The teacher could tell that I was distracted and said so. At times I could tell that she was staring at me. I didn't really care because I knew that in less than an hour I was going to meet with a woman monster. I felt like I couldn't back down, because if I did, she would really bully me for the rest of the year. After my last class for the day I walked slowly over to the gym. I was hoping to run into one of my friends. I figured they could be a witness if she threw the first punch. I saw no one that I knew. I was screwed. I walked behind the building and she wasn't there. I waited for a while with a pounding heart. I was truly scared, but also mad as hell. I had missed my bus waiting for this lunatic teacher, and couldn't help but feel that she was watching me from afar, laughing herself silly because I had shown. Then I thought she really couldn't hit me because that would be against the law. I had gone from being very scared, to very mad, and let's face it, I was now relieved.

I skipped school the next day saying to my mother that I didn't feel well. I really didn't know what I was going to school for. I had personal problems that seemed to overwhelm me, and the school was in shambles because of the lack of discipline from both teachers and administration. My math teacher who was also a shop teacher didn't teach the class. We would all walk in and he would be sitting with his feet up on the desk reading a newspaper. Every once in a while he would write a problem on the board and tell us how to do it. He would then give us four or five problems and tell us to hand it in at the end of the week. That was it! He would go back to reading his paper. I would sit there and get very sleepy because at home there were many nights that I just could not sleep. This was the perfect atmosphere for falling asleep from exhaustion. My sleep deprivation would catch up with me. He didn't like it if I went to sleep, so he would clear his throat and tell me to do homework. Out of a class of twenty-five there were only about nine kids who passed math that year in my class. He was questioned and fired. That was his final year there, and none of us missed him.

One day in class, I saw that Meagan was outside of the school crying her eyes out. I proceeded to leave class to go and see her. My English teacher, who was really a nice guy, insisted that I not leave the room. I was really mad because this was one of my best friends and she was in distress. The saying "One for all and all for one" was our motto amongst each other. We leaned on each other and depended on each other. I ignored him, left the room and went to her anyway. We were both sent down to the principal's office. My friend quit school right there that very day. There were bad problems at her home and I told her she could probably move in with me. She thanked me for the offer, but said that she thought it best if she stayed home, because maybe she could help her parents with their problems. She thought that she might be a part of the problems. This to me sounded totally ludicrous because I had been to her house many times, and knew that her parents were responsible for their own issues. I let it go. She had driven to school that day, and because she was over sixteen she didn't need her parent's permission to quit, they just had to approve it. One by one as the weeks followed I became aware of quite a few kids quitting. Alison was next, then Helen, who we didn't see much of anymore, because she hung out with other kids we didn't really know. Nothing was discussed before they quit, it just happened. I wasn't surprised. Laura and Kelly however were still in school. I believed that Kelly would make it, and she did so because even though her parents were very strange acting, they were more on top of her than the rest of our parents. Kelly was one of us and we all got along well, but in our hearts we knew that she was much more cared for than any of us were. Even if we felt that her parents didn't like kids, we knew that they thought her education was important. We also knew that they would think that it was a reflection on them!

———

CHAPTER 34

One night there was a knock at our door and there stood Laura with a suitcase in hand. Someone had dropped her off and she asked if she could move back in. I asked my mother and she said, "Yes." Mom asked no questions and didn't care whether Laura's mother called or not. My mother was kind of good that way. She would help people if they needed it and not ask questions. She figured if they showed up at the doorstep, they had enough problems and didn't need her to give them more. It also made things easier on my mother because I would have someone to talk to. You might say everyone benefited by it. In the time that she was gone, my mother and I had nothing to really say to each other anyway, so the idea of she and I getting close was non-existent. My mother and step-father lived for the business and that was all. My brother and I really did bring ourselves up, although for the seven years that my grandparent's lived with us, he had it made. I always felt that my mother was always shoving me off on other people rather than dealing with me directly. Laura and her parents had a big fight and they said that she could live with me forever if she wanted to. We were not unhappy with that decision because we both needed each other for company. It's amazing how you can live around people and still be lonely.

One day Laura said to me "Let's skip school and go to Newark." This seemed very strange to me, but I said all right. We waited for the school bus to come and go and we walked towards town and hopped on a city bus to Newark. I told her that all I had was a couple of dollars and she said not to worry because she had plenty of money. I had no reason to not believe her. It was a very cold winter day and I wished that I was dressed a little more warmly. In those days kids still wore skirts to school. I asked her what the attraction was in Newark. She said "Trust me, you'll like it!" We talked all the way there and the ride went quickly. Once we were there we walked around and around and I was getting really cold and a little mad. I asked, "What's this all about?" She confessed to me that she was running away! I was shocked, and asked her "Where do I fit into this picture?" She said "Come on Carol, you aren't happy either we all know what kind of life you have had and still have, so why stay there?" I got mad and said that it should have been my decision to make and if I was running away, I would have planned it much better than this. We were mad at each other and it became an uncomfortable situation. I was cold and starting to get hungry. We stopped in a donut shop and had a cup of coffee and a muffin. I was almost broke after that and was shocked and dismayed that she was too. She had lied to me. This is not what our group was about and I felt like slugging her.

We walked around for hours looking in shops just to pass time. I finally told her that I was going to have to call home and tell my mother what was going on, and once we got back home Laura could pack her bags and leave. I was that mad. She said "Let's go to the bus station." There would probably be some guys hanging out, and they might help us with the money we needed to get back home. This whole thing was a nightmare to me and made no sense. It was dark by that time and I wanted to get back home. I was willing to take the punishment for the crime committed, just let's get back instead of being out on the streets cold and broke and not knowing what to do. We hung around Penn Station for quite some time and no one approached us. I was really getting nervous because it was starting to snow, and it was getting late. Suddenly a man approached us and he said that he was from the Police Athletic League and he wanted to know if we needed help. I blurted out what had happened and he said to get on the bus and he would pay for both of us to get home safely. I thought great! We waited for the bus and he took Laura aside and spoke to her privately. I thought this was kind of odd but didn't care at that point. All of a sudden the bus arrived and we three boarded. The two of them went to the back of the bus and I again thought that to be strange. I sat up front. Every once in a while I would turn and look at them and I knew that they were too chummy. But I didn't care because I wanted to get home. The guy was in his thirties and I had a complete description of him. When the bus stopped at the plaza that was nearest my home, I turned and looked at Laura and she said, "I'm not getting off, I'm going back with John!"

I didn't know what to do, so I got off. It was a pretty long walk home and I knew that it was around eleven o'clock. I was so cold that I couldn't feel my legs as I walked the long road to my house. I was cold, scared, hungry and worried about my friend. When I got home my mother was really mad, but composed. She had called over at Laura's house to see if we had gone there instead of coming home, and of course I had a bad story to tell her. She wasn't really mad at me anymore after I told her everything, and she said that we had to call the police. They came over and I told them everything that I knew, and now she was considered to be missing. Many days went by and there was no sign of my friend. The police were looking everywhere. We were all very fearful that she might be dead. Laura would have run away even if I had not been with her, I came to realize this so I did not feel guilty, but I knew that she was in trouble. Helen would run away at times, but she was much more resourceful than Laura. Laura was the least bright one of our group and we all feared for her safety.

One night I was up in my room with the lights off and my door locked. I was on my knees saying prayers for my friend and suddenly I felt a hand on my shoulder. I was afraid that I had forgotten to lock my door and my mother had come in. I was made fun of by this side of the family because I believe in God. My mother who was an atheist had once said to me, "Carol you and I are too different, we will always have a problem getting along." She was right, how sad. To my surprise there was no one in the room, I was alone. One time my mother found rosary beads under my pillow and she and my brother and step-father made fun of me for weeks at the dinner table until I was reduced to tears. I was then made fun of for crying. I had always turned to the Catholic Church for comfort and felt that I belonged there. I may have mentioned that a large part of my family was Catholic and I was considered to be protestant, but I converted years later.

The next day there was a knock on the door and there stood a police officer. My friend had been found alive, but she had been raped and put out on the streets for prostitution. She also had been shooting up heroin and by this time was addicted. This addiction was of course to make her want to go out on the streets so she would not get dope-sick and make money for the pimp. Laura was returned home and stayed there for a couple of weeks. When she came back to school she told me that her parents said that she couldn't hang out with me because I was a bad influence! I was a bad influence? I was furious with them and I was also furious with my friend. It was her idea, not mine to run away, and I was made out to be the bad guy? We weren't friendly after that and the rest of the girls in our group decided that they didn't want to be friendly with her anymore either. She had put all of us through hell and back again with her antics, and I got blamed. Not long after that I decided I had enough of school too. The gym teacher kept giving me threatening looks and I said, "No More! I quit!" The guidance counselor called my house that evening and my mother said that it was all right for me not to go back. She did however insist that I get a job. I thought that was a good idea and I would take my G.E.D. test sometime in the future. I did get a job at the dime store with the thought that I would get something better later on. I had to walk to the bus station to get to work and back home again afterwards. It was cold, but I did it. I had dreams about school and would wake up in the morning thinking that I was late only to remember that I had quit. I really felt bad about it only because if the circumstances were different, I knew that I could have done well. I once asked my mother if I could attend another school and she of course said no. I made friends at my new job and was assigned to the candy section. What a mistake! There are not many things that I like better than malted balls! I ate too many and the supervisor ended up moving me to staples! I was very embarrassed to say the least, but I didn't blame him because I was eating far too many of them! I stayed there under a year, and finally got tired of the low pay and quit. I was also tired of having to walk to public transportation and home again after getting off the bus. I never understood why my parents couldn't find it within themselves to help me a little bit. Jimmy was always so catered to.

———

CHAPTER 35

My step-father's greenhouses were made out of steel and glass panes. Many times glass would break because of windy conditions. For years he would try to repair the greenhouses himself by replacing the broken glass, but it took time away that was needed for the business, so he hired a man to do the job. I noticed that he was kind of nice looking, and when he was on break we would talk. One day he asked me if I would like to go out with him on a date. I told him that I would think about it. I asked my parents what they thought and they both said to go ahead. I saw him the next day. He asked me again and I told him all right. We made plans for the following weekend. I called a couple of my friends up and told them. I was hoping that someone was having a party so my date and I would have some place to go. That was not meant to be.

The weekend came and I put on a nice skirt and heels, which I had bought while working. I know that I looked good. When Brian showed up he gave me a look of approval and out we went. I asked him where we were going. He said that he knew of a nice bar near his house and they wouldn't card me because he knew the people. We would go and get something to eat later on. It all sounded innocent enough to me and I thought maybe we would have a good time. The bar was not right around the corner, and I noticed that he was a lot quieter than when we just stood around and spoke at the greenhouses. I thought too that he was acting a little strange, but decided that I was just being paranoid.

We arrived at the bar and went inside. I saw nothing special about it and no one acted as if they even knew him. I wasn't carded so that part was true. He ordered us both a drink and when it was brought to the table he gulped his down and ordered another one before the barmaid had a chance to leave! I thought this is not good. I quietly drank my drink, and with no conversation between us, he ordered me another one. I wanted to go home! I felt that there was something wrong with this guy. He had a problem that was now surfacing. I also noticed that his face started to change. He had a nasty expression on his face. I started to get scared. Just as I was thinking about going to a phone and calling Meagan up to come and get me, he said, "Let's go!" I got up and was going to suggest that we get something to eat. My thought was that he may have had these drinks on an empty stomach and that was his problem, but he said, "Let's go to my Uncle's house." I thought that was a good idea because if he continued to act weird, there would be someone there that could help.

We left and we drove around and around. I looked at him and said, "Brian, I want to go home!" He said, "Not until I see my Uncle first!" We arrived at a house outside of town and when we got there I started to get out of the car and he said, "Wait, and let me see if he is home first!" I thought all right, but this is the last chance he is going to get. I felt that something was very wrong, but I didn't know what it was. I waited about five minutes and he came out alone. I was not happy.

He got into the car and he drove away. I had enough. I demanded to be taken home. He just simply said, "No!" I was in trouble! He was heading back towards town and I thought that if I saw a cop, I would flag him down. But as the saying goes, "Where are they when you need them?" We went through town and houses were getting few and far between. We were heading into what seemed to be a wooded area. I started to feel panic mode setting in. I demanded he take me home and he refused. I noticed that his face was twisted in a look of anger and I felt that my life was in jeopardy. I turned around and looked on the back seat of the car, and I saw ropes, a saw, a hammer and other tools. I knew that he used some

Chapter 35

of these tools on the greenhouses, but I suddenly had a sense that he was going to use them on me!

As we drove I noticed that the houses were getting even further apart and somehow I knew that I was going to have to jump from a moving vehicle to save myself! I didn't even give it a second thought! I very slowly put the strap of my pocketbook over my shoulder and waited for the right time to open the car door to jump. I noticed a curve in the road and common sense told me that he would have to slow down. As we approached the curve and he pushed on the brakes, I opened the car door and jumped for my life!

I heard him slam the brakes on and his car made a squealing noise, but he didn't back up. I looked up from the street and saw three houses. I had banged my knee up pretty badly, but I had no broken bones that I knew of, even though I had rolled over several times. I got up and went to house number one of the three that I had seen, and banged on the door. The people refused to open the door. I looked down the road and realized he was watching me to see if anyone would help me. I went to the next house and banged on that door and no one responded. I was getting frantic as I approached the last house. I banged on the door and a lady opened up a window and asked me what I wanted. I was crying by now and quickly told her I was in trouble and needed to use her phone. As I was speaking another lady opened the front door and let me in. I heard him speed away. The lady who let me in was a nurse and she had just gotten home from work. She took one look at me and told me to come in and sit down. I gave a sigh of relief and proceeded to tell them everything that happened that night. When I told them the name of the guy I was with, both women shrieked! Brian and his uncle were questioned the week before about a murdered woman they found up in the woods that bordered their street, but the police couldn't prove it so they weren't charged!

I believe that people do have a guardian angel that watches over them. Maybe they can't stop all things from happening to you, but I think they try. That night one was definitely with me. I called my mother and she and my step-father came and picked me up. What a night! We all thought that he was so nice! Boy, were we wrong! Both of my parents were shocked. He made sure not to ask me out until the greenhouse job was done and he was paid. The last day he was employed by my step-father is when he asked me so he would not have to come back to the green houses ever again. It was all planned out!

I ran into Laura one day in town. She apologized for her behavior and we resumed our friendship. After a week she moved back in! My mother said that we both had to be more grown up and she was right. Laura had quit school too and now we both had to get jobs. I told my mother that we would and out we went the next day bright and early to put applications in. We went to a nearby factory and applied for jobs. They made piano keys. We were both given a test and I passed with flying colors. I got the job and was to start the following Monday. I didn't know that I was going to be a supervisor at the old age of seventeen! Most of the people that would have to answer to me were twice my age. At the end of the week Laura and I decided to get a hold of Meagan to see if there was a party going on. We hadn't seen her in a while. Indeed there was, and it was good to see her because after she quit school, she had more or less gone her own way. Everything was changing in our lives, and the fab five had sort of drifted apart because of circumstances and just plain life in general.

The two of us went to Meagan's party and met a lot of new people there. A new crowd of misfits is what we were. The hoods found out about the party and halfway through the night they crashed it! I never saw so many guys fighting before in my life. Bottles were being smashed and a couple of the guys were trying to use them as weapons! This was *very* bad! The police were called and what a mess. This time Meagan's parents didn't have a fit on her, they were too mad at the hoods. We got a ride back to my house totally disgusted with how the evening turned out. My mother took one look at me and she knew that I had a couple of beers and she flipped out. She ordered both Laura and I out of the house never to return again! I told her that I had a job coming up, but she didn't care and she didn't want to hear about the night and what had happened. We were to leave right then! I only had a couple of dollars and she was saying horrible things to me. She was saying that I was no good, a horrible person, and that I was just like the other side of the family. I looked at her with shock because I thought that it was only my grandparents who felt that way, and started to cry. She made fun of me so badly for crying that I went into what had been my brother's room and flopped down on his bed. I lay there sobbing feeling totally rejected by my mother. Next to his bed on the floor was a piece of broken glass. I picked up the glass and put it to my wrist cutting as hard as I could. "My mother saw me do it and she said "Good, do it again, do it right!" Laura pushed her way from the bed and pulled me upward by the hair and said, "Let's get out of here!" She then shoved my mother out of the way and we ran down the stairs and out the door. My arm was bleeding pretty badly, but not as badly as it could have. The glass was dull and hadn't done that much damage. It did however turn into a faint scar later on. We had nowhere to go and no money to speak of. We had enough to get a cup of coffee. Here we go again!! This time it was both of us out on the street. We ran down the driveway to where the flowers were cut and bunched. There was a medicine cabinet, and we found gauze and tape. Laura helped me bandage up my arm and we left. We walked up to the town diner for lack of anywhere else to go.

Laura and I sat and gazed at a guy who was seated nearby. He knew that we were staring at him, but I didn't care. He was a few years older than us, and looked like a movie star. I felt like he was looking back at me more than Laura. Laura giggled and said "Alright, he's yours!" I thought to myself, "If this guy can look at me in the condition that I'm in, it'll be a miracle." In a minutes time mister wonderful came over and sat down next to me and introduced himself. Larry had the greenest eyes that I had ever seen, and with his black hair he was striking. He made Sonny look bad and Sonny was good looking. I was in love! We started to talk, and before I knew it we were telling him what had taken place that night. He shook his head and told us that he lived at home with his mother and father. There was no way that he could bring us home. He did say that I could have his car for the night. All I had to do was drop him off and he could get a ride the next day for work. I had to return his car the next evening before he got off work, and hopefully I would have figured out a solution to my problem. I was touched by this gracious gesture of generosity from a complete stranger. He never asked me for my driver's license, and I didn't offer the information that I didn't have one. I had no car and no one offered to buy me one. I was however expected to work and take public transportation, which was not right down the street. I walked to the bus stop in all kinds of weather, and I did resent it. The bus stop for public transportation was over a mile away from where we lived. Jimmy had cars given to him since the age of thirteen. God, parents can be weird!

We dropped Larry off. In his driveway I saw a blue Cadillac and a Harley Davidson, both of which were his. I know that it sounds silly, but I saw myself on the back of that bike already. We left and drove his car around for a while, but where were we going to go at this hour? We were two young women in trouble. I didn't want to bother my other friends at this hour. I even thought about going to my brother's apartment, but I wasn't sure where he lived. He didn't really keep in touch at all, and I heard that he had a girlfriend so we would be intruding for sure. We were driving through town and all of a sudden the car stalled right in front of the local police station! I tried to start it several times, and no way would it start. It wasn't out of gas, it had just broken down! We both panicked because it was in front of the police department and neither one of us had a license. We were almost in the middle of the street and we knew that we were in trouble. We looked in the glove compartment and to our amazement we found a gun! I didn't know Larry's last name, so I thought I would look at his insurance papers and run to a phone booth and try to call him. When he introduced himself he only used his first name. Laura said, "Oh my God, we have to get out of here!" We ran around the car trying to be very quiet and using a rag that we found in the car, we cleaned our prints off inside and out. This guy had a gun, and even though he was gorgeous and gracious, we knew nothing about him. We were freaking out! We started to run down the street as fast as we could.

We decided that we would go back to the workroom in my parents' florist shop, which was adjacent to a greenhouse, until it got light out. We would then call one of our friends for help. That seemed like a good idea.

Just as we reached the border of the town we lived in we heard a siren and the police stopped and picked us up. We were screwed. At the police department we were asked the usual questions, and my mother was called. Laura had told them that she lived with us so her parents were not called. My mother showed up very shortly and was told that I had driven a car without a license and had abandoned it. Larry's house was called as well, and within minutes he was there with his mother. Larry was a few years older than me, and it seemed odd that his mother came too. He was in trouble for letting me take the car without seeing if I had a driver's license. Also, because they found the loaded gun, there was a problem. Luckily for him, he had just gotten it registered, but he was not supposed to carry it in the car. We were all allowed to go. Larry and I were issued summonses for our infractions, and we both had to appear in court. On the way back to my house my mother refused to talk to us. She just stared straight ahead. We got out of the car and went to my room. We didn't feel comfortable being in the house because we were not welcome there. I was only seventeen and I really had no home. My mother did not want me, and I felt like she never did. What kind of mother tells her kid to cut harder and do it right? I must say, certainly not a loving or caring one. Those words that she spoke that night still ring in my ears to this day.

The next day we stayed out of her way because we didn't know what else to do. We just played it cool. When she went out we snuck downstairs and made sandwiches and drank some milk. I was to start my new job that next day and had no money to catch the bus. I called Meagan up and told her everything, and she came over and gave me ten dollars. It was a loan and I was to pay her back as soon as I got paid. I called work and told them that I could start the following day, and they said that was fine. We hung out for a while. Soon my mother came back into the house to make dinner.

We had no idea if we were going to be allowed to eat or not. We could smell the food cooking, and we were very hungry.

All of a sudden there was a knock on my bedroom door and there stood my mother. She said in a cold voice "Come and eat." We went downstairs and sat very quietly at the table and started to eat dinner. There was no mention of the night before. I caught her looking at the bandage that Laura had made for my cut, and when I felt she wasn't looking, I looked at it too. It was soaked with blood. I felt very self-conscious for some reason, and hid my arm for the rest of the meal. When we were finished eating, my mother said, "Get your ass up and go to work tomorrow so you can pay the fine you're going to get. Start your new job." I told her that I would and she told my friend to go back home.

After dinner we went to my room and I told Laura that I was sorry for all that had happened. She told me that I had nothing to apologize for. After what I had gone through she thought that maybe her house was not so bad! We both laughed because it was true. It was really Laura who always wanted to run away, and her parents never really threw her out. It was her choice because she didn't want to follow their wacky rules. They did in fact go too far, but maybe she could sit down with her mother this time and find some kind of compromise. That's exactly what happened between Laura and her mom, and we never really hung out too much afterwards. I was happy for her because she and her parents finally came to some sort of agreement that they could all live with. I wished that could happen in my home, but it wasn't meant to be.

The days went by and I didn't really see any of my friends. Everyone was getting a little older, and even though we kept in touch by phone, things were different. I was doing all right at my new job, but the employees resented the fact that I was so young and they had to take orders from me. It wasn't long before it started to cause trouble. I also received notification that I had to go to court. All day long I thought of Larry. I wondered if he hated me. I know it sounds dumb, but I was looking forward to court just so I could see him. I counted the days. At times Meagan would drive over and we would go by where he worked hoping to see him. Boy was I goofy or what? I did see him at a distance a few times, and I felt myself blush. I was able to save money from work to pay Meagan back and to have money for court. I had no idea how much I was going to be fined. Court night came and I got dressed up as though I was going on a date. I also had bought myself some clothes. My mother did go with me in case I didn't have enough money; she said that she would help but I had to pay her back. I thanked her, but thought none of this would have happened if she had just been a little more reasonable that horrible night. I made another vow to myself that when I have children, to be kind to them, and to listen when they are in trouble.

I sat in the courtroom and looked around to see if I could spot Larry. He showed up with his mother, and she was glaring at me from across the room. I felt myself flush again. I saw Larry standing near her and he was not looking my way. I thought to myself that he hates me. I heard our names called not long after court was in session. My heart was pounding and I was scared and embarrassed as I stood up. I could feel all eyes on me and I started to blush profusely. I was about to have a panic attack right there! I looked over at Larry and I was surprised to see that he was looking my way and was giving me a reassuring smile. I calmed down a little and didn't really hear what the judge said! My mother poked me and said, "Sit down." The judge only said that I couldn't apply for my driver's license until I was eighteen. I was also charged thirty dollars for not driving with a license, and leaving a car abandoned in the street! Larry however, did not do so well. He was charged with having the loaded gun in the glove compartment, and for allowing me to drive without a license. He was fined a lot more. As we were leaving the courthouse his mother approached me and said, "You stay away from my son!" I was angry to say the least. I was not the beast here, and I was mad at Larry too. He should be old enough to make up his own mind. As it turned out he was. My mother and I were walking towards our car and he came over to us and asked me for my telephone number. I gave it to him and he winked at me. My mother had to admit he looked like a movie star.

Two days later he called me and I was on cloud nine. We went out that Saturday and he picked me up on his bike! What fun we had. It was cold out and I dressed warmly in pants and a sweater and a warm jacket. We drove for a while, and then stopped to get something to eat. I had a comb in my pocket and my hair had grown long. I was very happy for the first time in a very long time. As the days went by and turned into weeks, we saw each other every single night after work, and all weekend long.

One night he said that on Saturday we were going to go into the city, and he would treat me to a wonderful dinner. He knew of a French restaurant that was very good. I knew that I had to dress nicely for this and this time I had clothes because I was working. My mother even allowed for me to wear her long beige fur coat. I felt like a million dollars. Larry picked me up in his Cadillac and we drove away in style. After we arrived in the city we were walking down the street, and I actually got some whistles. This was all very good for my low self-esteem. We were in love. We walked hand in hand and I felt like a new person. I wanted this feeling to last forever. Larry also took me to Sardis' on another New York City excursion. He made me feel very special. If we were not in the city we were riding his bike and were having the time of our lives. His mother invited me over for dinner. She saw that her son was in love and finally resigned herself to the fact that we were an item, and I was going to be around for a very long time. I was nervous about going over there, but was assured that everything would be all right.

The night arrived and we had a fine time. The dinner was very good. Larry's older sister and brother-in-law were there, as well as their young daughters. They really looked like a normal happy family. I didn't really have too much to compare them with, but thought that this is how families should be. Larry's mother made me feel very welcome and said to forget about court night, it was obviously meant to be. We all laughed because it was a strange way to meet.

One Saturday morning Larry came over to the house and had a very sad look on his face. It was during the Vietnam War and so many of my friends were getting drafted. Larry came over to tell me he had received a draft notice and was to report to downtown Newark in a couple of days for his physical exam. We were sick at heart. He confessed to me that he had received one earlier that month and ignored it. The last thing he wanted was to go off to war. We both sat down and cried. He suddenly stood up and pulled a little box from his pocket and he asked me, "Carol, Will you marry me?" My tears turned from tears of sadness to tears of joy. Of course I said, "Yes." We both went and told my mother and she smiled and said, "Congratulations." We also told her about the draft notice. I promised that I would wait for him and never cheat on him.

A couple of days later my period didn't come, and I just knew that I was pregnant. We hadn't used any protection. We decided that we really didn't care if I got pregnant, because we were in love. In his family children were welcomed. I went and had a test at the doctors, and sure enough the results came back positive. Larry and I were very happy, even though it was bad timing. Larry went and had his physical and passed it. He had a little time before he had to report for duty. We planned on getting married after basic training. My mother refused to give me a wedding because I was pregnant, but said I could live with her until Larry's return. I laughed to myself and thought that she would not have given me one anyway. Who was she kidding? Larry and I both gave notice at our jobs as our lives had dramatically changed.

The day finally came. Larry and I parted our ways crying our eyes out, but you can't fight the army. My mother took me to visit him at Fort Dix a couple of times during his basic training. When it was over he had a short leave before being transferred. He came home to my house and we got married by the justice of peace. My mother gave us no party, no money, and not even a card. She allowed for me to wear a very plain white dress of hers that she had worn when she married my stepfather so many years ago. The dress was so old in style that it actually came back in style. I washed it and wore it. After we were married, we went over to Larry's mother's house. They had a big cake, a family dinner, and a nice party for us. His mother gave me a beautiful negligee that was wrapped in a pretty box. They made me feel very welcome to the family. The next day we went to Atlantic City for a very short and rushed honeymoon before he had to leave. We didn't have much money so we stayed in an ordinary motel. We walked the boardwalk and we were happy and sad all at the same time. We spoke of the future and the coming of our baby. He or she would be a year and a half old when he got back. We didn't know where he would be permanently stationed. We prayed of course that it would not be Vietnam.

Every night everyone looked at the role call on the news to see if someone had died that they knew. It was horrible. I had friends that went to war and I was scared to death that I would see their names. As it turned out, Larry after being stationed in Georgia for a short time would be finally stationed in Korea. Korea is very far away, but at least he wasn't going to Vietnam. We were sad but also very thankful. Before Larry went to Korea, he managed to get a leave of absence. He was allowed to see me for several days before going to Korea. During this time I went into labor. Our son was born just as Larry entered the hospital to be with me. What timing! We were very happy, and my mother was happy to have a grandson. She had been nice to me during this time, had bought baby clothes, and when she knew it was a boy, was even happier and went out to buy more things for the baby. Larry and I had a couple of glorious days before he left. This was it, and knew that we would not see each other for a long time. He left with tears in his eyes. I was crying very hard, and continued crying off and on for a couple of days.

I knew that I had to pull myself together for our son's sake, but I was in fact very depressed. My job was to take care of baby and cook meals and clean. In my mother's eyes I now served a purpose in the house. I never went anywhere or did anything with the girls. Alison would come over on Friday nights for dinner, but other than that I saw no one. Each one of my friends went their separate ways and had similar weddings like I did. Like us, they started their own families. I looked back at the times when we girls had shared our lives. I remember how we clung to each other for support. I would think of the good times that a couple of us had at the lake. My son kept me going with hope for the future, and I knew that I wanted more children. For some reason I was meant to be a mommy — that was one thing that I was sure of.

It was very hard to write Larry everyday because nothing ever changed. I did though, only missing once or twice. I think that at one time he got into trouble over there because they were holding his mail, and he thought that I wasn't writing him for weeks. One day I received a letter saying, "I called you Tuesday, I hope I got you!" He wrote as if he was under the influence. What I didn't realize is that Larry was now drinking all the time. We both did a lot of drinking when we were dating, but I stopped for baby and he didn't. I didn't know to what extent until later. He was drinking heavily, and unfortunately he continued to even after he returned home.

The time went by very slowly and I was very depressed. I wasn't drinking or smoking now. I have to admit that when I had found out I was pregnant, I cleaned up my for the baby's sake. I didn't even drink wine. I was very clean cut and my mother would have killed me anyway even if I had an occasional drink. Since all I had to do was stay home, clean and take care of baby, I didn't feel the need to drink, but I must admit that I was very bored and longed for friendship from someone.

My mother and I played cards every night, and during the day she would sometimes take baby on delivery with her. She was the one who delivered flowers to the nearby florists in her big station wagon. She was very proud of her grandson and showed him off to everyone. I admit that I was surprised to see how much she could really like kids. I was never treated this way. Maybe it took her years and the right situation for her to act loving. Who knows, but I was thankful that she treated my son so well.

CHAPTER 36

After a year and a half my husband came home. I didn't know exactly what day he was due back, he wanted to surprise me. One night around eleven o'clock there was a knock on the front door. My mother answered it and let out a small gasp. There stood Larry! He said, "Hello Ma'am." I heard his voice and jumped off the couch and ran to greet him. My husband was home! We took one look at each other and something didn't feel right. The man I had been waiting for all of this long time didn't look pleased to see me! I knew that I looked all right. Even though he was gone and I was depressed, I kept up with my appearance. We just stood and looked at each other for a minute. We asked him if he wanted to come in and sit with us in the living room. The whole house had been done over while he was gone, which he noticed and commented about. He sat on the opposite side of the room. My mother started to ask Larry about Korea and he just quietly replied that he didn't want to talk about it. He did say that American women are very spoiled and there is no way he could describe what he saw.

It was getting late and my mother excused herself from the room giving me a strange look. I felt strange as well. Who was this man that I had been writing to for so long; a man that I never cheated on and waited and dreamed about for the day of his return? I had many times daydreamed about the day that he would come home to me and our son, who was now walking and saying Da-Da. What I was expecting was nothing like this! He was very cold acting towards me. I walked out into the kitchen and poured us a cup of coffee, and hoped that he would start to talk to me. He instead drank a few swallows of coffee and went upstairs to bed. I was shocked with his behavior. I lit a cigarette for the first time in ages, and sat down with a feeling of sadness and disappointment that words can't describe. I didn't have a drink for almost two years, but sure felt like having one now. My husband, the man that I loved and adored seemed like a stranger to me, and not a very nice one.

I finished my coffee and went upstairs to find him fast asleep. I thought that perhaps the next day would be better because maybe he was just bone tired. When we woke up I looked at him, and told him how much I loved and missed him. He barely answered. I got up and went to our sons crib and picked him up. He was awake and quietly looking at us. I changed him and brought him proudly over to see his daddy. Larry looked at him and managed to make a little fuss over him. Our son David didn't know his father, and that was to be expected. Larry smiled when David said Da-Da, but these two were not ready to be buddies yet. We both laughed at David, and knew that it would take a bit of time. We went downstairs and I made breakfast for us, but there was still an awkward silence between us. Finally I asked him what was wrong and he said that we would talk later when David was due for his nap. In the meantime he wanted to call his mother and let her know that he was back. She wanted to see him and I could understand that, so he left.

My mother let him borrow a car. He said that he would have someone drive her car home, and he would bring his caddy back to our house. When he left, my mother and I sat down and we both agreed that he was very different acting. I waited all day for him, and finally at dinnertime my mother actually gave me money and said "Go out with him for dinner and try to talk to him." I thanked her and that is what we did. He said very little about Korea. He mentioned that he did very well for the most part, and had even managed to be awarded medals. One was for expert marksmanship when there was a problem around the DMZ, because he was put on duty there for a while. Two other medals were for bravery and performance. He was about to become sergeant when he got discharged. He really seemed like he was still over there. I congratulated him on his efforts and for a job well done. Our dinner was almost cordial.

When we got back home we watched the television and had very little conversation. The next day after David was put down for a nap, we went outdoors on the back patio. All of a sudden he started to yell at me. He could not believe that I hadn't cheated on him, and he became physically abusive with me! He grabbed me by my shoulders and started to shake me like a rag doll, trying to intimidate me so I would tell him what he thought was the truth. There was nothing to say. If I were smart I would have left him right then and there. He continued to yell at me and I was so shocked and mortified that I couldn't answer him right when he would ask me these outrageous questions. As it turned out he had cheated on me, and he couldn't believe that I would stay in the house all of this time and be faithful! That's what I got for being good! He insisted that I hit him in the face. I hit him, but it wasn't hard enough for his liking, so I hit him again and again until he said "Enough!" I guess he finally felt it. The bastard! All this time of waiting and dreaming of a good life with Larry was now gone. I felt numb.

As the day unfolded he told me about the women over there. They hardly ever had any soap to bathe themselves with, and for the most part conditions were deplorable. I said that I was sorry for them, but that had nothing to do with us! I also told him that his behavior was scaring me, and after I said that I remember seeing a little smirk come across his face. I thought this is not the man I married, and I don't know what to do about it. My mother made it very clear that as soon as Larry came home we were to start looking for our own place. Under most circumstances that would be the right thing to do, and also a happy thing for a couple to look forward to. I started to feel an old feeling come back from years gone by. I started to feel fear. My mother had been pretty supportive while Larry was gone. She didn't ask for any money when Larry sent money once a month from his check. That was for me to save and use for rent and furniture. She did take care of a lot of the baby's needs. She bought most of his clothes and all of his diapers.

She was very fond of him, which was quite apparent. I once said to her, "Hey Mom, What if David was a girl instead of a boy, would you love him as much?" She didn't answer that question; she just looked the other way.

Larry's mom was having a party for us. My parents were invited too, but they declined saying that they had far too much work to do. Somehow I wasn't surprised. The night came for the party and we went over there. We were having a good time and everyone wanted to see David. I noticed that Larry was drinking too much, and he was dancing with his sister. It was a slow song and he really should have been dancing with me. I don't know if it was because he was drunk or what, but he started to hold her too tight. She became annoyed and started pushing him away. I finally saw a look of real annoyance on her face, and now she shoved him away roughly. I was shocked at what I saw and went over to him. I told him we had better go home because David was getting fussy. We left and I drove. I had gotten my license while he was gone. I didn't mention what I saw, but knew that it was strange. It was too strange for comfort.

After David was down for the night, we went out back to the patio, and he continued to drink. He was saying nasty things to me. I finally asked him what his problem was and he admitted that he missed Korea!! I was so shocked and mad that I felt like spitting in his face. My guess is that he had a girlfriend there and missed her. The next day I came out and asked him if that was the case, and he denied it. I asked him how he could miss a place that was so dirty, a place where people ate cockroaches as a delicacy, and I told him that he was not the same man that I married. I got slapped in the face for this. It was a good hard slap. That was to be just the beginning of much abuse from Larry over the years to come.

We had found a place to live in Elizabeth, NJ. It was in a pretty dumpy area, and in a four family house. Not only that, but it was upstairs and we had to walk up and down. We also had to put bars on the windows so David would not fall out! I remember being near the Nabisco cookie factory and I could smell the cookies being made. That might have been the only good part of where we lived. Larry got a job in a film factory, and every day when he came home he had to shower immediately to get the chemicals off of him. It was a horrible job, and at times he made me feel very sorry that he had to do this kind of work for a living. Larry had changed in every way a person could change. Every night was filled with fighting and many times he was shoving me around. This was a far cry from the young man that would pull a chair out for me to be seated in fancy restaurants, hold doors open for me and even open up the car door for me to get in. I guess if things look too good to be true, they are. He worked the three to eleven, or the midnight to eight graveyard shifts. It wasn't easy, but it was not our fault. Little Dave was afraid of his own father and it was obvious to see. They had real no relationship.

One morning after he got home from working the graveyard shift he forgot to lock the door. In minutes I heard a strange noise in the kitchen and woke Larry up who fell asleep the minute his head hit the pillow. All of a sudden a man walked into our bedroom with a loaded gun and pointed it at us. The only thing that I could do was pull the covers up over my head! I didn't want to watch him pull the trigger. As I went under the covers, I yelled, "You have the wrong apartment!" Larry, as far as I know did nothing, but who could see? I heard the guy say, "I think you're right!" and he left. After the guy left Larry got out of bed and locked the door. I told him that we had to find another place to live; it was too dangerous around there. He told me if I didn't like it to go back home to Mommy!

The next night was the end of his night shift. When he came home the next morning he started to drink instead of eating breakfast. By the days end he was yelling at me and yelling at the baby. I called my mother but she wasn't home. I was entertaining the thought of going back home, but I knew that if I did she would rub it under my nose. That is just the way she was. She was good to my son, but lousy to me. That night we had rough sex. I didn't want him to even touch me because he was drunk and nasty. He wanted to shove things up my vagina, but I wouldn't let him. He did his dirty deed. It wasn't a loving sex between husband and wife, it was brutal and he made me cry. What had I gotten myself into? I became pregnant with our daughter soon after that. Larry insisted on having sex well into what we thought to be the ninth month, and the doctor was furious with us. I begged Larry to stop forcing me for the baby's sake. We had sex two days before our baby was born, and our daughter was born breech and had no heartbeat. I was so frightened that I started to shake. Luckily, after what seemed to be a lifetime, my daughter started to cry and I was so thankful. I named her Michele Lee after the famous dancer. My children were always a blessing to me and I thank God for them every night. They turned out to be responsible upstanding citizens and I am very proud of them to this day.

Larry and I had years of a horrible relationship. There were many times that I thought of leaving him, but I kept trying to make it work. I wanted my kids to have their mother and father. Look at what I went through! I went through sexual abuse at the hands of an uncle, I was kidnapped and raped, I was hungry and dirty, and I didn't want my kids to suffer like I did. I took the beatings and the insults, and after a while, no matter how many names Larry called me, I didn't hear them anymore. I just heard noise. My mother would have made my life miserable if I moved back home, and my life was already miserable. I would go home for short periods of time when things got too bad with Larry, and she would say things to me that felt like a cutting knife. What she said hurt more than what Larry said, for whatever reason.

I left Larry three times and would go back home each time. Then I would go back to him. He always made so many promises and I wanted to believe in him. We had bought a house through the GI Bill Of Rights, and we lasted together there for about two more years. One night Larry was out at a local bar and he came home so drunk that he couldn't make it into the house. It was raining so hard that the ground and dirt driveway was completely covered with water. Larry fell out of the car on his face and laid face down in water. He was pretty heavy those days because he drank a lot of beer and ate like a horse. He now worked as a mechanic on the three to eleven shifts and then he would go to the bars. He made good money as a truck mechanic and we could and should have been all right, but we weren't. He also started to gamble at card games and lost a lot of money. I ran outside after watching him through the window. I knew that he was in trouble because he might drown. The whole thing reminded me of so many years ago when Aunt Glady had fallen down the steps and she needed my help, but because she treated me so poorly, I hesitated. I thought to myself, this is one way to get rid of him! Does this make me a bad person? He was beating me many nights a week, making the kids and I eat canned meatballs, mayonnaise sandwiches and sometimes ketchup sandwiches when things were really bad. He ate while he was out, and judging by the looks of him, he ate better than we did. He wore a size forty-two pants. I weighed in at ninety-five pounds. The kids were pretty skinny too. There is that fine line between right and wrong, sane and insane. I could have just let him stay there and whatever happened would have happened, but I would have to live with that for the rest of my life.

I walked over to this large man, and with all of my strength managed to move him a little. He was dead weight. I moved him enough and figured he was out of trouble. I also made a deep trench like crevice that would take the water away from his head, and then I just left him alone. I did give him a good kick in his leg (Oh that felt good) then I went into the house and went to bed.

Sometime later he came in and passed out on the couch. I didn't hear him enter the house. I was able to get a few hours sleep before the kids woke up and for that I was thankful. I was very skinny, sleep deprived and a nervous wreck.

Larry didn't hit the kids, in fact if anything he ignored them for the most part. At times he would hold Michele on his lap and they would watch cartoons. Over the years I found out that Larry came from a very bad background. One day after school when Larry walked into the house, his mother told him to go upstairs and check on his father. She told him that he wasn't well. When Larry got to his parents room he found his father on their bed unconscious. He had tried to commit suicide by drinking and taking a handful of pills. I was told that Larry, who was only eleven years old, screamed for his mother to come upstairs and she refused. She just called the police, and they called an ambulance, and took him away. His father had to go to a mental facility for some time, and from what I was told his mother was not happy when he was released from the facility. Larry's parents fought a lot too. I never saw any indication of this until years later. They hid their problems from other people very well.

It was New Years Eve and I decided to have a party! I invited all of my friends and had a lot of fun talking to them on the phone again. A couple of them showed up for the party, and my father-in-law came as well. We also had a couple of neighbors who stopped in for a few hours. I had made a lot of food. Larry wanted to impress everyone, so he was generous with money for once. I made fried chicken, lasagna and a big salad. We also made finger sandwiches and chips and dips of all kinds. It was very cold out and everyone ate heartily. By the time the ball was about to drop, Larry was so drunk that he had opened the den window and was hanging out of it passed out! I was told to leave him there by the guys. That's what I did. Everyone including the kids was having a good time, and David was running around the house like a little Indian. Michele was in her playpen playing happily with pots and pans. I thought to myself how I played with pots and pans when I was little. I had only a few toys and so did these kids. That thought made me sad for a minute, but I quickly dismissed it because they seemed happy. When the ball fell, I went over to Michele and told her to hit the pans together as hard as she could and that made her laugh with glee. While Larry hung out the window in the ice-cold weather, everyone yelled, "Happy New Year!" Not long after that everyone except my father-in-law left. They had traveled a long distance, and I think they were turned off by Larry and just wanted to go home. They saw no humor with his behavior and acted disgusted with him. I cleaned the house up, and put the kids to bed, who were exhausted. My father-in-law tried to get Larry back in from the window, but he was dead weight. I tried too, but gave up. I went to bed, and Pop, Larry's father, went out to his camper. I didn't know what to do with Larry hanging half in and half out of the window, and I knew if I did manage to get him back in and he came to, he would just call me the usual filthy names and tell me how stupid I was. The thought of his usual behavior just made me sick. Who needs that? I already felt inferior to everyone and secretly hated myself, and so for once I thought, "Too bad Larry, just stay there!"

Suddenly I heard a loud crash and jumped out of bed. Larry had finally gotten himself back in the house and had fallen on a table. The table was not very big and he smashed it to pieces. He also managed to knock over a lamp that crashed to the floor. I ran down stairs to see if he was all right, and in the kitchen he stood like a monster that was swaying back and forth because he drank so much. He came over and got behind me and managed to get me into a chokehold. We were standing next to the stove and I was able to reach for a knife and I grabbed it and held it in my hand. He was strangling me from behind in a chokehold that I could not get out of, he had me good. I could feel myself losing consciousness and I thought to myself, "It's either him or me!" I didn't care where I stabbed him, I just knew that I had to or I was going to die. I lifted my arm out from my side getting ready to stab him anywhere I could. Suddenly I felt something knock the knife from my hand. Then quick as a flash my father- in- law had broken the hold around my neck. He screamed at Larry and slapped him in the face. He ordered me to go upstairs to the bedroom and lock the door. I listened and was able to get myself up the stairs. I went into the bedroom and lit a cigarette. I heard shouting downstairs, and then silence.

I went to bed and slept for a couple of hours before the kids got up that morning. I was afraid to go downstairs, but knew I had to. My little Michele started to walk at the ripe old age of nine months, and she was able to climb out of her crib if she wanted to. She decided to that morning. When I went downstairs my father- in- law was in the kitchen and Larry was back in the den sleeping on the couch. He had made coffee and he said very quietly to me, "He is my son, but after what I saw a few hours ago, you had better sell this house and split up." He was right, and even though he was a drunk himself, he was always good to the kids and to me. We liked

him and he was a lot of fun. I listened to what he had to say and I
knew in my heart that he was right. I had something to work with
this time. We owned a house and even though it needed a lot of
work we had made some improvements. Larry had made the den
and was very handy with carpentry. He made other improvements
as well. I knew that we could sell the house and make a profit. We
would get separate checks at the closing, and I would have enough
money to get an apartment and a little furniture. The kids would
have their own bedrooms instead of sharing, and I would sleep
out on the couch in the living room. I had it all worked out. When
he woke up, his father came into the kitchen and the three of us
spoke. We agreed that we had to split up before something really
bad happened.

———

CHAPTER 37

In late February we were sitting in the real estate office with the lawyers. They were getting all of the necessary papers together for us to sign. Due to hostilities, Larry was sitting several seats away from me. When the checks were cut we each received one. The deal was done and we would go back to the house and prepare to go our separate ways. When we got back to the house Larry took off, and I didn't care. He was gone. I called my mother and told her everything that happened. She sighed, and said that the kids and I could come back home. I would have to straighten things out soon though, and could tell she was not a happy person, but would be supportive. I packed as much as possible of the clothing, toys, personals, and whatever else I needed that seemed important. The neighbors in the back asked for some of the furniture that was going to be left behind, and I gave it to them. After all, I didn't have a moving truck, and space was limited in the station wagon. I left behind things that would have been of value today, but at the time who would know? The only thing that I knew was that again I was half starved, beaten and told that I was ugly and stupid. This was going to be the last time for that!

I had fifteen hundred dollars to start a new life. That is how much each of us received from the sale of the house. I was told later on that there were so many beer cans in the basement that the new people who bought the house, cut the cans in half and glued them to one of the walls in the house! It was actually considered to be very artistic, and the wall was photographed by the local newspapers. Someone from that area told me that a magazine was even interested in taking pictures! Is that nuts! I think so. It was almost a smack in the face. I didn't know where Larry had gone, but my mother said that he should pay child support. I liked the idea of that, because I remember the lousy meals that I was forced to feed the kids, and how our clothing came from the general store down the street. I had enough money to go put down on an apartment, buy some furniture, but I didn't know if I could afford a two-bedroom unit. The kids were so young, if they had to share for now, then so be it. I would buy one of those couches that opened up to a bed for me to sleep on. I was just happy to be away from another monster in my life. I was suffering from such low self-esteem and I still couldn't make eye contact with anyone. At this point in my life I did think that I was ugly. Larry had done a job on me mentally and spiritually, which was the very last thing that I needed. As far as the kids were concerned they surely didn't need this abuse either. What were their egos like? Although they were young children, they hurt as much as I did. I remembered the nights I watched my parents fight and how I felt. I *think* my kids were asleep most of the times, but there was terrible tension in the daytime when Larry wasn't working. I know they felt that. My son did have bad nightmares and my daughter was very hyper.

My mother and step-father were very good to the kids and helpful to me. My mother and I always had a strained relationship, and unfortunately that never really changed. It hurt me all the years of my life to think that my mother didn't love me as she should have. Jimmy, who did so little to earn her love, had it. I remember one time when I was fourteen years old, my mother was vacuuming in the hallway of our house and I walked up to her and put my hand on her shoulder. She looked up from what she was doing and I said, "I love you Mommy," she looked shocked when I said that and just said, "Thank you." I so wanted her to say it back. I guess that she just didn't have it in her.

My mother took me out for days to look at apartments, and we finally found a landlord who would accept a woman who was separated with two kids. I had a wad of money and money does speak for itself. I put down six months rent and the landlord was happy. I went and bought the kids what they needed, and my mother took me to a second hand shop where I was able to get a couch, chair, and a couple of end tables for not much money. I certainly didn't have a pretty apartment, but it was neat and everything was new to me. My mother bought the kids some more clothes that came from a regular store, and I bought myself a jacket. I then went food shopping and got a lot of groceries and toiletries. After all of that, I still had money left. Money went so much further in those days. I was happy, the kids were happy, and we had a new start. Things were looking up! It was a bittersweet kind of happiness. I was happy not to be hit and screamed at, but I also knew that I was going to be lonely.

My mother gave me a car my brother had brought home from the junkyard. It ran and looked good. My brother was able to get cars at times that were luxury cars, because some people hadn't paid their car loans or whatever. He would take the cars to my mother and give them to her. My mother actually liked that arrangement, because he gave her a couple of fancy cars. He had moved out long before, but always needed money. I think he was able to get these cars for a song and dance, and then when he needed money because of problems with jobs, he would always say, "Look what I gave you!" It worked for him. Over the many years to come my mother showed me her checkbook, and my brother, because of legal issues and just plain money for living, received tons of money, before she said "No More!"

The kids made friends very quickly and so did I. I also got in touch with Meagan and we attempted to contact the old gang. We managed to find a few of the people we hung out with. It was good to find old friends. Most people our age were married, settled down with kids of their own, and you tend to lose contact with old friends because of this. Meagan had split up with her husband and we were like free as birds with no place to go. Once a week, Meagan and I would get together for a little fun. I would get a sitter and we would go out. We didn't meet anyone worth knowing. When the old gang did get together once in a while, that was a blast. I decided that I should start pursuing Larry for child support, and someone said that I should get on welfare. The thought of applying for welfare and food stamps blew my mind, but my kids came first. I remember going into the store with food stamps and feeling embarrassed. I already felt uncomfortable because I was sure that people were looking at me. I had not lost any of my phobias or panic attacks. I would go into stores with the kids and get out as soon as possible. David was old enough to somewhat understand food stamps. He said to me one day, "Mommy, are we real poor?" I felt like a leper. I didn't come from a poor family and now I was poor.

To try and find a full time sitter for two kids was very hard back then. My little Michele had developed tantrums like you wouldn't believe, and I was afraid she would cause problems with baby sitters. There was actually one sitter who said Michele gave her the "evil eye," and was scared of her! I almost laughed myself silly! Tension affects kids in all different ways, and this is how my daughter responded to all that had happened in her little life. My son became a very inward and angry person. This caused me concern because he didn't want to socialize with his peers. I hadn't gotten my GED yet, and that didn't help my cause either. I knew that someday I would get it, and perhaps even more education.

I was really feeling depressed. If only Larry could be a decent husband and father none of this would be taking place. Larry was located, and he had to pay a certain amount each week, but it didn't help me very much. I really didn't have enough to live on, and my mother gave me money for the items that welfare didn't provide for. Why do they feel that people don't need to wipe their butts? The kids and I went to my mother's a lot just to hang out, and at the end of the month she would make a "care" package until my check and stamps came. I felt like a fool and hated all this. I knew that I couldn't make enough money to survive if I got a job, not with two kids. I felt stuck.

One day there was a knock on the door and there was Larry! He took the kids out for a ride. When he came back to the house

I offered him to join us for dinner. He asked how I was doing, and said that he was lonely too. I told him that I could *not* be beaten anymore, or screamed at, and the kids needed and deserved better care than what he had given. He promised to be good and begged for another chance. I told him that he could come over and we would date for a while. He had to show me that he had changed. I was very leery. Everyone thought that I had lost my mind to even consider it. Of course, they were right.

Larry moved in two weeks later after that knock on the door. I stood there and didn't feel happiness. I don't think enough time had gone by while we were separated. To be lonely is one thing, but to be abused is another! I was supposed to stand there with open arms or something and I couldn't do it. I knew that I should notify welfare, but gave it a couple of days. I then called and said that he was there, but I wasn't sure that it was the right thing to do because he was abusive. The caseworker told me that I had a week to make up my mind, and she thanked me for my honesty. I was to call her either way. She seemed very sincere. She must have had second thoughts, because one day right after he moved in there was a knock at the door, and there stood a caseworker from welfare! I didn't know if someone called their office or what. I was scared to death. The lady looked at me and she walked around the apartment.

Her name was not the same as the lady's name that I spoke with a few days before. She asked me if anyone else was living with me. I didn't open my mouth to answer. I just shook my head no. Larry still had his clothes out in the car only because he had not yet unpacked. She opened up the closets and all she saw was my meager amount of clothing hanging in there. She looked in the closet for the kids and they too didn't have much. She was satisfied and left. Before she left she told me that there would be periodic checks done, and I wouldn't know when they would be.

That night when Larry got back to the apartment I told him he had to leave because I wasn't going to live like this. He and I got into a big fight. The kids just got out of our way because they didn't know what was going to happen next. When we lived in the house most of the fighting occurred late at night and they didn't see too much, because they were sound asleep. This apartment was not that big and the walls were thin. I remember the people in the back pounding on their walls telling us to shut up or they would call the cops. They also pounded on the walls when my daughter had her tantrums. What a life! I told him he had to keep his clothes out in the car, and he could stay a couple nights a week, but that was all for now. That seemed to satisfy him, not that I owed him anything. I just wanted to have things work out and be a family. He was helpful with the kids and he helped out with all the items not covered by welfare. My mother wasn't too happy covering expenses and this was a break for her. We tried to be a couple for about a month and finally I couldn't take it anymore. He was still drinking heavily. I was a nervous wreck and had started drinking too. I knew that I couldn't drink too much because of the kids. I was controlling my drinking.

One night the fighting was so bad that the police were called, but who ever called didn't give the exact address. I saw the patrol car. I ran inside and told Larry that the police had been called and he had better shut up. I didn't want trouble or any investigations, because I certainly did not want to lose my kids. The patrol car circled the building several times and then left. The next day Larry was gone. We couldn't handle seeing each other for even a couple days a week without problems. We stayed separated for well over a year. In that time I had become friendly with the owner of the apartment complex. He had a major crush on me, and more or less told me that he wanted to take care of me. Of course I was expected to be his girlfriend. In this case it would have been his mistress. He allowed for me to move up into a vacant house that he owned on the property. I declined his offer to be his mistress, because he was married and had children. He said that someday I would change my mind. The house was more rent, so I moved in a friend from the complex who had a young son. There was plenty of room and I cleared it with welfare. This arrangement lasted a while. We would get a babysitter once a week and go out to the bars hoping to find Mr. Wonderful. I never had to buy a drink because by that time I had gained back my weight and had long blonde hair. I must say that I looked pretty good. My friend on the other hand was plain looking and no one bought her drinks. But she still wanted to go out and try to have a good time. When we went out to the bars she had to pay for her drinks and sometimes she'd get mad. I would give her a couple of mine. We never left with anyone, but we did get a lot of attention. Once in a while I would see someone that I went to school with, but everyone was married.

Our house was quiet but lonely of male companionship. It was a bad age for both my friend and I. I did meet a couple of men and invited them over to the house for dinner, but nothing came of it. We just didn't hit it off. Or maybe they didn't like the fact that I had kids. My friend and her son stayed for quite a few months, and then she announced that she had a new place to live. We parted friends, but somehow I knew that we would never meet again.

———

CHAPTER 38

One day the phone rang and it was Larry. I was shocked to hear from him because we had not spoken in quite some time. He told me that he had been sober for many months, was living with his sister and wanted to see me. He claimed that he had turned over a new leaf and had found the Lord. I was dumbfounded. He said that he belonged to a religious group who had helped him and he wanted his family back. I was invited to his sister's house with our kids for the next weekend, and we would talk at that time. I thought, was this a joke or something? I hesitated for a few minutes because I just didn't know what to say. He reminded me that it was his right to see the kids, and I reminded him that he had failed to do that for quite awhile. He was not going to give up on me. He asked me what would be the worst thing that could happen if we all got together. I finally gave in.

The week went fast and he called me almost every night. He really seemed very sincere. I listened to what he had to say concerning the group that he and his sister belonged to. Saturday came, and at one o'clock the kids yelled, "Here comes Daddy!" I had mixed emotions when I saw him. The kids on the other hand seemed pleased. They never saw too much of the fighting until the last blow up when I told him he had to leave. This is the man that called me foul names, told me that I was ugly and stupid, and abused me physically also. He almost killed me and now he tells me that he's different!? How can I believe that! We all got into his car and he complimented me on the way I looked. I thought, "Yea, the kids and I are eating now!"

His sister Sara lived almost two hours away. He also had another sister that the kids and I liked a lot more. Her name was Patty. She could play the guitar, and Larry told me that at times she played for the group while they sang religious songs. I always believed in God and always will. I believe that I would have been killed several times in my life if He were not watching over me. Too many bad things happened and I came out standing on my feet. I still had quirks that seem to plague me. They had held me back because of panic attacks and low self-esteem. I still had nightmares and a habit of looking over my shoulder. In fact, I still do. I don't know if I will ever be totally comfortable with myself. I slept with a night light on at that time, and still do to this day.

When we arrived at Larry's sisters' house, she and her husband Phil came out to greet us. Their children were already out playing in the yard. Even David and Michele's grandparents were there. We got out and they all ran over to us. Everyone was hugging us and giving us kisses. I felt very awkward to say the least. Outside of Patty and Pop, I had no good relationships in Larry's family, because of all of the trouble over the years. Because of words said in the heat of the moment bad feelings had developed. There was going to have to be a lot of healing in this family if it was going to be whole again. I was very skeptical to say the least. My mother told me that if I went back with Larry she would never help me again. I was very grateful for the help she had given me over the years because we needed it so badly. She made sure that my kids had clothes when I told her that they needed them, and she did help us with food when I told her we were in trouble. When we lived in our house that we had gotten through the GI Bill Of rights, we lived far away from her and she only knew what I told her in dribs and drabs. I felt though, if Larry had really changed then maybe we could be a family at last. It was too hard trying to make ends meet the way I was living now, the kids needed a father, and yes, I wanted a husband. It all made sense. I was going to use caution this time though. I needed to feel the family out and see if what Larry said was really true about being sober.

We had a great dinner. Afterwards his sister Sara took Larry and me into the living room to sit and talk. The kids were glad to be with their cousins after not seeing them for such a long period of time. Patty came in too, and the four of us sat and spoke for about two hours. The three of them told me about the prayer group that they were involved in, and how it helped many people every day with many problems. They also went on to say that people were expected to go out into the community and help out voluntarily in nursing homes, hospitals or working with troubled youth. We would work at any place where we could be helpful. This is of course if everything was in order in your own home. That meant that your family had to have a good foundation with no major problems other than the normal ones that arise in regular homes. I thought "Boy it would be a freaking miracle if Larry and I ever reached that point in our lives." Patty played guitar in the nursing homes and Sara who was not musically inclined did other things to help the old people. It all sounded too good to be true, but I was ready for a change in my life, and if things could work out for us, the kids might have their father back for good. I thought, could I really forgive him enough for this to happen? All I ever wanted out of life was a normal home with normal people around, and normal friends. It seemed like that was always too much to expect in my life. I stayed overnight and felt strange sleeping with my own husband in his sister's house. Everything seemed to be so pure around me, people included.

The next evening I went to my first prayer meeting. I must admit that everyone seemed so happy and together. We sang and the leaders stood up and preached. There was also a priest involved in this prayer group. People spoke in tongues and the minute that I heard that I started to get my nervous giggle and I had to excuse myself. Larry and Sara came out and tried to coax me to go back in and I refused. I said that I was standing next to someone who sounded like Daffy Duck, and that was enough for me! We went home and Larry told us to gather up our clothes because it was time to go back to my house. I thanked everyone for their hospitality and I was sure that I would see them again. They said to come again next week and try another meeting. When we got home I noticed that there were police cars at my house. We quickly got out of the car to see what was wrong. When we left the house we forgot to close the windows and the curtains were hanging out. We also forgot to lock the doors. Nothing was touched in the house and I really didn't have much to steal. As it turned out my neighbor across the street thought that something really bad had happened to us. The police even looked down the well to see if bodies were down there!! I thought are all of these people crazy? I got complimented on having such a neat house. You can't really have a sloppy house when there is nothing to be sloppy with. I thanked my neighbor for her concern, and looked at Larry and told him to pick us up early next time. He smiled and agreed. We said our goodbyes as he left. I spoke to the kids the next day and asked them if they would like to try and make it work again with their father. They both said yes and I made up my mind. One last try with a sober Larry! Time will tell, but I had my fears and doubts.

The week went by slowly and Larry called every day. He seemed so changed and loving. Is it possible that he'll act like he did before he went into the service? I felt that I had died and gone to heaven at the thought of that being true. I found it to be amazing that people could change so much. I was far from convinced that this was for real. After all that had happened, it was going to take a lot more than sweet words and behavior that appeared to be normal. I did start to go through our things and again throw away clothing that no longer fit right. My actions reminded me of so long ago when Mommy went through our closets and did the same thing, only days before our lives of my brother and I knew, it changed. One thing that I was sure of was I would never leave my kids and make them live with other people no matter what! Saturday came and the kids were excited about going to see their cousins, and yes, to see their father as well! I still had mixed feelings and felt a little mad because I had taken so many beatings in my life, not just from Larry, but other people as well. A part of me was mad at myself for not being able to start over again without having to depend on someone else for help. How about meeting someone who there was no history with? It's very hard for a woman to start over again when she has children; but things do happen for a reason and I had to wait and see how this all worked out.

Larry pulled up and the kids ran outside to greet him. He seemed so shiny and new. He looked like one of the nicest people in the world. He hugged both of his children and then looked at me. He smiled and asked, "Hey pretty lady, are you ready to go?" He never called me pretty, even though at this point in my life I figured I looked all right because I got a lot of whistles. We locked the windows of the house, and the doors, and we went on our way. There would be no curtains flying this time and hopefully no cops on the property when we returned. I was feeling more hopeful.

We drove the two-hour ride and pulled up in his sister Sara's driveway. Everyone ran out to see us. We had a great time just talking, and after another good meal we went to the prayer group. The kids stayed home with Pop again. This time I tried to really look at the people in the group. They collected money for the needy every other week, and that week it came to the leader's attention that a family needed money for oil. It was starting to get colder out, and that family was having financial difficulties. The leaders told them to come up, and right there and then they gave the husband money for his house, and money for oil. I was quite impressed and was told that this was common practice for the group. There were over two hundred members in this prayer group. That impressed me. The prayer group also helped any family in need, even outside of their own group. People in need of food or clothing were helped. This was something that I had never seen before, but sure wished that this group were around when I needed help! I was getting to like the people and found myself getting sucked in. I decided that their speaking in tongues was a gift as mentioned in the Bible, and it did come from the Lord. I also made up my mind that the kids and I certainly needed a positive change in our lives, and wanted to be a part of a group that helped other people. I did grow up that way if you think about it. My mother and step-father helped a lot of people over the years. One time when I was growing up they allowed for a homeless man to live in the garage next to the greenhouses. Every night at dinner time my mother would make up a huge plate of food, and we would take turns taking it down to him. We also made sure that he had enough blankets to keep warm. My mother just had a problem with me!

After the meeting was over, which lasted about two hours; there was time for people to socialize if they chose to. We stayed for a while and I met some people. I decided that I liked what I saw. Larry asked me if I wanted to get back together and move down to Red Bank with the kids. I was convinced that these people in the group had something that I did not have, and I wanted it. For one thing they were genuinely happy, and I wanted to be happy too!

The next day when we went home I had to tell Leon that I was moving. I had Larry with me. At first he seemed a little nasty, but when I said that the kids needed their father, he melted. He agreed that all kids need both parents; he let me out of my lease and wished us well. He asked that I leave the house clean, and I did.

I said goodbye to my friends down in the complex and the kids said goodbye to theirs. We didn't have that much to move. None of the furniture that we had was anything that good, so we had put it out for garbage or for anyone else to take who needed it. I left the curtains up so the place didn't look empty. We packed what we could, including clothes, and we said goodbye to that area in which the kids and I lived for a couple of years. I knew that I had to get them registered in a new school and I thought, "Hear we go again." I prayed that I had made the right choice. We stayed at Sara's house for a week, and Larry found a house for rent, through the group of course. We had a new start!

My mother was furious when I called her and told her. I hadn't told her about my intentions regarding Larry at all. I was after all a grown woman and I sure hoped that this time things would work out. My mother was lucky when she met my step-father. Their marriage was made in heaven and they enjoyed each other for many years. I never knew of such a perfect marriage. I believe that their type of marriage comes along only once in a while. I decided that I wanted to take my G.E.D. really soon. I always felt bad that I quit school and decided it was about time to get that straightened out as well. It seemed like I was always trying to "straighten" out my life. I was spending a lifetime doing that, and believe me; I was getting tired of it. I sure hoped that this was not a mistake, and not just another time that I would have to go through hell. My mother told me that she would not visit. She also told me that if this was another mistake, I was on my own. Jimmy made one mistake after another in his life and he was always taken care of. He was married twice and both marriages failed. Nothing was ever said to him that was hurtful. He always received moral support and money when needed. He had one child, a daughter. I told myself that my kids are both very precious to me, and they will get all of the love and help that they need as long as I can help them, and I will never make them feel bad about it. When parents show such favoritism, the one that suffers from it hopefully learns from their parent's mistakes, and does not repeat them with their own children.

The next weeks were spent getting our new house together and getting the kids back in school. I have to admit that the school was rough and the kids were not that happy with it. The only other school they could go to was a Catholic school and they had to wear uniforms. The kids called my mother, and the last thing that my mother wanted to hear was that the kids had to go to a Catholic school. Ha Ha! She heard their stories about the public school, and after a few weeks she decided that she would help only because the kids were miserable. The kids had not yet been baptized and it was time to make a decision. To me it was a no-brainer. The kids started to go to CCD and I went for instructions. The school accepted the kids and we all converted to Catholicism. We were baptized in front of the whole congregation in St. James Catholic Church in Red Bank N.J.

CHAPTER 39

Larry was having a hard time getting work. He was working as a painter's helper and had jobs to do, but the man who was in our church group was not paying him! I saw this with my own eyes and I felt sorry for Larry. He was working very hard and deserved to be paid. His boss was a friend of his sisters, and she did after a while talk to his boss's wife about the situation. Larry felt foolish, but thought that his sister could be more instrumental. I have to say that it did no good. I guess there always has to be one rotten apple, and his boss was the one. I was glad that summer was coming because then we wouldn't have to worry about oil for our house. I started to see how the people in the group felt when they needed help. They were glad to get it, but felt embarrassed as well. Larry and I started to get a little picky with each other. I prayed that this was not the beginning of bad times to come.

One day someone in the prayer group approached me and told me about a group called the V.I.P program. That stood for Volunteers in Probation. She thought that with my rough background I could be very helpful with troubled youth. I figured she was probably right. In order for me to get a good job anytime in my life I had to get my G.E.D. and get some kind of background. I was so happy that I became a part of this group. It did change my life and help me. I joined the Volunteers in Probation program, and after a while I had over twenty kids that I was working with. I went into their homes and did assessment and evaluation; I worked one on one with these kids, and became a part of the Rahway Lifers Program — Scared Straight. This was the beginning of my background. Larry continued to struggle with gainful employment, but insisted that the work that I was doing was important and good for me, even if it did not pay money. I was learning, and maybe someday I would find a paying job, and then have a lot of back ground and experience to offer. I was very thankful for this opportunity. I got my GED without even studying for it. I passed with sixteen more points than what was required. One of my probationers' parents let me use their car to go to the school where the test was being held, because our car was not working, and we couldn't afford to get it fixed. Larry was proud and wouldn't ask for help from the group. His father finally helped us, and yes, we could use some food too.

One day there was a knock at the door and in walked two people from our church group. They had over eleven bags of food to bring in! I don't mean cheap meals either. There were roast of all kinds and everything you could think of. I was dumbfounded but very thankful. They left and just told me to go to meetings every Thursday night. I had skipped a few and Larry had skipped many. I was a little mad at him because he was the one who introduced me to the whole thing to begin with. I must say that this prayer group was everything a prayer group should be. Our group really did help people, and all of the people that I came to know well were good people who came from all walks of life. I loved being a part of the group. I felt that my problems with low self esteem were improving because instead of being told how bad or stupid I was, I was now being told just the opposite by people who were very sincere. I know that I will never get over all of my problems completely, but at least I like myself today, and realize that the people who hurt me all throughout my life were sick and I happened to be their victim. Because I had seen so much, and had been abused in so many ways, I was very instrumental in helping troubled teens. For once I was feeling productive and good about myself. All of the help that I gave came back to me and I did heal in some areas of my life. I call it identification.

I continued to work with the kids, and one day while driving down the street one of the boys who I was assigned to that day asked, "Hey do you drink beer?" I was floored. In the ashtray were bottle caps. I knew that I was not drinking and it had to be Larry's. Larry had gotten a job at a factory, and I noticed that many times he was late getting home. We were starting to argue about the smallest things and he was always chewing gum. It seemed like he wanted to pick a fight. He wasn't paying attention to the kids again. I was furious. Time had gone by and we should have been happier, but we were not. I cooked and cleaned, and one day our vacuum cleaner broke. I told Larry that we needed a new one. He said no. I had to go around the corner for months and borrow his sisters. I suppose I could have told the group, but I was embarrassed. They had already bought us food before Larry got his factory job. He never would show me his pay checks so I didn't know how much money my husband made! He paid the bills and would not let me near the checkbook. I felt like he was a bully, he was very controlling. I kept my mouth shut though, because he supported my work with the kids, and I knew that this work was one of the best things for me. I went to the group on Thursday nights and they would always ask where Larry was. I was starting to get embarrassed because at one time they thought so much of him. We ate over each other's houses and at times socialized. Larry had lost interest in the group. Our group was growing all of the time and now had over two hundred people in it.

Across the street from where we lived was a family that had five children, and these kids were very abused by their mother. She was so bad that even her husband, who was a big man, feared her! They had a closed in front porch made out of glass. He would stay out there at night with the light on, and he would sweep and sweep the porch and talk to himself. Later, even when it was very cold out, he would sleep in the car. What a wimp! I didn't want him to hit the lady, but I sure wanted him to get control of the situation. She would hit the kids and scream at them. One night during the summer, one of her girls got sick to her stomach, and was in the bathroom throwing up. I went outside and walked over to the side of the house and I could see the young girl. The witch was standing behind her yelling, "Throw up like a lady!" She was truly an awful person. My heart ached for these kids. I told the group about the problem and they knew of the family. They had many complaints against them at the police department, and nothing was really being done about it. Every night they had hot dogs for dinner and who knows what else. These kids were very angry kids and they took their frustrations out on the streets. That meant they hit the neighborhood kids. They hit my kids. I was furious, but I would get out there when I heard a fight brewing, and try to stop things from escalating. They had no respect for any adults and that included me. I was able to calm down a couple of the girls by sitting and talking to them. I understood their anger and knew that they were not really bad kids at all, they were abused.

I told my mother about this family and she thought that she could come down and get order. Ha! Was she in for a surprise! Every day there was trouble on the street while the parents were at work and my mother came down to see what she could do, and also to see if I was exaggerating! My mother came down the road in her pretty car, got out of the car in her pretty clothes, and walked into our house. She asked, "Where are the kids?" I told her that they were outside playing. I made her a cup of coffee and she walked around inside my house. She thought that it was all right looking, but she saw that we needed a new couch badly. She told me she had one that I could have, and all of a sudden there was a loud scream coming from outside. One of the Corey kids had hit Michele in the face. My mother put her cup down on the counter and said, "I'll fix this!" My mother went outside and started to yell at the Corey kids and she ran towards them thinking that she could scare them. They just looked at her and laughed and called her an old bag. My mother showed her teeth by pulling back her lips, just like she did when I was a kid, and they laughed at her even harder and called her a foul name. All of a sudden one of the girls bent over and picked up a piece of clay pipe from the sewer on the road and ran towards my daughter, she was going to hit her in the head. My mother reached out and grabbed the pipe just in time which taught Michele to never turn your back on a fight. I knew these kids, and I told her she had better run because these kids meant business! My mother said "Jesus, these kids are too tough for me!" I must admit that while she was running away from flying debris, I was laughing my head off. My mother had met her match! She ran into my house, went into her pocketbook and pulled out a Valium and took one. My mother usually took halves a couple times a day and only five milligram in all. On this particular day I'm sure that she took ten milligrams. She looked at me and saw that I was laughing. At first she was mad and then she started to laugh too. My mother shook her head and told me that we should move. I liked the group and my work so much that I surely didn't want to do that. The kids came in all rosy cheeked and excited. They said, "See what we mean Nena, they are even tougher than you!" We all laughed. It really was no laughing matter though. I told her that many times people called the police and nothing happened. This is why they had no respect for authority or adults. She asked me what could be done. I thought for a minute, and then decided to talk to father Bill at the church. I thought that he was one of the coolest priests that I ever knew. My mother scoffed at that. She stayed for a while longer and gave the kids a few dollars to put in their piggy banks before her long ride home. I thanked her for coming. Maybe I should have asked her for a vacuum cleaner!

That evening when Michele went to her bedroom she made a sad discovery. She went to put her money away in her piggy bank and discovered that the money she had collected for her Brownie group was gone. Michele had sold calendars and had done pretty well. She was devastated and so was I. I told Larry about it and he just shrugged. I was furious. We hardly ever had any other kids in the house, and I knew there was something fishy about this. I of course couldn't prove it, but I knew he had taken it. I was getting to the point that I couldn't stand him again. He hadn't changed. Any father that would do this to his daughter, knowing that she would get into trouble for it, was just too low for me.

I went to the church a few days later, and after confession I requested to speak to Father Bill. He invited me back into the office that he shared with the secretary and other priests, and I sat down. I told him of the story of the Corey kids. I felt like I could help a couple of the girls, but nothing could be permanent under the conditions that they were living in. This is one family where I wished that Child Protection Services would get involved. He promised that in a couple of days he would pay them a visit. That was on a Tuesday, and sure enough by Thursday when I was out on the sidewalk trying to get some order with the kids, I looked down the street and there walked Father Bill. Father Bill was a tall Blonde man who walked with a lot of confidence. The sun was behind him as he walked down the street, and as it shone on his longish hair he looked just like an angel. My mouth dropped and the kids looked to see what had my attention. Their mouths dropped too, and the Corey kids went running across the street into their house. Father Bill didn't say a word to me and hardly looked my way. He went to the Corey house and walked right in with out knocking. We stood outside watching the Corey house for about an hour, and finally gave up and went inside. I'm not sure when he left because I had to make dinner. The only thing that I can say is that the whole neighborhood had peace for almost a month. The Corey kids went to school, but didn't speak to anyone, and when they got home they went inside the house. The mother even acted a lot better. For that month we didn't hear any yelling, and the husband went inside the house at night instead of sweeping a porch that couldn't possibly have dirt on it. It was almost like a miracle! This lasted for about a month and then things went back to normal.

One night at the prayer group, one of the ladies walked up to me and told me that the Juvenile Detention Center was going to need help soon. It would be a paying job and we surely could use the money. By that time I had my GED and a lot of experience working with troubled youth. I told Larry about the job and he wasn't supportive at all. This shocked me because he approved so much of my volunteer work. I think he was just being nasty. We weren't getting along anymore at all. I was starting to feel nothing when I looked at him. He wasn't hitting me or even yelling at me like he had in the past. Larry ignored all of us. He now treated me the same way that he treated the kids. No relationship.

He stopped paying the bills and we received shut off notices for the electric. I also noticed that he was walking around with a paintbrush doing touch up work on the walls etc. That struck me as strange behavior. I told him that I appreciated it though, because in some places it needed it. The kids would wrestle or just horseplay like kids do and the walls needed to be touched up. I asked him again for a new vacuum cleaner and he just said no. His sister had gotten tired of me borrowing hers and yet no one offered to give me one. During the winter we had no more oil in the tank and Larry was burning all kinds of things in the fireplace for warmth. It wasn't working, we were still cold. Some pieces of wood that he found had paint on it and I was afraid of the fumes being toxic. I mentioned this, and he ignored me. I went up to the attic and looked for anything that I could think of to put on the kids beds for warmth. I found heavy curtains and used them as extra blankets. I got mad at him and he told me to shut the hell up. He went out and bought an electric heater for our bedroom and nothing for the kid's rooms. That did it!! My kids were suffering. I went to the group and asked for help. The next day the oil truck pulled up and filled our tank right to the top!

It was almost Easter and I wanted to get the kids some candy. Larry took thirty dollars out of his pocket and threw it on the floor. I hate to admit it, but I picked it up because it was enough money to buy candy, and maybe even a new blouse for Michele and a shirt for David. We stood there and just looked at each other. I suddenly realized that as I stood there, I had to again make different plans for the kids and my life. I admit that it saddened me, but I'm sure he felt the same way. I had done so well with the group. I had bettered myself in the almost two years that we were there. I think instead of being happy for me, he may have been jealous. I received many phone calls from parents who wanted me to try and work with their troubled kids. I had my own caseload! I don't believe that Larry thought that I would do so well. The group knew that we were in trouble and two of the leaders came over one night and wanted to know if our marriage was in trouble. I must admit that Larry was annoyed that they came over. He felt that they were intruding, and when asked if the problem was because I was so busy with probation, he said no. I know that the leaders were trying to be helpful, but they had no right to impose their will on me, or to come in as they did and question. I was also mad because they told everyone to find their niche and do what they could to help those in need. Our marriage, which I admit was in trouble, had nothing to do with my work. I didn't neglect any of my wifely obligations or duties. The house was all right, but could have been better if I had a vacuum cleaner. I was using a broom instead, and cleaning the kitchen floor on my hands and knees with a bucket and rag like they did in the old days. I didn't have a mop either, and I didn't ask for one.

One afternoon there was a knock on the door. There stood my friend Alison. We were so happy to see each other. I hadn't seen her in years, so this was a treat. I always hated myself for not having a sense of direction and lacking the confidence to drive outside of my comfort zone. It was once explained to me by a psychologist that I had this problem after I showed the cops where I was raped as a child. My mind suffered trauma and I never healed from it. I believe this because once I get out of my safety zone, I can still suffer panic. I must have someone in the car with me if I am going somewhere unknown. I am scared to death of getting lost. This is one of the left over quirks that I speak of that originated from the abuse I experienced. A kid *cannot* go through what I have gone through in my life and not have lasting damage!! I'm sure that the Corey kids have damage too. That's just the way it is.

Alison and I spent the entire day together and I told her about Larry and my failing marriage. She wasn't surprised. She was happy that I got my GED, and I told her about all of the experience that I had acquired through probation as a volunteer. She said, "Now you have something to work with!" We were given certificates of completion from probation for courses taken, and I knew that would help. I could now feel confident applying for a job. I went home and Larry was acting very ugly because I was with Alison for so long. Alison said goodbye and told me she would call me soon. That night Larry and I had an awful fight and I knew that we weren't going to make up from this one.

The next day I received a phone call from my Aunt Priscilla, and she told me that my beloved grandmother had died. I was totally blown away. I admit that Larry was also sad, because he liked that side of the family. I had no real coat to speak of so I went to the thrift shop the next day to get one. The only thing they had was a long maxi coat. I bought it for thirty cents and took it home and cut a lot off of the length and sewed a hem by hand. I took and iron and a wet wash cloth and held the cloth on the hem and ironed. It worked, the coat looked new and in style. I wanted to look good for my grandmothers' viewing. When Larry and I arrived at the viewing, we were the only ones that showed, except for my Uncle Jack! My grandmother lived to be eighty-four and had lost touch with people over the years, and I'm sure that most of them had died or were incapacitated. My Uncle gave me the ring and a watch that my grandmother cherished, and he told me that she loved me very much. I was very touched and felt so bad. Grandma had never judged me in any way and I knew that she loved me. It was a big loss for me. I was also going to receive fifteen hundred dollars inheritance, as was my brother Jimmy. I said a long time ago that my grandmother was fair and that was one reason why I loved her so much. I knew what I was going to do with that inheritance, I was going to leave Larry for good and start a new life with the kids. This time was for good, we couldn't even fight anymore! I would be able to work for money and be more self sufficient for the first time in my life.

It was Thursday night and time for the prayer meeting. I went and approached the lady who told me about the job at detention. I explained about Larry and she shook her head saying that she wasn't surprised. The job would be available in a few weeks. I had to get things together quickly. I was thankful that the job was not available when she first told me; I still had a little time. I told Larry my intentions and I must say that he begged me not to go. I was shocked. I told him it was too late, because so much damage had been done. He walked out of the house and came back in with a big bottle of booze. He had graduated! No more beer! I wasn't shocked that he had started to drink again, because of the bottle caps found in the car. I was more hurt that after all we had been through; he would again ruin it for us. My children weren't meant to have him as a father, and he and I were done. No more excuses, no more lies and no more hope.

My uncle told me that in a few weeks I would be getting a check. I already was starting to make plans as to how to spend it. I was no longer going to be the subject of Larry's abuse, and I didn't want the kids to continue to be neglected by him either. I wanted to be able to buy clothes from a real store for the kids and myself. Larry never cared that his clothes came from the thrift shop. I knew in my heart that he could have done better by us if he wanted to. I didn't quite understand where the money went, and of course I wasn't allowed to know how much he made. I found out later that he was gambling and drinking even more than I realized. He must not have been a good gambler. We had to go to a family wedding and Larry told me to go to the thrift shop to get a dress for myself, and some clothes for the kids. While I was there, if a suit in his size could be found, I was to get it! I came back with clothes for everyone and I showed Larry his suit. He claimed it was fine and it fit. The day of the wedding he wore his suit, and when we were at the reception, one of the guys there made a snickering comment to Larry and said "Nice suit if it was fifty years ago" and then the man laughed. Larry blushed and I didn't feel sorry for him. We ate and he insisted that we go because he was embarrassed. That night he forced himself on me and we had rough sex. I wanted to vomit, just like the old days from when I was very young. Larry had gotten very drunk that night, but that was no excuse for his behavior. This incident did however motivate me to try harder to look for an apartment. I got out of bed after he passed out, and got the newspaper and started to search for a new place to live. Again I had the same amount to work with like I had years ago, but this time money was different, fifteen hundred went a lot farther then. I also planned to take furniture, the kid's beds, and anything else of use with me. This way so much would not have to be purchased. I went to the church and spoke to Father Bill. I told him everything and he was disgusted with Larry. Father Bill was one of the priests involved in our prayer group, and he knew that Larry was not attending church or prayer meetings. He told me that God doesn't want his children to be unhappy, and I had proven myself to be of good character in everyone's eyes. He said, "Gather up your children and start a new life. Don't forget all that you have done for the needy, and when you can in your life, continue to help those who need you." He gave me his blessings!

Very shortly after that conversation my check arrived. Father Bill told me to take it and run. I called my mother, and that afternoon she came over with the station wagon and we made several trips to her house. My brother even helped me move. That was a miracle. I knew that all I had to do was find an apartment, so the stay at my mother's house would not be for that long. As I was going from bedroom to bedroom I noticed that our bed was gone. While we took a load to my mother's house, in a few hours time, Larry had purchased a new bed and a television for the bedroom. I looked a little closer and I noticed that on the nightstand next to the bed was an unused condom still in its package! I now knew that Larry had a girlfriend. He had not expected us to come back for another load. I caught him! I suddenly heard whimpering noises in the closet of our bedroom. I don't know if he was hiding in there crying, or his girlfriend! I didn't investigate. I was totally disgusted and how would it look to the kids? I brought my mother into the bedroom and pointed to the condom, and to a presence in the closet. I didn't tell the kids what we saw until many years later.

The kids were delighted to go to my parent's house because they were treated well there. None of us would be cold or hungry. I felt a feeling of anger the size of Montana, and once the last thing was packed I didn't even look back. Red Bank was now history. The Corey kids were standing out in the street and they were giving us the finger as we drove away. They were true to form.

The next days were spent with finding an apartment that would take the three of us. I was able to find one but it was still occupied for a few weeks. I decided that I had better go and apply for a job at detention pretty quick. I was very nervous because this was going to be the first real job that I could be proud of, and I wanted the interview to go just right. For several days I practiced out loud as to what I was going to say when I got there. The day of the interview I was feeling really nervous and scared. I was very annoyed with myself. I did after all have experience now and yet I still had that panic problem starting to build in my gut. I told my mother and she said, "Just go do it!" She allowed for me to take her car as I was again without one. I had gotten a new outfit and I looked good, now if only I could speak well. I arrived at Juvenile Detention right on time and marched in hoping not to lose any confidence that I had. I was taken into the director's office and after all of that rehearsing, any confidence I had flew out the window. I suddenly felt very small. I also felt like running away. We eyeballed each other and I said, "You have a job opening here and I can do the job, when do I start?" He looked at me with shock, and any paperwork I had with me I plopped down on his desk! He looked briefly at it and said, "Hired!" I was so thankful that I almost fainted. I went back to my mother's house and told her what happened, and she laughed and said "What do you care how you sounded, you got the job!" I was told that I had to purchase detention center uniforms out of my own pocket, and then if I made it through my probationary time, anything after that would be covered.

Within days the kids and I moved into our new apartment. I enjoyed working there for a while, but the pay was too low. As head of the household there was no way that a single mother with two kids could make a living. This job was fine as a supplemental job if I had a working husband, but I didn't. I now worked with troubled girls that I could identify with. Their backgrounds were similar to mine. They too had been molested, and one of the girls had been brutally raped. I felt such compassion for these kids. Two of them had turned to booze and other drugs. People who are abused often do that to numb themselves to try and block out the pain, and other feelings that only people who have been molested and raped can truly feel. I told them of my past, and they were shocked that I had come so far in my life. They were going to psychologists, and felt they were not getting that far with their therapy. I told them not to give up, because I was sure that if I had some sort of therapy in my life, I might not have suffered so much, and perhaps I would have made better choices for myself. I also told them that I did benefit a lot from helping others. That helped to give me starting points in my life. As time goes by you get a feel for the type of work you want to do. I worked there a little under a year because of the low pay. I saw a job in the paper that interested me. It was working in an alcohol detoxification facility as a counselor. This was something I had a passion for, and they paid somewhat better. I gave my notice, and when the job at Detox started, it was a whole new experience for me.

Day one as a counselor at Detox was quite inspiring. I was one of ten counselors hired. We were told that we were going to have to work rotating shifts, as we were part of a hospital that was located directly across the street. We were to work with hard core off the street addicts, who were addicted to both alcohol and drugs. Anything that alters the way you think or behave is a drug. That was rule number one. Too many times people make the mistake of saying "Oh, he or she only drinks." Friends or family members are relieved that they are not doing heroin or cocaine or whatever. They fail to realize how dangerous alcohol is and what it does to the body. God knows, I did my share of drinking in my life. This job required that you have experience with counseling and drug abuse in general. They considered my work with juveniles to be very helpful. The Rahway Lifers Program experience helped me a lot also. My involvement was acknowledged as solid background. Because my own life had so much turmoil in it as a child, the people that I would be dealing with probably would have the same kind of past and problems as I had. I was fascinated with the job, and was able to identify with a lot of the clients and their needs. We were state funded and in those days programs for drug addicts and alcoholics could be a year long. Understandably, people who went inpatient for a year were likely to have a higher success rate. Today programs are much too short, and people have to have good insurance programs to cover them. I knew someone who went into a detox program and was ordered to leave after three days by their insurance company! What can that do to help an alcoholic recover effectively?

We also had to attend school for courses, and then be certified to continue to work there. As the weeks went by, and turned into months, we were all called into the director's office for a meeting. We had to draw straws to see which two staff members would attend Princeton University Tech for courses. I was one of the lucky ones and a nurse was the other. She drove and I paid for gas and treated her for lunch almost everyday. We weren't allowed to miss more than two days during the entire program. It was considered to be a seminar, but it was the longest seminar that I ever attended. We learned a lot, and did a lot of role-playing. It was great fun, and we had many professors who taught classes. Of course, I was chosen for role-playing one after noon. I was not a happy camper. It was really a little ironic because my role to play was that of an abused housewife who had an alcoholic husband! How did this guy know me? I lived as a child watching my parents, and then married into it. This by the way is not at all uncommon for women to do. We too often make that mistake in our own lives. There are times we do it more than once. To break the chain is very difficult. You first have to recognize the character of the other person, look at their habits and where they come from. You need to have high expectations for yourself and the other person, or you end up doing the same thing over and over again until you learn. Learning can be painful because you also have to look at yourself and love yourself. You know the old saying "If you don't love yourself, how can you love others?"

The day came that we received our certificates and we were allowed to wear a badge that said counselor. It was another accomplishment for me. I loved the job, and made a name for myself for being a pretty darn good counselor. I ran many rap groups and at the end of these sessions clients would applaud. Some of the counselors were told to observe me as I ran group. Everything was going well until one day I was in the middle of running a group, and "Boom!" I felt a panic attack come on! I thought I had that conquered, only to find out that I really hadn't. I quickly excused myself and ran upstairs to the bathroom. I was shocked and disappointed. For the remainder of the time that I worked there, I didn't run group nearly as much. Nothing was ever said, I think everyone just knew. With all of my training that I had now acquired, I became acutely aware that the past was still the present! Some things never change; they might improve, but leave their mark.

CHAPTER 40

I had met Marty two months after I moved. He was married, but on the verge of separation. His wife had told him to leave many times, and she refused to go with him for counseling. They had never had any children and I had my two. I hired babysitters for second and third shift, and it was very hard on me to work these stressful hours, even though I did love the job. Marty and I met through mutual friends and became friends right off the bat. He would come over and speak about his unhappy marriage. I spoke to people who knew him, and they had to admit that his wife was very difficult. I knew that it was only a matter of time before they broke up. He was different than any guy that I knew, and I had my guard up, because I didn't want to get hurt again. We remained friends for a long time before we considered it to be anything else. At times Marty, with my permission, would sneak over to my apartment in the morning to check and see if the kids went to school, or if they were playing hooky. Much to their surprise, he did catch them a couple of times. They were not happy. From a parent's point of view, I needed to know if they were behaving or not. It was very hard to try and work with no help from others. I was damned if I did and damned if I didn't. I needed to know if the kids were safe and doing right. I knew that if this was ever to turn into a real relationship, the kids would have to get used to him and he would have to get used to them.

In time our relationship got much more serious, and I told him that I was not going to be his girlfriend. I needed more of a commitment. It wasn't fair to me or his wife. Two days later he showed up at my door with suitcase in hand. I had already made space in my closet, because somehow I just knew that he was going to be a part of our lives. I opened the door and he went straight to my bedroom and told me which side of the bed he prefers! I had never lived with a guy before, and it went against my beliefs, but he certainly was no stranger to any of us. I had tried the conventional way and look what happened! The only difference was that he now slept here. The kids just shrugged and went about their own business. I have always allowed the kids to decorate their own bedrooms. I felt that it was a way of self-expression and they were both busy fixing their rooms when Marty moved in. It did take a long time for them to get along well. It would have been a lot easier if things went smoothly from the start, but in the end as time went by, they came to accept each other. I know in my heart that Marty loves my kids and he has expressed it many times. We had a different kind of background and different religious beliefs, but that never got in the way. There were a lot of personality clashes and behaviors that needed to be changed before everyone could get along. We all had to learn respect for one another. It was a period of adjustment that we all had to make, and we did.

One day when Marty was at work, I received a phone call that he had been in an accident while working. Marty was an electrician by trade. He had been badly burned in an explosion while working on the building's main electrical distribution panel. There were electrical problems in the building that he was working in. The wiring was not up to code and he had been called in to work on it anyway. As he was working, suddenly there was an explosion, and he went flying through the air. A 2000 Amp main circuit breaker failed to trip. He was burned badly on his face and arms. He was hospitalized, but refused to stay because of poor nursing treatment. I picked him up the next day and ended up caring for him at home. My job suffered. A counselor from the clinic was sent over one day to check things out, and to see how we were doing.

He was shocked when he saw Marty's face and said that he was foolish for leaving the hospital, Marty thought otherwise. I ended up quitting my job to care for Marty. We also decided that a move was in order. Marty's parents had recently died just a few months apart from each other, and he and his brother were left a sum of money. We wanted to buy a house in the country. Where we lived now wasn't in a good area for the kids. The complex had turned tough and there was trouble all over the place. The kids didn't seem to mind the move, and we started to pack again. We ended up buying a home near Hackettstown, NJ. To this day my daughter and son and their families still live in that area. Marty and I divorced our spouses after we moved to Hackettstown, and a year later the justice of peace married us shortly after. My parents refused to be a part of it. They gave us enough money to buy a *used* lawn mower for the property and that was it. The day my mother gave us a few bucks, she said "Make sure it's used!" What's the hell was that about? My brother on the other hand, when he had gotten married his second time, was given a beautiful lawn wedding on the property and my mother even bought his bride a beautiful wedding gown! Go figure! My brother divorced some years later. Marty saw right through my mother, and never considered her to be anything more than a cruel person to her daughter.

My new husband struggled to get work at first, and finally landed a job working for the New York City Housing Authority as an electrician. It took a while before he was able to save any money at his new job. I got a job working with emotionally disturbed girls and after a while I became supervisor of my shift. Things were improving monetarily for once, but there was a lot of friction in the house. The kids really needed their mother to stay at home. All of the moves from school to school, and home to home had taken a big toll. I worked there for about a year and quit. By that time Marty was making better money and I could stay home. Our home was not beautiful, but we had what we needed. Our clothes did *not* have to come out of the thrift shop anymore.

We lived near Hackettstown for around five years and the kids were becoming grown up by that time. My daughter had made me a young grandmother and I must admit that I was shocked. I did however get very excited after a while, and I adore my grandson. In time we had to move again because Marty was very far from work, and it was very hard on him driving every day to the city, so we decided to move much closer to his work. We ended up in Dover, NJ. Marty and I stayed there for eighteen years.

Soon after our move to Dover it wasn't long before our son met his future wife, who already had a son of her own. Within two years they married. Some years later they had a precious little girl. It's not that we loved Dover, it was just convenient. During that time living in our two family house; we decided that it was much better for me to stay home. Marty was making good money, and the upstairs rental unit brought in good income. I took care of the painting and spackling of our old plaster house, and watched over our part of the neighborhood. However, I managed to work for a few years during that time. I worked at a mental institution for a year, and then several years at a methadone clinic as a counselor. I can only say that all through the years, the jobs I chose to work at had a close similarity to the life that I knew personally. Life is about choices. With the abuses that I have experienced all through my life, I could have chosen to throw in the towel and say the hell with it all. I desperately wanted to be an upstanding citizen, be happy and contribute to society. The only thing that I could think to do all of these years was to work with those in need and share with them what I learned. I do know that those people out there who have had abusive backgrounds can either learn from it as I did, or not. I once read somewhere a quote that I firmly believe in, "Forgiveness does not change the past, but it does enlarge the future!"

I don't believe for one minute that people who sexually abuse others can use the excuse that it happened to them, so therefore "This is why I am the way that I am!" Not good enough! I have never abused a child or anyone else for that matter. I'm sure that there are a lot of people out there who have been abused as I have, and they are doing their best to be decent people. I had the occasion just the other day to speak to a lady who had been sexually abused as a child. I told her about this book that I am writing, and the subject content. We both agree that abuse of this nature never goes away — you just learn to push it aside. It leaves ugly scars, whether it is a relative or a stranger, or as in my case both. You have to find a way to live and move on and survive all of the nasty memories of being violated. If you don't do this, you become emotionally crippled for the rest of your life.

One of the reasons for writing this book is to share with whoever reads it, that you can be abused in all different ways, and there is help for you. I listen to the news and other programs and hear about people who sexually abuse young kids and get away with it. I want to scream! It's said that perhaps the molester or the pedophile had a bad life. I ask what about the life of the child or the person who has been violated? Rapists and molesters *ruin* people's lives. For years I had to live with all kinds of phobias, panic attacks, inferiority complexes and more. I hear stories about the offenders receiving a slap on the hand and probation! What kind of a world do we live in that allows for people like that to go free? What kind of justice system allows for those terrible people to walk the streets and continue to stalk the unsuspecting and young? I would love to sit down with any of these judges who allow for this, and ask them questions like "Isn't the punishment supposed to fit the crime?" A judge is a public official. At one time, if I met a judge I would have been impressed. I can't say that all judges are bad, of course. I can only say that judges, who allow our citizens to walk around in fear because they have *not* done their job, should be made to step down. And I say to those judges, "Shame on you!"

Today I am a lot better than what I was years ago, but it took a long time getting there. I look back at all of the years of abuse that I endured sexually and other ways — because I had no voice. I only knew fear. I no longer hate myself. I don't even hate the people who were the abusers; I just want justice to be served, so all of the rest of society can feel safe.

Wake up people! We have the right for freedom of speech; we have the right to vote and on and on it goes; and yes, we have the right to be safe in our homes and on the streets. Anyone who may compromise our safety, no matter what position they hold, should be questioned and disarmed! They too are dangerous people, because they jeopardize our rights, our security, and our freedom from fear.

Today's children are tomorrow's hope! People speak up! _Demand_ better laws! Let's stop this atrocity!

Carol D. Levine

———

I did some research on the Internet and found that children who are sexually abused can suffer from panic attacks; panic disorder (repeated panic attacks). Hyper vigilance and panic attacks often go hand in hand. Both of these are just some of the effects that make up Rape Trauma Disorder (RTD) and Post Traumatic Stress Disorder (PTSD).

As it appears, one of the most effective forms of treatment is talk therapy.

Child abuse may also cause Social Phobia (which I suffered from) Agoraphobia and PTSD. Oftentimes victims of child abuse and sexual abuse suffer with alcoholism. Not surprised with that one either!

There is hope for we who survived and suffer. Therapy and self-help groups can be found easily. Contact your local hospital; many times there are counselors who run groups in the hospital. The Internet or in the phone book under Guide to Human Services offers some information. It's different today, you can get help. Don't hide, don't keep quiet, don't be embarrassed, *get angry!* Remember, you're okay; it's the violator who's screwed up!

———

Megan's Law

At the time of this writing there were more than 14,000 convicted sex offenders in New York State alone. Megan's Law, which addresses sex offenders and child molesters, was signed by President Clinton on May 17, 1996. It was the brutal rape and murder of Megan Kanka by a previously registered sex offender that prompted the public demand for broad based community notification. Megan's Law mandates that every state develop a procedure for notifying residents of sex offenders in their area. Each state differs on how they report the information, but there are many useful web sites that have easy access to local information.

Megan's Law requires convicted sex offenders to notify authorities of their current address. Every time a convicted sex offender moves they are required to notify local police of their new location. This allows the public to know where the sex offenders live at all times. However, this requirement is not always permanent and many convicted sex offenders are only required to report for ten years. Megan's Law is not enough. All too often sex offenders are back on our streets to commit crimes again.

Jessica's Law refers to the Jessica Lunsford Act passed in Florida which mandates a minimum sentence of twenty five years and maximum of life for the first time child sex offender. Paroled sex offenders wear a GPS positioning unit so police can keep track of them all of the time. Research shows that criminals who prey on young children tend to _repeat_ their crimes.

People who are sexually abused need to get mad and speak up. Write your congressional representative and demand that more be done so our children can be safe. There are approximately seven states that have not passed Jessica's Law. I unfortunately live in one of them. What's wrong with people who don't support laws that protect our children from sexual predators? I say, wise up! Rape can happen to anyone, at anytime, and any place. All states need Jessica's Law. Children deserve to be safe. We all deserve to be safe. Sexual offenders should lose his or her rights the minute he or she sexually violates a child _or_ an adult.

Lightning Source UK Ltd.
Milton Keynes UK
27 September 2010

160416UK00001B/288/P